Make no little plans, they have no magic to stir the blood and probably themselves will not be realized. Make big plans; aim high in hope and work, remembering that a noble, logical diagram once recorded will never die, but long after we are gone will be a living thing, asserting itself with evergrowing insistency.
—Daniel Burnham

David Taylor

This book honoring participants in the first twenty years of University Research Park is dedicated to David Taylor, Celanese research chemist and administrator, director of University Research Park from its first year, president and chairman of the park longer than anyone else, while serving overlapping terms as chairman of The Foundation of The University of North Carolina at Charlotte and president of the Charlotte Chamber. His uncommon combination of vision, commitment, persistence, executive acumen, and quiet persuasiveness render him a public servant *par excellence.*

UNIVERSITY RESEARCH PARK
THE FIRST TWENTY YEARS

Dean W. Colvard
Douglas M. Orr, Jr.
Mary Dawn Bailey

DISCARDED

Urban Institute
University of North Carolina at Charlotte

Funded by University Research Park, Inc.
Charlotte, North Carolina

ISBN 0-945344-00-7

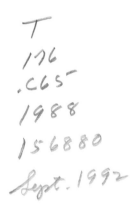

CONTENTS

PREFACE AND ACKNOWLEDGMENTS

Those involved with the University Research Park from the beginning know that community cooperation and faith in the future are the cornerstones upon which the park was built. Those who joined the project during its early years know that vision and enlightened leadership — by individuals, private enterprise, government, and academia — led to its ultimate success. They know that support from Charlotte's banks enabled the project to get underway; that the Charlotte Chamber of Commerce, now the Charlotte Chamber, originated the idea of a research park and has continued its support and leadership. They know that very extensive cooperation among members of City Council, County Commissioners, the City/County Planning Commission, the North Carolina Department of Transportation, and their staffs has not only been a source of strength but might be regarded as a rare occurrence in many communities. And they know that The University of North Carolina at Charlotte (UNCC) has been a constant and supportive partner of the park's development.

In 1987 the net result of this impressive community cooperation and visionary leadership is not only the University Research Park, but also the designation of the northeast part of the county as "University City," a mini-city within a city planned to insure orderly and high quality development in the area surrounding the park and the university.

Planning and voluntary coordination of agencies over the years has resulted in the creation of the dynamic community of which the University Research Park is a part. UNCC commissioned Odell Associates of Charlotte and Caudill Rowlett Scott Sirrine of Houston, Texas as professional planners; park directors engaged J.N. Pease & Associates of Charlotte; professional planners on the City/County Planning Commission were active from the beginning; city, county, and state engineers planned utilities and roads; geographers' studies of research parks and the factors contributing to their success or failure helped to make sound decisions; urban planners, demographers, and model towns in Europe gave direction to University Place; planning by the Health and Hospital Council (no longer in existence) and the Charlotte/Mecklenburg Hospital Authority brought University Memorial Hospital into being. Some plans were based on economic analysis and known market needs; others relied on projections of future needs and trends; in most instances visions and judgments of how urbanization, new technologies, computerized management of information, and educational requirements would merge dictated the courses charted; practical and political considerations influenced but did not dominate decisions.

Soon after Seddon "Rusty" Goode, Jr. became president of University Research Park in 1981, I sent him a copy of a transcribed interview conducted with W.T. (Bill) Harris who is regarded, more than any other individual, as the "founding father" of the research park. Goode suggested that additional interviews be sought with Harris' successor, David Taylor, and with John A. Tate, Jr. and Claude Q. Freeman, Sr., who played very prominent roles in the park's development. Having been involved for a short period of time in the planning of the Research Triangle Park in the Raleigh/Durham/Chapel Hill area and having been involved with the University Research Park from its beginning, I set about to accumulate additional documentation of the extensive high-calibre leadership so necessary to the success of projects of this magnitude. Interviews with J. Norman Pease, Jr., who was very much involved with planning, and with President Goode were also recorded. Excerpts of all interviews are included in the appendix.

As one thing led to another, President Goode encouraged me to record the story of the park's development. He expressed an interest in honoring the distinguished leaders who brought it into being. We agreed that our story might be of interest to others considering launching a similar park. To provide the most complete picture possible the charter and bylaws are included in the appendix.[1]

I have recorded both exciting successes and periods of discouragement. The time span covered is approximately twenty years, from the date of the park's origin in late 1966 through 1987. Unfortunately, some of the stalwart leaders during the first years had died, thus depriving us of their personal recollections. Such forceful leaders as General Paul Younts, William M. Ficklen, Patrick N. Calhoun, and others made important contributions and are mentioned in the interviews. This underscored in our minds the importance of including specific information on the quality of leadership so generously contributed by so many people.

---

[1] It should be noted that University Research Park modified its charter and zoning to permit high-technology manufacturing and information management, as well as research, to be performed in the park.

When, on April 1, 1966, I became the first chancellor of The University of North Carolina at Charlotte, the fourth campus of the Consolidated University of North Carolina, it seemed clear that the university, in addition to its prescribed academic functions, should be concerned with the town/gown relationship. For several years community leaders had worked closely with Dr. Bonnie Cone in actions leading up to the creation of UNCC. My first public appearance in Charlotte was at a welcome banquet hosted by the Charlotte Chamber of Commerce in cooperation with Mayor Stanford Brookshire and attended by a large number of local and state leaders. Though I came with no clear plan, had no knowledge of the program under discussion in the Charlotte Chamber of Commerce, and had only begun to visualize how UNCC could interface with the community, my comments to that group revealed my interests in economic and cultural exchanges. Among other things, I said,

> "My purpose is not to enunciate long-range plans, but rather to place emphasis on planning. We shall strive to keep the thinking and planning ahead of the action. Our goal is to provide vitality in this university, equal to the vitality of this community and equal to the requirements of society for trained minds and understanding people. My hope is that UNCC will be in the midst of real life in North Carolina and Charlotte. Town and gown are mutually interdependent."

Had I known about the work plans of the Charlotte Chamber of Commerce, which included the idea of a research park, what a fine example that would have been! As the content of this book will reveal, my successor, E.K. Fretwell Jr., and members of his staff have added greatly both to the vision and the action.

The payoff for efforts such as those which created Research Triangle Park and University Research Park may be measured by what happens to the economy and the quality of life of the state and the regions most directly affected. Per capita income has increased, both actually and relatively; quality of life is improved; the ability of the state and the regions where the parks are located to respond to changing forces in the economy and the society are enhanced.

As the drafts of several chapters began to take shape, I called upon my former colleagues at UNCC to assist with the editing. Vice Chancellor for Development and Public Service Douglas M. Orr, Jr. and Associate Director of the Urban Institute Mary Dawn Bailey began to contribute in such important ways that I was pleased to invite them to become co-authors. Ms. Bailey provided important content and was responsible for all pre-publication aspects of the book. With the support of the Urban Institute and The Foundation of the University of North Carolina at Charlotte, arranged by Dr. Orr and approved by Chancellor Fretwell, the Urban Institute's publications program editor, Dr. John McNair of the English Department, was engaged as editor of the book. Dr. Orr was responsible for working with President Goode in publishing the document. He and Dr. James Clay were primarily responsible for envisioning, launching, and developing University Place and for the content of Chapter VIII dealing with University Place.

The park office has made all of its records available. The most important single source was the official minutes covering most of the action and auditors' reports. In a few instances, the lack of an office of its own in its first years may account for gaps in the story. Other sources include the University Research Park files from The Charlotte Chamber of Commerce, David Taylor's files while he served as president, Ed Latimer's files covering the original plan of financing the organization, my own files from the UNCC Chancellor's Office from the beginning through 1978, newspaper clippings, and special studies and reports used in formulating policies.

The authors express their special gratitude to Linda Labat who has assisted with the research, done the typing, and skillfully manipulated the word processor through numerous revisions.

We also extend our appreciation to my daughter, Carol Cason, graphics designer of Reston, Virginia, and to Sharon Moss, Charlotte, for the design of the cover and to Al Mahoney for his help with photographs.

This book is full of names, dates, and events. The opportunities, indeed the probabilities, for mistakes are somewhat frightening. As omissions or errors may be discovered, they will be noted in the records of the University Research Park and the archives of the UNCC library where all of the files have been placed. More time will be required for the history of the park to be written. My hope is that the information herein assembled will be helpful.

Dean W. Colvard

FOREWORD

Seddon "Rusty" Goode, Jr.

University Research Park is a successful concept — a public corporation where technology to solve problems of the future is researched, developed, and perfected to benefit society. Its directors are leaders in the Charlotte business community who volunteer their time, influence, and energies to direct the park and promote its benefits around the county and, indeed, the world. We who serve the park are committed to providing the setting, atmosphere, and backup which enhance a company's operations. We work well with the community, the university, and our neighbors.

The park's 20-square mile neighborhood is University City and we are proud of our role as the epicenter for the new burst of development which the area is experiencing. The park in 1988 reflects the energy of the market which it serves.

University Research Park is a non-profit corporation. Located adjacent to The University of North Carolina at Charlotte, the beneficiary of the corporation, we have a close working relationship with the university's administration and faculty. It is fitting that their people should write our story.

On behalf of the board I would like to thank the authors, particularly Chancellor Emeritus Dean W. Colvard, for taking the time to research, write, and publish this important book. The unique 20-year history of the park demonstrates that the Charlotte community has created a place where new ideas and approaches can flourish. Reality has indeed exceeded the most optimistic predictions of 1966. University Research Park, located in University City in Charlotte, North Carolina, is tomorrow's place for success. It has a bright future.

Seddon "Rusty" Goode, Jr.
President, University Research Park, Inc.

UNIVERSITY CITY

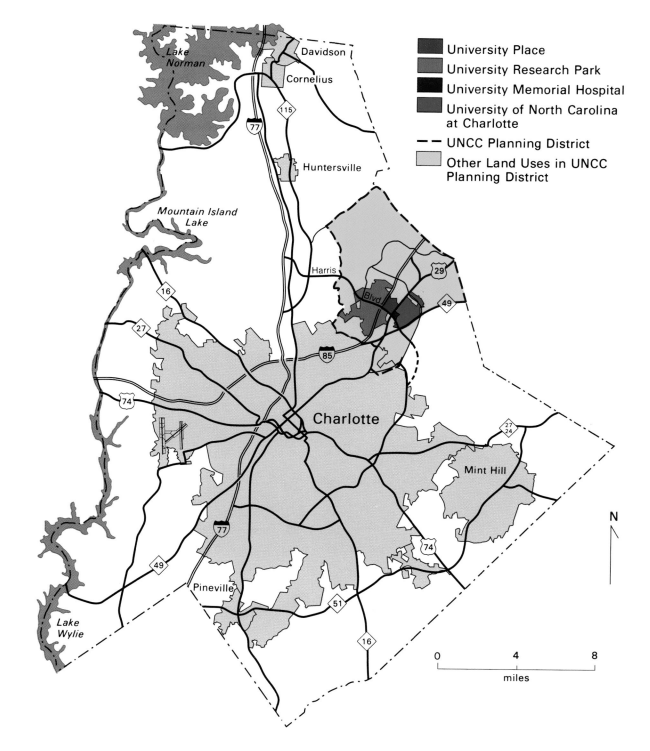

University Place
University Research Park
University Memorial Hospital
University of North Carolina
at Charlotte
– – – UNCC Planning District
Other Land Uses in UNCC
Planning District

Lake Norman

Davidson

Cornelius

Huntersville

Mountain Island Lake

Harris

Blvd

Charlotte

Mint Hill

Pineville

Lake Wylie

N

0   4   8
miles

UNIVERSITY RESEARCH PARK IS BORN

"We have taken a giant step toward a greater future for Charlotte and Mecklenburg County. I believe this park is destined to have a tremendous impact on the city's economic, cultural, and social life."
—W. T. Harris

When W.T. "Bill" Harris, president of the University Research Park for its first ten years, was asked[2] what had inspired plans for the park, his response clearly revealed the concerns of community leaders at the time. For years, he said, businessmen who had explored locating research and development firms in the Charlotte area had found that the region simply did not have allurements competitive with those in the North Carolina Research Triangle, Atlanta, and other cities. Therefore, he lamented, the community had failed to attract some very good companies. He added, "We had to face up to the fact that if we wanted to increase the level of the take-home pay of the people of this community, we had to move away from the total warehouse distribution type of business and get more research and people with more education. We also felt pretty strongly that if we could bring quite a few people in here with PhDs it would help the university to develop and, between the two, this would be a worthwhile project."

W. T. "Bill" Harris

Research Triangle Points the Way

A decade earlier, similar thoughts led to the establishment of Research Triangle Park in the Raleigh/Durham/Chapel Hill area. Soon after Governor Luther H.

Hodges was sworn into office late in 1954, he gave public expression to his concern about the low ranking of the state in average income. He commissioned The University of North Carolina at Chapel Hill and North Carolina State College to make a study of the per-capita income of the state. The report[3] revealed that the state ranked eleventh in total population, tenth in the number of people employed in manufacturing, first in farm population, and forty-third in per-capita income. It further emphasized the need for more high wage employment.

Also early in 1955, Romeo H. Guest, a building contractor in Greensboro, North Carolina, had conversations with Governor Hodges, President Gordon Gray of The University of North Carolina, President Hollis Edens of Duke University, and other state officials concerning his views of how research oriented industries might be encouraged to locate in North Carolina, particularly in the area near the three major universities — The University of North Carolina at Chapel Hill, Duke University, and North Carolina State College. Guest's company, C. M. Guest and Sons, had been involved in building and renovating facilities for the textile industries of North and South Carolina. He was concerned because the relocation of conventional industries from New England to the South was slowing down. As a

---

2 See Appendix C, page 1. (Copy in Dalton Rare Documents Room, UNCC Library.)

3 *Studies of Per Capita Income in North Carolina*, A Report by an Interinstitutional Committee of North Carolina State College and The University of North Carolina at Chapel Hill, March 1956.

graduate of the Massachusetts Institute of Technology and somewhat familiar with research operations in that area, he concluded that the future of his contractual business would be more promising if research institutions could be attracted to the South. He also believed that research would generate new industries. Through his service as a director of the Textile Foundation, which supported research at North Carolina State College's School of Textiles, he became acquainted with Textile School Dean Malcolm Campbell. Their association reinforced his views of the compatibility of research industries and universities.

To focus attention on North Carolina as an attractive location for research activities, Guest published a brochure emphasizing that "research fits North Carolina like a glove." The brochure pictured the bell towers of Duke University, The University of North Carolina at Chapel Hill, and North Carolina State College and used the label "North Carolina's Own Research Triangle." This was the beginning of a systematic effort to depict the region's unusual concentration of research personnel and equipment as a unique North Carolina resource providing a setting in which research specialists would like to live and work.

Guest was also a friend of William P. Saunders, Governor Hodges' director of Conservation and Development. He discussed ideas with Saunders as well as Brandon P. Hodges, state treasurer and one of the state's most articulate industry recruiters. The three urged the governor to assume strong leadership in developing the Research Triangle idea. This he did.

Governor Hodges established two groups to advise him on the initial development of the Research Triangle Park. Nine prominent business leaders[4] composed his Research Triangle Development Council. Another group of nine,[5] the Working Committee, consisted of three academic leaders from each of the major universities in the area. Dean W. Colvard was one of the three deans of North Carolina State College serving on the Working Committee. In 1955, a major assignment of the working committee was to make an inventory of research personnel and equipment in the area.[6]

In the triangle area (the sides of which varied from twelve to thirty-five miles in length) were located two medical schools, two schools of dentistry, two schools of forestry, a school of agriculture (including an agricultural research service with sixteen branch stations scattered over the state), a school of public health, a school of business administration, an institute of experimental statistics in which was located the world's highest concentration of professional research statisticians, an institute of government, and a number of other specialized schools and institutes. In this small area were three outstanding libraries of more than two million volumes and scientific journals covering almost every field of research.

Professional staff and research specialists in these three institutions numbered more than eight hundred and fifty. There were few locations in the United States that could match this concentration of research talent, laboratory equipment, and library holdings. In the academic year 1954-55, these three universities conferred two hundred and eighty-two doctor's degrees and two hundred and thirty-five master's degrees.

The University of North Carolina at Chapel Hill, which had been in existence 160 years, had an enrollment of 6,500 students in a town with a population of 5,500; Duke University, which had been in existence under different names for 117 years, had an enrollment of 5,100 students in the town of Durham, with a population of 70,000; North Carolina State College, which had been in existence for 68 years, had an enrollment of 5,000 students in Raleigh, a town with a population of about 80,000 people.

Governor Hodges and those working with him made a strong and convincing argument that the universities concentrated in a relatively small area represented an underutilized resource for attracting research and development firms. As a result of the studies and counsel, an organization called the Research Triangle Committee, Incorporated, was created on September 25, 1956, by Governor Luther H. Hodges, Robert M. Hanes, chief executive officer of Wachovia Bank and Trust Company in Winston-Salem, and Brandon P. Hodges, then serving as state treasurer. The name was changed to the Research Triangle Foundation of North Carolina on December 23, 1958. Leadership was then vested primarily in top officers of the three universities and businessmen from Durham and Raleigh, including George Watts Hill of Durham and G. Akers Moore, Jr. of Raleigh.

---

4 Robert M. Hanes, A. Hollis Edens, Brandon P. Hodges, William C. Friday, Robert Armstrong, E.Y. Floyd, Grady Rankin, C.W. Reynolds, and William H. Ruffin.

5 From North Carolina State College: J. Harold Lampe, chairman, Dean W. Colvard, and Malcolm Campbell. From Duke University: W.C. Davison, Marcus E. Hobbs, and W.J. Seeley. From The University of North Carolina at Chapel Hill: Henry T. Clark, Jr., Arthur Roe, and Gordon W. Blackwell.

6 *An Inventory of Selected Resources of the Research Triangle,* Subcommittee on Inventory: Marcus E. Hobbs, chairman, R.J.M. Hobbs, W.C. Davison, Dean W. Colvard, December 1955. (Copy in Dalton Rare Documents Room, UNCC Library).

Several leaders in Charlotte had been involved in the Research Triangle Park planning and understood the compatibility of universities and research industries. Robert Armstrong, vice president of Celanese Corporation, was a member of the governor's Research Triangle Development Council. Realtor Claude Q. Freeman, Sr. had worked with Romeo H. Guest when he was involved in assembling land for the Celanese Corporation which located a new plant in Charlotte. This association led to Freeman's appointment as a director of Pinelands Corporation, formed to buy land for the Research Triangle. John A. Tate, Jr., a former partner of Freeman, was a banker with North Carolina National Bank. J. Paul Lucas, vice president of Duke Power Company and Charlotte College Trustee, and others had varying degrees of knowledge and understanding of the Research Triangle Park and its purposes.

Charlotte Chamber of Commerce Takes Lead

In 1966, W. T. Harris became president of the Charlotte Chamber of Commerce. He appointed J. Paul Lucas to head the committee to develop the work program for that year. The resulting 1966 work program emphasized two new concepts: (1) the development of a research park between The University of North Carolina at Charlotte (UNCC) and Davidson College and (2) planned development of a "university city" around UNCC. The work program also called for building a downtown convention and exposition center. In justifying the proposals, Lucas pointed out that Charlotte's population had grown from 134,000 in 1950 to more than 250,000 in 1966. He projected enrollment growth of UNCC from 1,800 at that time to 15,000 by 1980. "The shopping centers, restaurants, and stores that will go into this 'university city' can be combined with the university to form a harmonious whole if planning is begun now," Lucas concluded.

The discussion was undoubtedly enlivened by the announcement in 1965 that International Business Machines Corporation (IBM) would build a $15 million facility employing about 2,500 persons in Research Triangle Park.

Realtors Take Options on Land

At the same time Chamber of Commerce leaders were discussing creation of a research park, realtor Paul Younts was putting together a tract of land to entice a reputable national corporation to establish a research and service center in the area. Hercules Powder Company had expressed interest in a location. Younts was in the process of taking an option at $400 per acre. A public announcement relative to zoning caused the price to jump to $2,500 per acre. Although price of land may not have been the determining factor, this company chose to locate in Research Triangle Park. Younts did not give up. Using his own money, he took transferable options on some properties.

Younts and Harris conferred with John A. Tate, Jr., then vice president of North Carolina National Bank (NCNB) and responsible for Charlotte operations, concerning financing land options and purchases. In turn, Tate conferred with Addison H. Reese, chairman of NCNB and also former chairman of the Board of Trustees of Charlotte College. Reese and Tate agreed to underwrite the initial options Younts had taken and suggested that other banks be asked to participate. Concurrently, Harris was talking with attorney Joseph W. Grier, Jr. about the kind of organization that should be formed to shepherd development of the park.

The New University of North Carolina at Charlotte

By action of the North Carolina General Assembly of 1965, Charlotte College, led by Dr. Bonnie Cone as president, became the fourth campus of the consolidated university of North Carolina. In contrast to the universities in the Research Triangle area, its scope and resources were limited indeed. It was a small commuter institution. However, there was excitement in Charlotte stemming from the high expectations for this developing institution. It showed promise of introducing a new dimension of education to the Charlotte community. The University of North Carolina at Charlotte was expected to grow at a rate much faster than other North Carolina universities had experienced in their early years.

Charlotte College in 1961. NC Highway 49 in foreground, US Highway 29 and future site of University Place in background

The area of the new university was rural countryside. Charlotte College had occupied its first two buildings (later known as Kennedy and Macy) in 1961. By 1966, seven more buildings were in place or under construction. The student body consisted of about 1,800 commuter students. As a four-year institution Charlotte College conferred its first and only baccalaureate degrees, a total of twenty, in 1965. There were approximately seventy faculty. No graduate programs had been authorized. No funds had been earmarked for research.

UNCC got its water from three wells. In the summer of 1966 these wells failed to provide the water required for operation. This forced the institution to close until the supply could be augmented by hauling water in tank trucks. This emergency also prompted city and county governments to accelerate plans to extend a 20-inch wa-

ter line to the campus. A small sewage facility was operated in cooperation with county-owned Green Acres, a home for low income citizens. This waste-disposal facility was located in a valley which later became the site of athletic fields for UNCC. The Green Acres property, including farmland, was owned by Mecklenburg County and leased to a private operator. Cattle were grazing on much of the land the county had given to UNCC. The area which later became University Place, a part of the Green Acres conveyance to UNCC, was in cultivated cropland. Three dilapidated tenant houses were occupied but had only wells and outdoor privies for utilities.

Four-lane Highway 29 served as the main transportation artery from Charlotte to Concord, Salisbury, and other points north. Highway 49 was a two-lane road. Extension of I-85 through the Green Acres property was planned. Harris Boulevard had not yet been proposed. UNCC was served internally by a two-lane hard-surfaced road, Mary Alexander Boulevard, running from Highway 49 to Mallard Creek Church Road. The only paved internal lateral road extended from Mary Alexander Boulevard along the north side of Hechenbleikner Lake (where Rowe and Colvard buildings were later located) to a paved parking lot north of where the parking deck was later built. Across Highway 49 from UNCC, the Crosland Company had built the beginnings of College Downs, a residential area. These homes received their water from wells and were served by a small privately-owned sewer facility located on the west side of Highway 49. With the exception of a few small restaurants, motels, and service stations on Highway 29, the area was devoid of retail establishments. The only access to much of the land which became University Research Park was on foot, by horseback, jeep, or helicopter. References to UNCC as "rural college," "way-out-there," and the like, were understandable. Conversations about developing UNCC as an urban-oriented university sometimes generated skeptical responses.

In spite of the undeveloped status of the area, there were widely shared beliefs that the largest population center in North Carolina and a highly competitive economy moving rapidly toward greater reliance on management, science, and technology would inevitably provide the ingredients for research park development. The most obvious deficiency was the lack of a major university. The remark that Charlotte was the most "undercolleged" city of its size in the United States was heard in many discussions. Excellent private colleges with limited enrollment, and perhaps the strongest community college in North Carolina, were serving important roles but there was no major, diversified public university.

Faith in the Future

Dean W. Colvard's arrival as the first chancellor of UNCC on April 1, 1966, coincided with the timing of the first movement within the Chamber of Commerce toward developing a research park. Having been a member of Governor Hodges' Working Committee involved in formulating the Research Triangle Park some ten years earlier, it was a source of great satisfaction for him to see the steps which were being taken to involve UNCC with the community and with the state as a whole in economic development.

As was stated in an early brochure, "The Research Triangle was not planned," but grew out of the promising resources of three well-established universities. In contrast to the Research Triangle Park, which had been created to reap the benefits of an existing concentration of research talent and equipment in an area which had re-

lied primarily on governmental and institutional employment, University Research Park was born out of the vision of business leaders in the state's largest city and commercial center. The concept of the Research Triangle Park originated with people who lived outside the region. It had been promoted by a governor of North Carolina who was receiving advice from business leaders

Dean W. Colvard

from across the state as well as locally. By contrast, University Research Park was launched entirely by local business leaders in cooperation with a new university.

Although the leadership for the development of a research park was local, the vision for both the park and UNCC was that they would be a strong complement to the University of North Carolina system as well as to the Research Triangle Park. From the very beginning UNCC emphasized a commitment to urban affairs and community services. Its location in the largest population center of the state at a time when society was becoming urbanized provided an opportunity that had not existed when other campuses of the UNC system had been founded much earlier. Leaders were also motivated by the belief that Charlotte and the piedmont region needed a greater concentration of high-tech industry.

Leaders of the planning for the University Research Park shared the beliefs that had motivated developers of the Research Triangle Park. They believed that education and technology would become increasingly powerful tools in the future as the state's economy expanded. They were eager to see North Carolina share in the rewards of discovery. They wanted to provide attractive environments for high-wage enterprises rather than to continue almost total reliance on traditional industries. They also expected to see science, technology, and management play increasingly important roles in those traditional industries which had served the state so well.

William M. Ficklen

Park Development, Inc. Organized

The first meeting of record to consider forming an organization to oversee development of a research park was called by W. T. Harris on November 23, 1966. It was attended by William M. Ficklen of the Charlotte Chamber of Commerce, John A. Tate, Jr. and Cleve McGriff of North Carolina National Bank, Charles Rich of Wachovia Bank & Trust Company, Graeme Keith of First Union National Bank, Sid Hughes of First Citizens Bank & Trust Company, D. W. Jones of Duke Power Company and the Chamber of Commerce, and General Paul Younts, realtor. Also in attendance were Edwin L. Jones, Jr., John S. Stafford, and attorney Carlton Fleming representing the J. A. Jones Construction Company. Joseph W. Grier, Jr., attorney, met with the group and advised Harris on the legal

pros and cons of forming an organization. In an internal memorandum covering this meeting, Grier said, "For the time being I think our best procedure is to organize a corporation having as a stated objective the social, economic, and cultural growth of the community and to purchase the property in the name of such corporation . . . " Harris called another meeting for December 1 at 3:30 p.m.

In preparation for that meeting William M. Ficklen arranged a luncheon for himself and W. T. Harris, Edwin L. Jones, Jr., Patrick N. Calhoun, Russell M. Robinson (Jones' attorney), Joseph W. Grier, Jr. (attorney for the Chamber of Commerce), and Charles Crawford of the Chamber of Commerce. Prior to this luncheon Grier and Robinson had agreed on the general structure of the organization to be proposed. Also attending the 3:30 meeting were representatives of the banks, William McIntyre of the Charlotte-Mecklenburg Planning Commission, and several others. Grier read the document he had drafted. Edwin L. Jones, Jr. advised the group that he would not be willing to sell the approximately 610 acres owned by his company unless it could be appraised after the new interstate road was in place. He agreed, however, to pool it with other lands in the proposed park and to share in the expenses of development. This stimulated extensive discussion. The meeting was concluded on an optimistic note (with some reservations). Grier's conclusion was: "It seems clear to me that the appointment of a Board of Directors to take charge of the project is indicated and this should be done." Others agreed and Grier proceeded to draw up a charter. When the proper documents had been drawn up, Grier, Francis I. Parker, and James Y. Preston served as incorporators and to approve bylaws and elect officers. Grier was elected president; Parker, secretary-treasurer; and Preston, vice president and assistant secretary-treasurer. For fewer than three months the organization was called Park Development, Inc.

At the formation meeting of the new organization on November 23, officers were authorized to pay $650 for surveying the "Spencer property" and to negotiate with financial institutions for a loan to the corporation for $60,000.00 to execute a purchase agreement with Helen Saunders Spencer for a total of $181,022.38 as specified in a Younts's option. The option was due to expire on November 29, 1966. The down payment required was $52,496.48. The balance was to be paid in installments of $25,705.18 on November 29 each year for 1967, 1968, 1969, 1970, and 1971, with interest at 4 percent per annum. Authority was also given the organization's officers to execute an $18,000 note to Younts Realty and Insurance Company to cover the real estate sales commission on the Spencer land. This note was to be subordinate to the $60,000 note to the banks. It is clear that the organization was created for a purpose and that it got down to business very promptly.

In the interview with W. T. Harris on December 20, 1979, he indicated that although financial arrangements with the banks were not worked out immediately, Younts Realty and Insurance Company proceeded by putting up its own money to take an option on 160 acres owned by J. L. and Ada Pendelton. This property launched the park when it was sold for $2,200 per acre to Collins & Aikman Corporation for its science and service division. The Spencer property was held for future expansion as envisioned by the new organization.

John A. Tate, Jr.

Name Changed to University Research Park, Inc.

W. T. Harris was succeeded as president of the Chamber of Commerce by D. W. "Red" Jones. Jones asked Harris to assume leadership of this high priority part of the chamber's work program begun during his administration.

In a confidential letter dated December 20, 1966, Harris invited a few community leaders, including UNCC Chancellor Dean W. Colvard, to meet on December 27 for the purpose of making important decisions. At this meeting there was general agreement that the organization should be further refined. The group discussed the name, Park Development, Inc., which had been used by Grier

for purposes of incorporation and several other possible names for the park: "University Research Park," "University Research and Office Park," "University Research and Executive Park," "Spearhead Center," "Mecklenburg Office Park," "Interstate Research Center," "New South Research Park," "New South Center," "Charlotte Research Park," and "Piedmont Crescent Scientific Center."

The group agreed that another meeting would be held soon for the purpose of perfecting the organization. When Joseph W. Grier, Jr., president of Park Development, Inc., convened the next meeting on January 4, 1967, he had received recommendation from the Chamber of Commerce that W. T. Harris and John A. Tate, Jr. be elected directors. When this was accomplished, Parker and Preston tendered their resignations as directors and the following additional directors (essentially, the group that Harris invited to the luncheon on December 27, 1966) were elected:

> James G. Cannon, Vice President, American Credit Corporation
>
> Dean W. Colvard, Chancellor, The University of North Carolina at Charlotte
>
> J. Scott Cramer, Vice President, Wachovia Bank & Trust Company
>
> Buell H. Duncan, President, Piedmont Natural Gas Company
>
> R. O. Evans, President, Concrete Supply Company and Chairman of the Chamber of Commerce Industrial Development Committee
>
> Carl Horn, Jr., Vice President, Finance and General Counsel, Duke Power Company
>
> Graeme Keith, Vice President, First Union National Bank
>
> D. W. "Red" Jones, Vice President, Duke Power Company and President, Charlotte Chamber of Commerce
>
> Frank McQuilkin, Director of Manufacturing and Development, Collins & Aikman Corporation
>
> Harry J. Nicholas, Vice President, First Citizens Bank & Trust Company
>
> B. L. Ray, retired executive, Standard Oil Company
>
> John J. Ryan, Vice President, Southern Bell Telephone Company.

Another meeting was called for the following day, January 5, 1967. At this meeting Joseph W. Grier, Jr. submitted his resignation as president and director. This was followed by the election of the following officers:

President: W. T. "Bill" Harris

Vice Presidents: J. Scott Cramer, Graeme Keith, and John A. Tate, Jr.

Secretary: Carl Horn, Jr.

Treasurer: B. L. Ray

Assistant Treasurer: Harry J. Nicholas.

William M. Ficklen, Industrial Manager of the Charlotte Chamber of Commerce, agreed to provide custodial service for the new organization in his office. Following the election of officers, a principal subject of discussion was what the corporation should be named. Previously mentioned names were discussed. W. T. Harris read a letter he had received expressing the view that geographic terms such as "Charlotte," "Piedmont," and "Mecklenburg" should not be used and that the park should be construed as an extension of, and not as a competitor with, Research Triangle Park. University Research Park was the name chosen.

Necessary adjustments were made to the charter and bylaws. Other business transacted included the naming of North Carolina National Bank as the depository and authorizing officers Ray and Harris to sign checks. Action was also taken to reaffirm the action which had been taken in the first meeting of Park Development, Inc. and to amend Article IV of the Articles of Incorpora-tion by deleting "the corporation shall have no members" and substituting "the corporation shall have members."

The bylaws which were adopted included as their first objective the purpose expressed by W. T. Harris: "To foster and stimulate the physical, economic, and social growth and development of Charlotte, Mecklenburg County, and North Carolina for the benefit generally of the citizens thereof, by devoting funds, properties, and resources to the attraction of business-related enterprises to locate facilities in the City and County."

With the adjournment of this meeting on January 5, 1967, University Research Park, Inc. was duly constituted and in business staffed with officers and directors whose challenge was to activate and shape the organization in the immediate future.

CITY, COUNTY, AND STATE GOVERNMENT HELP PLAN

"There would be no research park if there hadn't been an unbelievable amount of cooperation and dedication by a large number of people. The spirit of Charlotte — that's what really made University Research Park."
—*John A. Tate, Jr.*

With the University Research Park organized and officers elected, the major tasks confronted in 1967 were (1) further refining the Articles of Incorporation, (2) publicizing the organization and its purposes, (3) developing a plan for financing, (4) initiating plans for roads and utilities to serve prospective residents, and (5) proceeding with studies of zoning and covenants to protect and govern development.

First Tenant — Collins & Aikman Corporation

Collins & Aikman Corporation purchased the tract that General Younts had assembled. Founded in New York City in 1843, Collins & Aikman was one of the nation's oldest corporations. Their major products were automotive upholstery, carpet, wall coverings, and related products. They planned to use only a part of the 160 acres purchased from J. L. and Ada Pendelton for a science and service division, a 65,000 square-foot building housing research and development laboratories, management information services, engineering, industrial engineering, human resources, corporate accounting, and support staff. Most of the company's pure research was to be done there. General Younts had pledged $80,000 to Collins & Aikman as a guarantee of water and sewer facilities. Providing these facilities gave the new board some specific challenges to negotiate with city and county officials.

University Research Park, 1967

University Research Park Committees Appointed

To accomplish such objectives, four University Research Park committees were appointed. The finance committee, chaired by John A. Tate, Jr., included James G. Cannon, B. L. Ray, and Carl Horn, Jr. This committee was charged with determining the funds needed for the first five years and with recommending guidelines for membership participation, bank loans, and methods of "stretching out" payments for land purchases. The area development committee, chaired by J. Scott Cramer, included Frank McQuilkin and R. O. Evans. This committee was assigned major responsibility for zoning, water and sewer lines, and roads. The property development committee, chaired by Graeme Keith, included Buell H. Duncan and John J. Ryan. The duties of this committee included providing topographical and highway maps of the area and proposing guidelines for land use, restrictive covenants, esthetic considerations, telephone services, and fire protection. The promotional committee, chaired by Harry J. Nicholas, included R. O. Evans and Dean W. Colvard. Its duty was to define and express goals and the "what" and "why" of the project, and to use this information to prepare promotional literature to help publicize and promote the park.

9

City, County, and State Government Become Involved

On January 24, 1967, President Harris and other officers met with Mayor Stanford R. Brookshire, Councilman Milton Short, City Manager William J. Veeder, County Commission Chairman Gus Campbell, Commissioner Robert D. Potter, and County Manager Harry Weatherly. President Harris explained the proposed University Research Park, its formation, the election of officers and directors, and the vital need for water to serve the area. Arrangements were made for a request for services to be made in open meetings of both groups.

There was also a meeting with William McIntrye of the City/County Planning Commission to ask for special zoning of property south of university land between Highway 29 and I-85 and an area west of I-85. The planning commission initially recommended that the research park be confined to the area between Highway 29 and I-85 but sufficient land in that area was not made available. Dean W. Colvard also met with McIntyre to request that planning for the UNCC area be coordinated with that for the University Research Park.

President Harris asked Highway Commissioner George Broadrick and State Highway Administrator William Babcock to make a study of roads needed to develop the

George Broadrick

area. Broadrick, vice president of First Citizens Bank and Trust Company, had been appointed to the Highway Commission as successor to Paul Younts by recently elected Governor Dan K. Moore. Directors J. Scott Cramer and Dean W. Colvard were asked to pursue the discussions pertaining to roads. Arrangements were made for highway officials to meet with representatives of Collins & Aikman Corporation about connecting roads to the new buildings the corporation was planning.

UNCC Becomes Beneficiary

Although University Research Park was designated as a nonprofit corporation, it was anticipated that it would accrue some assets. In the meeting of February 24, 1967, action was taken to amend the Articles of Incorporation to allow for this possibility. Article IX was amended to include the following: "Upon liquidation all of the assets thereof shall be distributed to The Foundation of The University of North Carolina at Charlotte and/or to and among such other institutions of higher education as shall be determined by the Board of Directors. Provided, no distribution shall be made unless such institution qualifies for exemption as an organization described in Section 501(c)(3) of the Internal Revenue Code as presently enforced and in effect." Several years later the Articles of Incorporation were amended again to make it very clear that The University of North Carolina at Charlotte was to be the sole beneficiary of such fund distribution and that The Foundation of The University of North Carolina at Charlotte would dispense the funds.

Purpose and Location

Harry J. Nicholas and his promotional committee developed a statement of purpose and created a brochure titled "University Research Park, Charlotte's Stake in the Search for Tomorrow." It succinctly defined the project, its purpose, and the reasons for its promotion.

The introductory section read:

"University Research Park, Inc. is a nonprofit corporation established to provide the proper setting and atmosphere to give birth to the new ideas and techniques that will lead Charlotte into the future . . .

This organization was sponsored and initiated by the Charlotte Chamber of Commerce to promote and develop a research and development park for business corporations. It is a community-wide project with its officers and directors prominent members of the Charlotte business community.

Research and development is a huge, multiplying industry of ideas which has grown fifteen-fold since 1930. The research park concept is an idea whose time has come for the City of Charlotte. But a research park will not emerge full grown of itself. We must provide the space and proper atmosphere . . .

A research park would have a tremendous, incalculable effect on the economic, social and cultural future of Charlotte. No other possible developments at this time could

10

Harry J. Nicholas

have such a powerful influence on the Charlotte of to-morrow...

The research park would mean much more than just the much higher than average salaries paid in the industry, more than the vast physical and financial investment, more than just a companion for Charlotte's young university...

A research park would put Charlotte in the big league among cities of this nation and insure its continued growth to greatness.

Thus, we should not wait to act, Charlotte's future will not wait . . . "

This was followed by an answer to the question "Where Is It?" accompanied by a map showing the location:

"University Research Park, Inc. presently has 450 acres of land fronting on the western edge of the extension of I-85 immediately to the west of The University of North Carolina at Charlotte. It is anticipated that eventually approximately 1,200 acres of land in this area will be zoned to permit research and development activities. One large tenant already has been secured for University Research Park — Collins & Aikman Corporation — which plans to build a large research and development and data processing facility at the park. This company owns 160 acres of land adjoining the eastern edge of the park and fronting on the extension of I-85. Other prospects have shown a

strong interest in locating in the park."

The brochure answered the question "Why does Charlotte need University Research Park?":

"Research and development are experiencing explosive growth. R and D, electronic data processing and other facets of what has been called 'the knowledge industry' are claiming an ever-increasing share of this nation's total economic output. These are areas of accelerating change, and Charlotte must move ahead with the times. The present and future benefits of a research and development park to this community would be tremendous, almost incalculable. Some specific reasons why this park must be developed:

1. The type of people attracted to such facilities have a higher cultural and educational level and would make a maximum contribution to our community.

2. The higher salaries due to the specialized knowledge and technical training will result in an average annual salary over $12,000. (1967)

3. The county would realize substantial tax benefits because of the proportionately higher investment that this type of technical facility requires.

4. Charlotte must secure its share of the firms locating in the Carolinas and the South. Research activities seem to gravitate to locations that provide the proper environment and atmosphere for these activities. Charlotte has been passed over by several companies that would have built multi-million dollar facilities because it could not offer them a fully-developed location that would be conducive to research and development activities. Charlotte has been losing bluechip research facilities to the Research Triangle area and the Clemson Ravenel Research facility.

5. Charlotte has certain advantages that would facilitate the development of University Research Park: size, cultural facilities, excellent air and highway transportation, a well-balanced economy, good climate, and the existence of a number of companies engaged in these kinds of activities.

6. The research park would complement and be a stimulus to The University of North Carolina at Charlotte. Research installations and centers of learning tend to enjoy a mutually beneficial relationship; the park would draw on university talent and the University can use industrial experts as part-time instructors. UNCC can provide the opportunity for continuing education for hundreds of technical and other park employees.

7. University Research Park, when fully developed, has the potential of generating an investment in the community of $200 million and creating more than 10,000 new jobs.

8. By establishing University Research Park, we can materially help to raise the income level of Charlotteans, broaden our tax base, retain and import brainpower, and continue to strengthen our overall economic foundations."

The brochure also emphasized that the project would involve and serve the entire community. The section titled "A Community Wide Objective" included the following statement:

"University Research Park is seeking the support of the entire Charlotte community. Private investors, realtors, and industrial development specialists are invited to participate in the development of this important facility. The corporation especially invites the support of those large companies whose success depends on the continued growth and development of Charlotte. It should be emphasized that University Research Park, Inc. has been established for the good of the entire community. Profits accruing to the corporation over and above that needed to develop and promote the park will be given to The University of North Carolina at Charlotte or other educational institutions. The corporation will have 24 directors, 10 of whom will be elected by the Charlotte Chamber of Commerce, 10 by the membership of the corporation and four by the chancellor of the university."

Tentative Plan for Financing

John A. Tate, Jr.'s finance committee came forward with a plan for financing the organization. The committee estimated that $500,000 would be needed the first three years. Estimated yearly cash flow requirements were prepared by Charlie Briley, a well-known CPA: 1967 — $215,000, 1968 — $122,000, and 1969 — $117,000, making a total of $454,000. Additional working capital of $46,000 for the three years was recommended, making a grand total of $500,000 capital to be raised. In making the above estimate, the committee conservatively assumed that: (1) major land development costs would be financed out of land sales and (2) the project should be in operation and well under way by the end of 1969. This committee recommended and the Board of Directors approved as sources of income: (1) $50,000 in $1,000 memberships, (2) $50,000 in bank loans, and (3) $400,000 in 6 percent ten-year debentures (callable without penalty). The debentures would be subscribed 50 percent in cash with 30 percent additional payable January 1, 1968, and 20 percent payable January 1, 1969. All debenture purchasers would be expected to take out at least one membership, payable over a two year period at the option of the purchaser. The corporations or individuals making commitments could choose whether to write this amount off as a "gift" or an "expense." Members would have the responsibility of electing corporation directors. The finance committee's plan was given tentative approval in March, 1967.

Utilities Planning and Land Adjustment

By this time, mid-1967, UNCC negotiations with city and county government to open bids for construction of a twenty-inch water line to the campus of UNCC had been completed. J. N. Pease Associates was employed to

work with city and county planners and engineers to develop plans to extend water and sewer facilities to University Research Park. A sixteen-inch line was extended from the UNCC line at the junction of Highways 29 and 49 along the right-of-way of Highway 29 to Green Acres and Collins & Aikman.

When I-85 was built it cut through the Spencer property which had been bought by University Research Park, leaving a tract of 10 acres on the eastern side adjacent to Collins & Aikman. This was sold to Collins & Aikman at $2,500 per acre.

Additional Directors

During these first six months it had become apparent that some persons with special talents and connections should be added to the Board of Directors. In the first discussions on the formation of a research park, Edwin L. Jones, Jr., president of J. A. Jones Construction Company, had been approached about selling to the new corporation a tract of approximately 600 acres owned by his company.[7] He had suggested that, as an alternative, he might enter into an agreement for development of the whole area according to a uniform plan. He indicated his willingness to dedicate his company's land to the park and to

Edwin L. Jones, Jr.

7 Internal memorandum of Joseph W. Grier, Jr., December 2, 1966.

contribute a *pro rata* share to the cost of planning and installation of roads, water, sewer, etc. Because this plan was being pursued, Jones was invited to become a member of the Board of Directors.

One of the vice presidents of the largest commercial research operation in the Charlotte community, Celanese Corporation, was Robert Armstrong. He had been actively involved in planning the Research Triangle Park, and Celanese had given financial support to initial research conducted by the Research Triangle Institute. David Taylor, president of Celanese Fibers, had provided leadership in both planning and operating their Charlotte facility. He had extensive experience in conducting and administering industrial research as well. Taylor was added to the University Research Park board in May 1967. Both Taylor and Jones, who was added in August 1967, were to play important roles in the park's development.

Because the idea of promoting University Research Park had originated in the Charlotte Chamber of Commerce, each successive president of the Chamber was elected to the Board of Directors. Likewise, representatives from the major banks and new residents of the park were included in board membership. W. T. Harris was president of the Chamber of Commerce when discussions were initiated. He was succeeded by D. W. Jones, whose health necessitated his resignation early in his tenure. First Vice President Patrick N. Calhoun succeeded Jones as president of the Chamber of Commerce and thus became a member of the board.

New Financial Plans

Also in 1967, Edwin P. Latimer, chairman of the board of American Credit Corporation and vice president of the Chamber of Commerce, agreed to serve as chairman of a campaign to raise the necessary funds proposed by the committee on finance. At the board meeting on August 2, 1967, Latimer reported that, in conversations with representatives of the banks, bankers seemed to prefer making loans of $100,000 each rather than buying a $50,000 debenture. The board accepted his recommendation and plans were made to confer with officials of the banks to pursue this plan. In a letter dated October 18, 1967, Latimer reported that the five banks contacted had made firm commitments to provide $90,000 each. Less than one year after the organization had been formed, the board authorized borrowing $450,000 from First Union National Bank, First Citizens Bank & Trust Company, Northwestern Bank, North Carolina National Bank, and Wachovia Bank & Trust Company. The resolution authorizing loans stipulated an interest rate of 1/2 percent above prime, but no less than 6 percent per annum. As security, a first lien deed of trust was authorized, cover-

Edwin P. Latimer

ing all property owned by the corporation. Edwin P. Latimer was to continue his solicitation of $1,000 each for memberships from a list of more than fifty firms. Some of these were asked to make additional capital contributions. Latimer assigned to several directors a list of firms for personal solicitation.

Zoning Emphasized

As the University Research Park was being planned and activated it was essential to adopt zoning proposals developed by the planning commission. President Harris asked Dean W. Colvard to appear before the city council on September 27, 1967, to request support of the plan which was then before them. Following is the statement made on that date:

"Mr. Mayor, members of the city council, ladies and gentlemen: As the chancellor of The University of North Carolina at Charlotte and as a director of the University Research Park, I am here to support the zoning of the University Research Park area for the purposes for which the park was created. There are mutual advantages which can accrue to the Charlotte-Mecklenburg area, the state of North Carolina, and The University of North Carolina at Charlotte as a result of such action.

1. The university campus and the park will form the core of the university city which is being planned and which is already emerging. The university is developing a master long-range plan for its campus presently involving about 900 acres. The University Research Park involves a somewhat larger area and is contiguous with the campus. Both areas need to be planned to limit their use to their respective purposes and to assure a proper environment.

2. Economic, industrial, commercial, and governmental enterprises are more and more dependent upon technology, research, and education. Specialized laboratories, computing and tabulating centers, executive management and analysis functions, and other activities designed to produce knowledge, understanding, programs, policies, and pilot operations are attracted to the university. Thus the university becomes an economic as well an educational asset. Its highly skilled and specialized personnel, its libraries, and its opportunities for continuous lifelong learning can become magnets which attract high salaried personnel to the state and the area. The University Research Park will provide an attractive home for enterprises wishing to locate near the university in order to make use of its resources.

3. The University of North Carolina at Charlotte will be strengthened by the presence of specialized personnel in the community. Such benefits will accrue in many ways. I will mention two. In the first place, certain technical and specialized personnel and equipment may be used by the University for instructional purposes. Some staff members of these firms may serve as adjunct professors. This not only supplements scarce talents available but it assures exposure of students to current problems of business enterprises. Secondly, this kind of relationship provides employment opportunities for students, both while they are enrolled in the university and after they graduate.

In my opinion, there is no better place in the United States to develop a first-class university than here. At a time when the university plays a central role in our society we need to lay our plans carefully to maximize its usefulness. I believe the University Research Park will provide an attractive setting for the kinds of research and managerial personnel the university will help to attract. Proper zoning is essential, inexpensive and in the best interest of the Charlotte-Mecklenburg area — and indeed of the state.

I could elaborate on this subject, and I shall be happy to do so if necessary to make clear why I am so enthusiastic about the future of The University of North Carolina at Charlotte and the University Research Park. My singular purpose now is to urge that action be taken to zone the University Research Park area as requested by the professional planners and officials of the nonprofit community development venture under consideration."

Active First Year

When the first year of operation ended Collins & Aikman Corporation was making plans to proceed with the first installation in the park. A financial plan was in place. Some land was optioned. Tract 12 of about sixteen acres held in trust by North Carolina National Bank was appraised. Tract 17 of 165 acres had been under option for $65,007.50 ($1,350.00 per acre) and the owner, Dr. C. W. Robinson, would not extend the lease, saying that he had been offered more money for it. The board authorized the officers to execute a loan up to $70,000 to consummate the purchase. Authorization was also given to purchase tract 11 of thirty acres, tract 16 of ninety acres, and the Morris property of 16 2/3 acres. The price for the Morris property was $28,000, or about $1,680 per acre. A partnership among University Research Park, Collins & Aikman, and J. A. Jones Construction Company had been formed and planning was under way. The financial statement from the beginning of University Research Park in late 1966 through October 31, 1967, reveals that it was not necessary to borrow the full amount authorized because payments to sellers of the land were spread out. The financial summary for the first year, Table 1, also reveals other aspects of the handling of purchases.

On October 12, 1967, Director Graeme Keith, working with J. Norman Pease, Jr. and his associates in developing plans for getting water into the area, reported that city engineers had recommended that a sixteen-inch water line from the twenty-inch UNCC line costing approximately $160,000 should follow Highway 29. Plans for sharing the costs were under discussion. The North Carolina Highway Commission was making plans to broaden Highway 49 from UNCC to Highway 29 into four lanes, to cooperate in building a four-lane entrance to UNCC (later named Broadrick Boulevard), and to plan a road from Highway 49 to Mallard Creek Road. Through the cooperation of UNCC, The Foundation of UNCC, Mecklenburg County, and University Research Park, a four lane right-of-way was provided without cost to the State of North Carolina. Plans were being made to construct the first two-lane section of a road later named Harris Boulevard. At that time plans had not been made for an interchange at the intersection of Harris Boulevard and I-85, then under construction. The importance of this interchange was discussed at the December 6, 1967, meeting.

During this same period the city and county were developing a sewage treatment plant along Toby Creek (north of the UNCC area). In June 1967 J. N. Pease Associates was engaged to make a comprehensive study of the entire area of the park. Their studies included topographic characteristics, land slope, optimal size of parcels, natural drainage, tree cover, soil types, transportation access, water and sewer distribution, power needs and distribution, and other pertinent factors. They also assisted in coordinating city, county, and state agencies. For the first several years they were called upon for reports at each meeting of the directors. In all of these transactions, Sydnor Thompson, a partner in the law firm headed by Joseph W. Grier, Jr., provided legal counsel.

The first year of the University Research Park was characterized by active involvement by officers and board members and extensive cooperation among county, city, and state agencies.

Table 1

Summary of Cash Receipts and Disbursements
From November 29, 1966 to October 31, 1967

Cash Receipts
Loans from bank
November 29, 1966 — on demand —
6% ... $60,000.00
May 3, 1967 — on demand — 6% ... 60,000.00
May 10, 1967 — on demand — 6% ... 44,000.00
Sale of land — Collins & Aikman ... 12,860.50
Rental Income
11 months @ $70 — R. J. Phillips ... 770.00
5 months @ $65 — C. B. Denny ... 325.00
U. S. Soil Bank Payment ... 535.70
... $178,491.20

Cash Disbursements
Payments on land purchases
Tract 10 — Spencer ... $54,738.10
Tract 11 — P. Barton ... 12,523.34
Tract 16 — Mrs. M. Barton ... 38,053.46
Tract 17 — C. W. Robinson ... 68,421.13
Appraisal Fees ... 275.00
Insurance ... 117.92
Interest — on $60,000 note through
May 10, 1967 ... 1,550.00
Repairs — Spencer house ... 32.50
Organization expenses ... 542.52
Legal expenses ... 750.00
Legal and survey expense — P. Barton
property ... 720.30
Pro rata share of Soil Bank Payment
due Dr. C. W. Robinson ... 178.56
... 177,902.83
Cash Balance, October 31, 1967 ... $ 588.37

Land — at cost (less reduction of $12,860.50
for portion sold to Collins & Aikman) — at
October 31, 1967 ... $573,646.31

Payables at October 31, 1967
Notes Payable — Younts Realty & Insurance
Co. (Commission on Spencer property) ... $ 18,000.00
Notes Payable — banks ... 164,000.00
Mortgages Payable ... 411,203.21
... $593,203.21

BREAKING GROUND FOR COLLINS & AIKMAN AND LAUNCHING THE UNIVERSITY RESEARCH PARK

"Charlotte-Mecklenburg has a rare opportunity to plan and guide the growth of a new University City as it rises out of the fields, farms, and forests that cover the area today."
—William E. McIntyre, 1969

Early 1968 saw the public launching of University Research Park and the groundbreaking of Collins & Aikman Corporation's science and service division. The date was January 11, 1968. In effect, this was also the groundbreaking for the park.

Governor Dan K. Moore was scheduled to participate in the groundbreaking, along with President Donald F. McCullough of Collins & Aikman Corporation, Chairman of the Board of County Commissioners Dr. James Martin (who served later as U. S. Congressman and as Governor of North Carolina), Charlotte Mayor Stanford Brookshire, President of the Chamber of Commerce Donald Denton, and UNCC Chancellor Dean W. Colvard.

President McCullough arrived from New York on January 10, in the midst of a very severe ice storm. Roads and runways throughout the state were closed. Governor Moore was unable to attend the ceremony. The only roads leading to the Collins & Aikman building site and the park area were unpaved and completely covered with ice. A luncheon had been planned at UNCC, but weather conditions were so severe that the university, which had only commuter students, had to be closed.

President Harris and some members of the board met with representatives of Collins & Aikman and decided that "the show must go on." The groundbreaking ceremony was moved to the Charlotte City Club. William M.

Donald F. McCullough and Dean W. Colvard at Collins and Aikman groundbreaking

17

Collins and Aikman

Ficklen, who was accustomed to making quick changes in plans, crawled under his residence and filled a bucket with dirt and brought it to the club. Dean W. Colvard, who had been asked to preside and to speak for UNCC, was asked to also speak for Governor Moore. A mortar and pestle were brought from a UNCC chemistry laboratory and President McCullough and Chancellor Colvard, dressed in white laboratory coats, crushed some earth in a warm, dry, and comfortable room on the third floor of the Charlotte City Club before a roomful of Charlotte's leading citizens. Chancellor Colvard's remarks reiterated the importance of university and industry cooperation:

"The official launching of the University Research Park and the beginning of construction by Collins & Aikman Corporation of its Research and Management Center in the park give reality to dreams many leaders in the Charlotte Chamber of Commerce have had and dreams which have been shared by The University of North Carolina at Charlotte.

Much of the energy generated by contemporary society is intellectual energy. The university is a generator of such energy. The tools of the university include books, journals, laboratories, computers, seminars, classrooms, and informal exchanges of ideas. These are also the tools of the industrial and governmental manager and researcher.

Students need exposure to and involvement in both theoretical and applied aspects of the subjects being studied. Management centers such as the one being built by Collins & Aikman and others contemplated for the University Research Park will provide nearby laboratories for practical involvement as well as for employment.

The scholar is involved in both teaching and learning. From his vantage point in the laboratory or the library he has something to learn from the arena where the action is. Likewise the action-oriented specialist needs to update and expand his theory. Scientists and managers in the University Research Park may serve as adjunct professors at the university. University professors may serve as consultants for industry. The advantages are mutual.

18

The University Research Park will serve the state and the community by helping to maximize the impact of the university upon the economic life of this region. Dr. Weldon B. Gibson, executive vice president of Stanford Research Institute in California, has said that, 'one of the first steps in an effective, regional development program is to strengthen the area's institutions of higher learning, gain their interest in participation in the greater cause of regional development, and then see that nothing happens to diminish the intimate relationship between educational and economic planning.'

This university, a creation of Governor Moore's administration, is committed to the kinds of involvement required of good universities at this time in our history. We are happy to see the development of the University Research Park which has been envisioned by leaders in the Charlotte Chamber of Commerce. We welcome the Collins & Aikman plant as the first research-oriented neighbor in the park. We expect to be involved in many kinds of cultural and economic interactions with the community and we believe that the time is right for full development, both of the university and the University Research Park.

And as we plan with these practical ends in mind, we urge that both the university and the University Research Park assign a high priority to the beautification of the entire area. Potentially the area comprising approximately 2,500 acres and including both the campus and the park is one of the beautiful areas of our region.

I shall not attempt to call the roll of all of those whose leadership has been felt in the early history of the university or of the University Research Park. My hope is that the results of your efforts will gain in visibility and be amply rewarding."

With a substitute speaking for Governor Moore, the ceremony became very informal. There was more ad libbing than had been planned, and comments made by other speakers were not recorded. At any rate it was a happy and significant occasion. The ground had been broken. The science and service division for a corporation operating 16 manufacturing plants in North Carolina and employing 7,000 people was exactly the type of installation University Research Park was designed to serve.

The day after the dedication, Donald F. McCullough wrote the following letter suggesting the spirit of the occasion:

"Dear Dean,

Just a short note of congratulations on your performance as a scientist the other day. I understand we came off quite well before the TV cameras!

Seriously, sincere thanks for the fine welcome. We very much look forward to becoming a part of the Charlotte business education community.

Thank you again.

Sincerely,
Donald F. McCullough"

Crossing his letter in the mail was the following note:
"Dear Don,

It was a lot of fun to share the platform with you for the indoor groundbreaking of your new center in the University Research Park. We shall look forward to seeing you when you come to Charlotte, and we want you and your associates to know that we are happy to have you as neighbors.

With kind personal regards, I am
Sincerely yours,
Dean W. Colvard"

On May 9, 1968, the Board of Directors passed a resolution addressed to Governor Dan K. Moore expressing appreciation for his support in launching University Research Park and connecting roads:

WHEREAS, the Honorable Dan K. Moore, Governor of the State of North Carolina, has displayed a strong personal interest in the advancement of The University of North Carolina at Charlotte, and

WHEREAS, Governor Moore, realizing the inter-relationship between education, research, and the future economic development of the Charlotte area, has lent the support of his office to the University Research Park, and

WHEREAS, Governor Moore has personally made possible the construction of an access road to serve The University of North Carolina at Charlotte and the Research Park,

NOW THEREFORE BE IT RESOLVED that the University Research Park Board of Directors hereby offers its sincere thanks and gratitude to Governor Moore and members of the Highway Commission for their support of the University Research Park and related development in the Charlotte area.

Contributing Members

By mid-year 1968 Edwin P. Latimer reported twenty-nine memberships at $1,000 each and extra contributions providing the park with a total capital fund of $51,000. The members and contributors are listed alphabetically in Table 2 on page 20.

This $51,000 represented the only capital contributed to the development of University Research Park in its first twenty years. There was extensive cooperation by governmental and institutional agencies but no outright appropriations to the park as a nonprofit corporation. Other capital was generated by loans and sales. The J. A. Jones Construction Company owned the land pooled with land bought by Collins & Aikman and land purchased by University Research Park with borrowed funds.

Table 2

MEMBERS AND CONTRIBUTORS

Members:

1. American Credit Corporation	$ 1,000
2. Belk Brothers Company	1,000
3. Celanese Corporation	1,000
4. Collins & Aikman Corporation	1,000
5. Concrete Supply Company	1,000
6. John Crosland Company	1,000
7. Duke Power Company	1,000
8. Fiber Industries	1,000
9. First Citizens Bank & Trust Company	1,000
10. First Union National Bank	1,000
11. Freeman & McClintock Company	1,000
12. Grier, Parker, Poe & Thompson	1,000
13. James J. Harris & Company	1,000
14. Harris-Teeter Supermarkets	1,000
15. International Business Machines Corp.	1,000
16. J. A. Jones Construction Company	1,000
17. North Carolina National Bank	1,000
18. Northwestern Bank	1,000
19. A. G. Odell & Associates	1,000
20. J. N. Pease Associates	1,000
21. Piedmont Natural Gas Company	1,000
22. Reeves Brothers, Inc.	1,000
23. Southern Bell Telephone & Telegraph Co.	1,000
24. Southern Real Estate & Insurance Co.	1,000
25. C. D. Spangler Construction Company	1,000
26. C. P. Street & Company	1,000
27. Vinson Realty Company	1,000
28. Wachovia Bank & Trust Company	1,000
29. Younts Realty & Insurance Company	1,000
Members Total	$29,000

Contributors:

1. Duke Power Company	$10,000
2. Piedmont Natural Gas Company	5,000
3. Younts Realty & Insurance Company	7,000
Total Contributions $22,000	
Total Memberships and Contributions	$51,000

Planning Extended

Most of the year 1968 was devoted to the execution of earlier plans and to working with J. N. Pease Associates, UNCC, and planners in the Charlotte/Mecklenburg Planning Commission to develop plans for the park and for University City. On June 5, 1968, County Engineer Ken Hoffman reported that a temporary sewage treatment plant would cost approximately $400,000 and that a request had been made to the federal government for 30 percent of the cost. He indicated that the county would provide $80,000 and University Research Park should provide $200,000 under the plan.

On December 5, 1968, directors of the park met with county commissioners for cocktails and dinner at the Charlotte Athletic Club. Several new commissioners had been elected, and it was thought that all the members of that body of county leaders should be kept up-to-date both on progress and plans. President Harris presided; William M. Ficklen reviewed the reasons for promoting the park; Dean W. Colvard discussed the relationship of the park to UNCC; Patrick N. Calhoun discussed organization and finances; J. Scott Cramer reviewed the vital importance of water and how extensions were to be financed; and Graeme Keith reviewed land use and sewage facilities. Throughout the planning period, efforts were made to keep all public officials fully informed.

In the meantime, UNCC was building two dormitories with a capacity of 1,000 students and other campus building which would require sewage facilities no later than the opening of the new academic year in August 1969. In effect, this established a deadline for having adequate sewage service in place.

Throughout these first years it was necessary to pursue vigorously the development of utilities and roads. Collins & Aikman, Queens Properties (a subsidiary of J. A. Jones Construction Company), and University Research Park shared the costs of extending water and sewer lines not covered by the city and the county. In early 1969 Governor Dan K. Moore approved $500,000 to be used for constructing Harris Boulevard from Highway 49 to I-85 and for a bridge over I-85. By July 1969 J. Scott Cramer reported to the Board of Directors that grading for Harris Boulevard had been roughed-in and that a contract had been let for the bridge. He also reported that an additional $697,865 had been made available to extend Harris Boulevard to Mallard Creek Road. George Broadrick, executive vice president of First Citizens Bank & Trust Company and a highway commissioner, participated effectively in these negotiations.

Toward the end of 1968 President Harris was authorized to appoint an executive committee composed of Frank McQuilkin, Edwin L. Jones, Jr., J. Scott Cramer, Patrick N. Calhoun, and Dean W. Colvard to work with him as chairman to make decisions between board meetings.

The Second Occupant - Reeves Brothers, Inc.

Under the leadership of William M. Ficklen of the Charlotte Chamber of Commerce, the second occupant of the park was in the process of making final plans. The following letter to the director of research activities of Reeves Brothers, Inc. illustrates Mr. Ficklen's role, cooperation among UNCC, University Research Park, and the Chamber of Commerce, and the necessity of convincing prospective occupants that UNCC was to be developed into a complete university:

"Dear Mr. Greenspan:

Mr. William M. Ficklen has shared with me, on a confidential basis, some of his recent conversations with you concerning your continuing exploration of the location in the University Research Park for your research activities.

On the basis of our recent contacts we have looked for-ward to the prospect of having you in the university com-munity, and I take this occasion to renew our welcome and to give you a brief report concerning the develop-ment of the university.

Both our physical plant and our academic planning are developing on schedule. We have two twelve-story dor-mitories, each providing accommodations for 500 stu-dents, under construction. They are scheduled to provide on-campus residential facilities for 1,000 students in the fall of 1969. Other buildings, including a large health and physical education facility, a fine arts building, an addi-tional classroom building, a major library expansion, and a cafeteria, are well advanced in the planning stages and are expected to be under construction by the end of 1968.

The academic program has been reorganized on a divi-sional basis, and a number of leadership positions have been filled in recent weeks. We are also moving into a major academic planning program aided by substantial gifts which have recently been made available from two foundations. Beginning on September 1, 1968, Dr. Paul Miller, formerly Provost at Michigan State University, President of West Virginia University and until recently Assistant Secretary (Education) of the Department of Health, Education and Welfare, is joining us and will give direction to our University Planning Studies. Our sum-mer school enrollment was about 38 percent above that of last year and we are projecting about 2,400 students when we open this fall. Our projection for 1975 is 8,000 stu-dents.

I shall not go into greater detail concerning the institu-tion, but I did want to affirm that any plans we may have discussed earlier with regard to relationships with spe-cialized personnel in the community are still a part of our planning. In fact, if there is any difference these relation-ships have been expanded.

If there is any way by which we may be of assistance to you and your associates, we hope you will not hesitate to call upon us. We welcome the prospect of having you in our immediate community.

Sincerely yours,

Dean W. Colvard"

This approach was taken with many other firms that had been contacted.

The site purchased by Reeves Brothers, Inc. was a 21-acre tract of the Jones property between I-85 and Re-search Drive. A relatively low price had been quoted by the J. A. Jones Construction Company to encourage de-velopment in that portion of the park. This purchase was closed in March 1969. Reeves Brothers, Inc. is one of the nation's leading diversified manufacturers of textiles, coated fabrics, polyurethane foam, and home furnishing products. Their plan was to build a research and develop-ment center to serve their industry. Construction did not begin until several months later.

Real Estate Committee Activated

Although acquisition of land for University Research Park was begun by realtor Paul Younts even before the chartering of the organization, efforts were greatly inten-sified after a financial plan was developed and the orga-nization was legally established. Three prominent real-

tors, Paul Younts, Ed Vinson, and Louis Rose, Sr., were added to the Board of Directors. The board executed an agreement with them which encouraged the cooperation of other realtors. By the end of 1969 several options to purchase had been executed.

Largely through the activities of William M. Ficklen, industry recruiter for the Charlotte Chamber of Com-merce, and the real estate committee, continuous efforts were made to identify prospective residents for the park. Brochures were mailed to Fortune's top 1,000 firms and to other selected corporations throughout the country call-ing their attention to what the community had to offer for relocation or expansion. Industrial recruiters of local banks, as well as most of the directors of the park, par-ticipated in recruitment. These efforts were coordinated through William M. Ficklen and President Harris. In March, 1969, Ed Vinson reported for the real estate com-mittee that a price of $5,000 per acre had been estab-lished.

University City Plan

Early in 1969, William E. McIntyre, Director of the Charlotte-Mecklenburg Planning Commission, released a zoning plan that had been approved for an area designat-ed as University City which included University Re-search Park, UNCC, and surrounding areas. In explaining this plan, he said "Charlotte-Mecklenburg has a rare op-portunity to plan and guide the growth of a new Univer-sity City as it rises out of the fields, farms, and forests that cover the area today." He estimated population of the area to be 38,000 by 1985-90.

This plan envisioned both single-family and multi-family residences and greenways designated as public parks. McIntyre described the Town Center included in his plan as "a delightful community magnet — a place where people come together not only to do business but where they gather to have group meetings, see exhibits, enjoy terrace dining, window shop in a pleasant atmo-sphere, see a movie, or engage in a variety of enjoyable activities." He added that the Town Center would in-clude a "carefully integrated concept of offices, stores, parking, courts, plazas, and pedestrian circulation — pos-sibly built on different levels with some high-rise build-ings."

McIntyre had worked closely with A. G. Odell who had been commissioned to do a long-range plan for UNCC. Included in their original plan was a pedestrian overpass between the area where the first dormitories were being built at UNCC and the shopping center on the opposite side of Highway 49. While the idea of "Uni-versity Place" between Highway 29 and I-85 had not been proposed at that time, there had been discussion among directors of University Research Park about the need for a hotel and continuing education center in the area.

The release of this plan provided additional assurance to park officers and directors that city/county governments were supporting their efforts in deeds, as well as words.

Financial Plan Becomes a Reality

The years 1968 and 1969 were crucial in putting financial plans into action. By July, 1968, Treasurer Patrick N. Calhoun reported that total indebtedness was $267,000 and that the bank balance was $12,700. Money was being borrowed from the banks as needed at an interest rate of one-half percent above prime, which was about nine percent. During these early years, University Research Park had no staff and no mailing address. A modest supplement was paid to the Charlotte Chamber of Commerce for the services rendered by William M. Ficklen and other members of its staff. Financial records were kept by the treasurer, an officer in one of the supporting banks. The rate of expenditures was increasing and the corpora-

tion had no income. Land which had been purchased and improvements made were the only collateral. The financial report through October 31, 1969, revealed total assets of $662,973.98. Of this, $591,074.09 represented property purchased at cost. Liabilities included demand notes payable to banks amounting to $415,000.00 and mortgage installments due in 1969, '71, and '72 totaling $246,722.25. This represented a deficit of $61,901.05 when commitments through 1972 were taken into account.

Although this project had represented an act of faith in the future of UNCC and the area, some directors had begun to express concern each time they approved borrowing more money to pay interest on borrowed money. This concern grew as economic pressure was being felt in much of the national economy. After two-and-a-half years of existence University Research Park had generated no income.

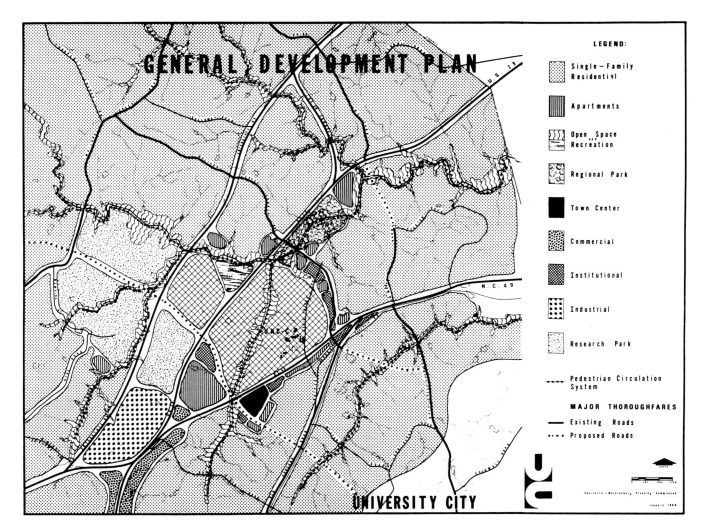

1969 University City Plan

BREAKTHROUGH AND FINANCIAL RECOVERY

"IBM was a tremendous catalyst for growth."
—David A. Taylor

An important stimulus to the future development of University Research Park and the University City area occurred on April 1, 1970, when a formal dedication and ribbon cutting was held for Harris Boulevard, the new road from Highway 49 to Mallard Creek Road. D. McLauchlin Faircloth, chairman of the North Carolina Highway Commission, was the principal speaker. Board Vice President Graeme Keith was chairman and presiding officer. Others who made testimonial remarks were Charlotte Mayor John M. Belk, Charlotte Chamber of Commerce President George Broadrick, and Mecklenburg County Commission Chairman Charles M. Lowe. Present, but not speaking, was Representative Charles R. Jonas. Open to traffic at this time were two lanes connecting Highways 49, 29, and I-85.

An extension west of I-85 to Mallard Creek Road was also under construction at this time. Commissioner Faircloth stated that Governor Moore had made funds available to initiate this project, that a four-lane right-of-way had been provided by UNCC, The Foundation of UNCC, Mecklenburg County, and University Research Park, and that construction of additional lanes was expected to come later. James B. McDuffie parked his panel truck near the ceremonies and displayed a sign protesting the use of highway funds to build Harris Boulevard.

Breakthrough: IBM Buys Land

When the directors met on June 2, 1970, they were told by President Harris that International Business Machines Corporation had taken an option, at $5,000 per acre, on about 450 acres of the land which had been purchased by University Research Park. IBM had paid $28,800 for the option. This long-awaited breakthrough was received with a mixture of relief and excitement. A request that zoning restrictions be modified to permit "light manufacturing" was endorsed for recommendation to the proper authorities.

George Broadrick, president of the Chamber of Commerce, and President Harris of University Research Park, made a public announcement that reflected the feelings of success and relief shared by park directors. Mr. Broadrick said:

"One of the underlying reasons for the establishment of the research park was that Charlotte had been bypassed on several occasions by some prominent research-oriented firms which had ultimately decided to locate in the Research Triangle and other locations in the Southeast. Another obvious reason was to further the economic development of the entire community by bringing to Charlotte the highest type of executives and scientific personnel. This personnel would, in turn, contribute to the intellectual growth of the community.

The Chamber of Commerce, through its industrial manager, Mr. William M. Ficklen, has been working on a confidential basis for the past three years this month with this firm. During that time, this firm and its representatives, under assumed names, have visited many people in our community, talking with representatives of both our city and county governments, the Planning Commission, other manufacturing firms, educational institutions, especially The University of North Carolina at Charlotte, and many business and civic leaders throughout our community.

To all of these people we would like to express our deep gratitude for their willingness to go beyond the call of duty in supplying the information that was needed in order to help this firm arrive at the decision to locate here in Charlotte. This has truly been a team effort, requiring the full cooperation of so many of our citizens; and to them, we are deeply grateful for they helped in so many ways . . . "

President Harris identified the company by saying:

"Indeed it is a happy day for us in Charlotte and, particularly, for the University Research Park. This is the day for which we have been waiting with much anticipation, and I would like to express my keen excitement and gratification over the announcement that has just been made by International Business Machines Corporation stating that they have taken an option on 450 acres in the University Research Park.

The University Research Park is a nonprofit corporation. Credit for the funding of the Research Park, which has been in excess of $1 million, goes to our local banks, as it was they who have put up the money for the purchase of the property and for providing the financing. We would be remiss in not complimenting them on the foresightedness, initiative, and enterprise which they have displayed in this project and in similar projects as well. We are indebted to our city-county governments for their help in the extension of the water and sewer facilities. We are grateful to the Highway Department for building a connecting road which provides access to the university from the University Research Park and from that area of the county west to I-85. This has all been done with the conviction that we, the citizens of our city, want to do our dead-level best to promote and create as many jobs for our community as we possibly can. With this thought in mind, we have put our financial resources, our energies, and our talents into this project so that we can provide a sounder and broader economic base for our community."

President Harris raised the question of what disposition should be made of funds remaining after repayment of all the loans which had been advanced by the banks and the remaining commitments to former owners of land. Some directors even hinted at the possibility of repaying all debts and liquidating the corporation. After three and a half years of borrowing money to pay interest on borrowed money while receiving no income, a feeling of uneasiness was evident. Furthermore, UNCC was expanding and surplus money which would have accrued to it through the UNCC Foundation if University Research Park were liquidated would have been very helpful. It was decided that there would be discussion with the chancellor of the university and others on this option and a decision should be made soon about another option, investment in additional land.

Notwithstanding the great feeling of relief which the announcement of the sale to IBM generated, it was necessary to pass a resolution authorizing officers to borrow up to $600,000 to keep payments to former landowners current until the IBM sale could be closed. The resolution was passed, although the bank balance was only $454 on February 4, 1970, and only $20,000 of unused credit remained in the $450,000 authorization. The interest rate was holding at about nine percent.

Additional Land Purchases Authorized

At the next meeting of the board on July 1, 1970, President Harris asked for further consideration about what should be done with surplus funds when full payment for the land sold was received. An excerpt of the minutes shows that the chancellor of UNCC,

"speaking for the university, expressed great satisfaction in what the University Research Park Board of Directors had done in assembling the research park and in attracting, in such a short time, such outstanding tenants. He felt this park was an extremely valuable contribution to the university, as well as the community as a whole, and

suggested, therefore, that in the long range he personally felt that it would be more meaningful to the university to have the Board of Directors, with its top leadership, working for the good of the community as a 'going concern' rather than liquidating it now. He felt, therefore, that we should invest in additional land, and perhaps, because we would now have equity in such property, the banks might be willing to assist in the purchase of additional land."

The officers were authorized to proceed with negotiations to purchase additional land. The possibility of purchasing some of the land owned by the J. A. Jones Construction Company (Queens Properties) and already included in the park for zoning and planning purposes had been discussed. The University Research Park purchased 156 acres of the Jones land. This property, extending attractively along I-85 and Harris Boulevard, was scheduled to have the utilities necessary for its future development. Edwin L. Jones, Jr. stated that his company had agreed to sell 150 acres at $4,000 per acre and that they would pay the realtor's commission. The board voted to exercise the option to purchase.

Renewed Enthusiasm

In contrast to meetings held a year earlier, the October 7, 1970, meeting generated feelings of success and achievement. After paying for the Jones land, the park still had some $200,000, drawing interest, which could be used at a later date for capital investment or for whatever purposes the directors might choose. President Harris' statement gave expression to the lift in spirit which was shared by the directors:

"Without a doubt the obvious highlight of 1970 was the successful completion and sale of 450 acres to IBM. This single sale not only took us out of debt, but placed us in a liquid position whereby we could invest in additional land. Most important of all, however, is the tremendously favorable impact IBM will have on Charlotte through the utilization of this property. There has been no new word from IBM as to when they will begin construction. However, I am sure that each of you join me in hoping that this announcement will be made soon. It is felt from information which we have that eventually IBM will place some six to eight buildings in campus style in the University Research Park and will eventually employ approximately 5,000 people.

Another major development during the year was the purchase of 32 acres of land by Allstate Insurance Company from Collins & Aikman. They plan to erect an office building of approximately 125,000 square feet and to employ some 500 to 600 people.

Work on Harris Boulevard has been completed and is now open for traffic. Also, the diamond interchange was completed tying in Harris Boulevard with I-85. This will be open to the public in July.

I feel that a very satisfactory beginning has been made for the park, and that because of the contributions made by this Board of Directors, our community will definitely benefit from an economic point of view. Its favorable impact will continue during the years yet to come, and I personally wish to thank each of you for the time and effort you individually have given thus far in making this University Research Park a successful project. There is yet much work to be done, and I know that each of you will continue to do more than your part as has been the case in the past, and through this type of cooperation we can bring additional firms to locate here. Again, let me thank you for your help and cooperation."

IBM had actually purchased 428.137 acres of land at $5,000 per acre for a total of $2,140,685. The financial report for 1970, Table 3, was much more satisfying than any to that date.

There was enthusiastic adoption of a resolution of appreciation to North Carolina National Bank, First Citizens Bank & Trust Company, First Union National Bank, Northwestern Bank, and Wachovia Bank & Trust Company for the great confidence they had displayed in advancing funds to operate the corporation since the first land purchases were made in 1967.

The increase in business to be transacted prompted the directors to resume monthly meetings and, on some occasions, to have special meetings. At the meeting on November 4, 1970, Attorney Sydnor Thompson reported that UNCC had received the necessary clearances to offer the park a strip of 13 acres of land adjacent to the park on the west side of I-85 which had been separated from the main campus tract by the location of I-85. Purchase by the park was authorized at the appraised price of $29,250. Because of a reversion clause in the deed from Mecklenburg County conveying this property to UNCC which specified that in the event the property was not used for the purposes for which it was given it would revert to the county, the chancellor recommended that payment be made to Mecklenburg County.

Table 3

STATEMENT OF RECEIPTS AND DISBURSEMENTS COVERING SALE OF LAND TO IBM

Sale to IBM of 428.137 acres @ $5,000 per acre		$2,140,685.00
Less option credits		50,400.00
Less cost of revenue stamps		2,141.00
Less pro rata share of N.C. ad valorem taxes		982.49
Net		$2,087,161.51
Disbursements:		
Payments of bank loans to NCNB, as Agent		
Principal	$600,000.00	
Interest	12,183.60	$ 612,183.60
Mrs. Helen S. Spencer		58,129.06
Mrs. Margaret L. Barton		39,324.38
Dr. C. W. Robinson		76,415.61
Paul Barton		13,217.09
Kenneth Griffin, Attorney		1,023.21
Jane Harris Nierenberg		67,195.25
NCNB, Trustee (Morris Property)		58,520.74
J. A. Jones Construction Company		93,128.32
Register of Deeds		590.50
Vinson Realty Company		50.00
Mitchell Clark		50.00
		$1,019,827.76
Balance		$1,067,333.75

Officers were authorized to purchase a tract of property owned by the Salvation Army on Morehead Street and to execute a transfer of this property to the J. A. Jones Construction Company in partial payment for the land being purchased from them. The financial report following the purchase from Jones revealed that University Research Park paid $99,900.00 for the Salvation Army property and paid J. A. Jones Construction Company an additional $525,908.88, a total of $625,808.88 for the 156 acres purchased, an average of $4,012.00 per acre. For the first time in its history University Research Park had no outstanding indebtedness against its real estate. In addition, it began the year 1971 with a bank balance of $65,745.00, a certificate of deposit of $200,000.00, and outstanding commitments of $66,018.00.

Allstate Insurance Company

When the 1971 annual meeting was convened on February 3, President Harris reported that Allstate Insurance Company had finalized its purchase of some of the park land owned by Collins & Aikman, which he had announced earlier, and was proceeding with building plans. Allstate Insurance was the largest stock company auto insurer and was expanding rapidly in other lines including homeowners, individual and group health, boatowners, and finance, as well as individual and group life. They planned to install sophisticated computer equipment capable of communicating with the Allstate home office in Illinois and other regional offices. They expected to serve more than 700,000 policies in force in the region. In the *Charlotte News* on January 7, 1972, Emery Wister described the four million dollar structure as "the third largest single company office building in Charlotte," exceeded only by buildings serving Duke Power Company and Celanese Corporation.

As was the case with most of the firms locating in the park, more good news was to come later. On May 29, 1976, Ted H. Ousley, Allstate's regional associate vice president, announced a major realignment of the company's regional office system in the South which resulted in the addition of about 200 employees in the University Research Park facility. The responsibility for servicing policy holders in Georgia would be transferred from Atlanta. The restructured regional center would now serve North Carolina, South Carolina, east Tennessee, and Georgia. Allstate's Mecklenburg payroll was estimated to increase by $1 million annually and total employment would reach about 700.

Other Reports

President Harris also reported that Harris Boulevard was open for traffic and that the interchange which Governor Moore and the Highway Commission had authorized to connect this new road to I-85 would be finished by July.

Although they had purchased their site in March 1969, it was not until late 1972 that Reeves Brothers, Inc. held their open house. With Allstate still under construction, Reeves Brothers, Inc. became the second operational tenant in the park.

For the first time, IBM had a representative on the University Research Park Board of Directors. Because they neither had initiated their building program nor had assigned any personnel to the anticipated development, they recommended John Temple, their branch manager in Charlotte, as their representative.

There was discussion at the meeting on March 3, 1971, of whether or not steps should be taken to find a hotel or motel developer interested in building a facility in the northeast corner of the intersection of I-85 and Harris Boulevard. The chancellor of UNCC pointed out that there would be a growing need for conference and continuing education facilities to serve the university, the corporations located in the park, the community, and the entire region. Further study was indicated.

Special Expenditures

When Harry J. Nicholas showed the board the brochure prepared three years earlier he recommended that a new one be developed at an estimated cost of $2,500 for 5,000 copies. It was agreed that he should proceed, with the understanding that Collins & Aikman Corporation and J. A. Jones Construction Company would pay $750 each and University Research Park would pay $1,000.

The increase in business since the sale to IBM created a new awareness of the work load being borne by the Charlotte Chamber of Commerce. As a partial compensation for its services, the board voted to pay $500 per month. Since the chamber had provided the office services and much of the leadership in seeking new tenants from the inception of the park, a motion was made and passed to pay that organization $7,500 for services previously rendered. An additional payment of $5,000 was authorized to pay William M. Ficklen for special services rendered in administering University Research Park and for assisting with the sale of properties.

Allstate Insurance Company

President Harris read a letter he had received from the chancellor of UNCC expressing his desire to establish an office of development to seek private funds for the university and requesting $100,000 to support that office. Also at this time, the Athletic Foundation at UNCC was being initiated. After discussion, the board authorized $100,000 for the development office and $6,000 to support the athletic program. These were the first grants made to UNCC by the park.

Hiatus in Development

In contrast to the action-filled board meetings of the last half of 1970 and the first half of 1971, the agendas of the meetings in the last half of 1971 listed only routine operating items. The deaths of two stalwart realtors brought replacements who were to become important contributors to the future of the park. General Paul Younts was replaced by Claude Q. Freeman, Sr. and Louis Rose, Sr. was replaced by Louis Rose, Jr. Freeman had been involved with Romeo H. Guest in assembling some of the land for the Research Triangle Park more than a decade earlier. The access road to Reeves Brothers' property was named Louis Rose Place in memory of Louis Rose, Sr.

J. Norman Pease, Jr. continued to report to directors on land-use studies. Concern about the lack of success in attracting new corporate tenants prompted the board to reduce the asking price of land to $2,500 per acre. At the end of 1971 the financial report showed total liquid assets of about $275,000 and land holdings unchanged since the purchase of the Jones property and the strip west of I-85.

Claude Q. Freeman, Sr.

Patrick N. Calhoun, W.T. Harris, Claude Q. Freeman, Sr. and Louis Rose, Jr. on IBM property, 1972.

SIX YEARS OF INACTION, UNCERTAINTY, AND PLANNING

"The potential for Charlotte's University Research Park is virtually unlimited."
—Patrick N. Calhoun

Although University Research Park, as a corporation, was free of debts to the banks, the lack of major new development from 1972 through 1977 was a source of great concern to the officers and directors. Collins & Aikman Corporation, Allstate Insurance Company, and Reeves Brothers, Inc. were moving ahead with their programs as planned, but inaction of IBM and failure to attract other tenants were sources of discouragement.

Status of IBM Development Uncertain

Early in 1972, IBM advised that they would not begin their building by September 23, 1973, the date specified in the sales agreement. They requested release from that commitment and offered to resell approximately 200 acres of their property to University Research Park at the price paid for it. IBM aroused even greater concern among park directors when they mentioned the possibility of selling all of their property. Near the end of 1972, the Billy Graham Foundation was given an option on 161 acres of the land which had been conditionally released by IBM as a possible location for a library and museum. After further study, a decision was made to locate that program at Wheaton College in Illinois. This did not cause great disappointment since there was some uncertainty about the compatibility of their proposed facility with the major purposes of the park. Their option funds were returned. Some other promising prospects were lost to locations where residential areas and other amenities were more fully developed.

Several actions were taken in an effort to improve effectiveness in recruiting new tenants. William M. Ficklen of the Chamber of Commerce was appointed executive director. A logo and new letterhead were designed, although University Research Park still had no separate address. The board was enlarged to provide for representa-

tion by Allstate Insurance Company and Reeves Brothers, Inc. A delegation[8] visited IBM headquarters in New York on March 30, 1972, to assure top executives of continuing support and to express the hope that they would find it possible to activate their plans. The great reduction in the size of computer components made possible by new technology was among the factors which decreased the urgency for IBM's expansion at that time.

North Mecklenburg Roads Studied

In May 1973 John A. Tate, Jr. reported on a study of roads in northern Mecklenburg County. He emphasized the importance of extending Harris Boulevard to I-77 (south of Davidson and Lake Norman) and of making it into a four-lane divided boulevard. The directors of the Chamber of Commerce were invited to a luncheon with University Research Park directors at UNCC to keep the leadership fully informed of the needs and the opportunities for developing the park and northern Mecklenburg County. President Harris was asked to appoint a committee to invite Billy Rose and Perrin Anderson (assistant secretary and local representative, respectively, of the North Carolina Department of Transportation) and members of the Charlotte City Council, the Charlotte/Mecklenburg Planning Commission, and the County Commissioners to a general meeting for the purpose of emphasizing the road needs of northern Mecklenburg County. Patrick N. Calhoun was asked to serve as chairman of the committee made up of John A. Tate, Jr., David Taylor, and Dean W. Colvard.

Chamber of Commerce Continuing Support Cultivated

When the directors of the Chamber of Commerce visited University Research Park on July 11, 1973, Patrick N. Calhoun, who had been involved from the beginning either as a representative of North Carolina National Bank, president of the Chamber of Commerce, or as treasurer of

---

Mayor John Belk, C.C. Cameron, Dean W. Colvard, and T.N. Storrs.

Patrick N. Calhoun

University Research Park, greeted them with words which reflected his unwavering enthusiasm for and commitment to the project. Neither the directors of the Chamber of Commerce nor of University Research Park suspected that only a few months later his failing health would force his resignation. His prepared statement was:

"Gentlemen, we are grateful for this opportunity to meet with you today, and I want to take just a couple of minutes before your tour of the University Research Park facilities to highlight some of the background of this community project.

Seven years ago, the Chamber Board of Directors, as part of its 1966 program of work, adopted a recommendation calling for action to be taken which would lay the foundation for a research park near The University of North Carolina at Charlotte.

A research park was deemed highly desirable for Charlotte for a number of reasons. First, we had no such facility and Charlotte was not in a position to compete with other communities in the acquisition of these sophisticated, prestigious, technology-oriented, new operations. As you know, research facilities attract a high caliber of trained scientists and administrators, create a high average personal income for employees, and are ecologically desirable.

---

⁹ Some of the IBM acreage purchased was outside of but adjacent to the park.

The Chamber of Commerce worked with the City-County Planning Commission on feasibility studies which justified the creation and development of such a research park.

In early 1967 a nonprofit corporation was organized with the financial support of Charlotte's five largest banks who committed for a term loan to provide financing for the acquisition of property located three miles northwest of the Charlotte city limits and near The University of North Carolina at Charlotte. Approximately 25 community-minded businessmen directed the project, and at this time I particularly want to single out one of them for his outstanding contribution to this venture. The man I am talking about is Bill Harris who had served as president of the Chamber of Commerce the preceeding year and who in 1967 took on the presidency of University Research Park. Through his strong support, his leadership and genuine interest, University Research Park has made and will continue to make a significant contribution to the community; and I believe Dr. Colvard would agree it is a valuable asset now and for the future of The University of North Carolina at Charlotte.

Al Pruitt is going to give each of you a brochure which lists the current officers and directors of the park and also contains some vital statistics plus other information of interest.

The park has excellent roads, all utilities and services, and desirable protective zoning. Its first tenant, Collins & Aikman Corporation, has been joined by Reeves Brothers Company, and Allstate Insurance. In addition, IBM has purchased 750 acres⁹ for future use.

The potential for Charlotte's University Research Park is virtually unlimited. Its geographic location is ideal and is greatly enhanced by the excellent transportation facilities in the area. Furthermore, its proximity to the fastest growing campus of The University of North Carolina system gives it access to an expanding reservoir of scientific brain power at UNCC.

Another factor in its potential is the growing number of UNCC graduate students who are available for part-time work as well as an excellent program of post graduate study for the scientific and research-oriented staffs located in the park.

Last but not least among its assets is the "University City" development. This zoned area should provide the attractive living conditions, cultural advantages, and campus atmosphere that are most desirable in a residential community today.

As you tour the research park this afternoon, we hope you can visualize its undeveloped state of six years ago and what it can be by 1980. We believe its growth will be significant."

Chancellor Colvard of UNCC reminded the board of the excellent plans for developing the area around the university, known as "University City." This area included approximately 1,100 acres owned by the University and 1,400 acres designated as University Research Park, as well as other adjoining properties. Directors of the park were invited to meet with representatives of Caudil Rowlett Scott, commissioned to make a long-range plan for UNCC in 1974. Concern was expressed about the lack of development of the proposed shopping center on Highway 49 and the fear that if the development schedules proposed were not followed undesirable growth could get out of hand. It was, however, an encouraging sign that as plans for the park and UNCC were developing, Mecklenburg County was planning an expansion of sewage treatment facilities with a capacity of 2,000,000 gallons for the Mallard Creek area.

Dauntless Leaders Lost

The loss of two key leaders in the planning and development of University Research Park was announced at the meeting of November 12, 1974. William M. Ficklen of the Charlotte Chamber of Commerce had died and Patrick N. Calhoun had resigned because of ill health. Both had given generously of their energies and talents during the first eight years of the park. Expressions of gratitude were recorded. J. W. Claud was elected to succeed Patrick N. Calhoun as treasurer, and Charles Crawford was asked to handle William M. Ficklen's duties until permanent assignments could be worked out.

At the annual meeting in February 1975, G. Jackson Burney of the Chamber of Commerce was elected executive director and secretary, the positions formerly held by William M. Ficklen. The chancellor of UNCC reported on some further explorations of the possibility of building a hotel on UNCC property in the northeast corner of the intersection of Harris Boulevard and I-85. No action was recommended to, or taken by, the board.

Research Triangle Institute and Research Triangle Foundation Discussed

Dr. George Herbert, executive director of the Research Triangle Institute, was invited to update the board on his organization and its plans to open a branch in the Charlotte area. He stated that the Research Triangle Institute employed about 600 people and had revenue in 1974 of $13,000,000. This research organization, begun in 1959, engaged in a broad array of research/contract activities. It had become one of the largest of 18 such not-for-profit organizations in the country. Dr. Herbert said that in opening a new branch in the Charlotte area, he would want to work very closely with UNCC. He made it clear that there would be no fundraising activities in Charlotte to support this new venture. Dr. James Cox, director of UNCC's Institute of Urban Studies (later UNCC Urban Institute), had been designated to provide liaison between this RTI branch and UNCC.[10]

The annual meeting held on February 4, 1976, featured an address by Ned Huffman, executive vice president of the Research Triangle Foundation. He emphasized that one thing they had learned from their experience was that patience was very much in order. Research Triangle Park, he said, had owed $1.3 million in 1965 and was considering selling its land. At that time their organiza-

tion had been in existence for almost ten years. Directors present, realizing that the University Research Park itself had been organized for about ten years, listened carefully to the success story of the Research Triangle Park in its second ten years. Mr. Huffman pointed out that in the last ten years employees in their park had increased from 700 to 11,000 and payrolls from $3 million to $165 million. New construction committed at that time was $140 million.

Efforts to Generate New Activity

Reporting for the real estate committee, Ed Vinson urged that it was time to "wake up" development efforts after several years with very little progress. A major limitation discussed was the absence of water/sewer facilities, which had retarded residential expansion. All seemed to agree that a new force was needed to break the development "log-jam." A proposed new hospital on Highway 29 and the shopping center provided in the plans on Highway 49 were mentioned as possible incentives which seemed about to be realized. Developments in health planning for the area seemed to favor building the next new hospital on Green Acres property (adjacent to UNCC) owned by Mecklenburg County.

Although members of the board may not have anticipated the impact of the brief meeting on April 2, 1975, the action taken paved the way for important leadership changes in the future. Seddon "Rusty" Goode, Jr., chairman of Interstate Securities Company, was elected to membership on the board. He was to become a major leader in the future reorganization and development of the University Research Park.

The meeting of February 4, 1976, was concluded with the appointment of a study committee chaired by Seddon "Rusty" Goode, Jr. and including David Taylor and Dean W. Colvard. The committee was to confer with Drs. Wayne Walcott, Nelson Nunnally, and Patrick Beaton of UNCC on new approaches to developing University Research Park. These faculty and staff of the UNCC Department of Geography and Earth Sciences and Institute for Urban Studies had been commissioned by University Research Park and the Charlotte Chamber of Commerce to make a study and propose strategies for targeting industries and firms for location in the park. It was apparent to all present that the time had come for a renewal of development efforts.

Another important action taken in 1976 was the appointment of Maurice Ewing as economic development representative to work with University Research Park and the Chamber of Commerce in seeking new tenants for the park and new industries or business enterprises for the Charlotte community. University Research Park and the Charlotte Chamber of Commerce shared the cost of Ewing's salary and expenses on a 50/50 basis. At a meeting of the directors on July 21, 1976, Seddon "Rusty"

---

[10] After about 18 months, the representative of RTI was recalled and the branch office was not developed.

Goode, Jr. recommended that the park commit $12,500 annually for this purpose and ask the Chamber of Commerce to match these funds with an equal amount for a period of two years. The outcome was that Maurice Ewing was employed as a staff member of the Chamber of Commerce and assigned specific responsibility for seeking new tenants for the park.

Although no new tenants were added to the park during 1977, there was evidence of follow-up on the studies of other parks and of existing opportunities which had been a topic of continuing discussion during the year. When President Harris convened the annual meeting on February 28, 1977, he called for a report from Maurice Ewing, who mentioned some promising prospects but had no firm commitments to report.

Leadership Changes at End of First Decade

At the February, 1977 meeting, President Harris stated that after serving for ten years, he should not be nominated for re-election. Since he had made his wishes known in advance of the meeting, an appropriate plaque expressing appreciation for his leadership had been prepared. The inscription read:

> "In special recognition of his leadership so willingly provided in the founding and development of University Research Park, Inc., and in appreciation of his qualities of dedication, persuasion, perception, and desire to make Charlotte-Mecklenburg a better place to live, and in gratitude for his generous and unselfish contribution of time and energies to make University Research Park, Inc. a significant part of the community and a bridge between business and The University of North Carolina at Charlotte, now therefore the Board of Directors of University Research Park, Inc. do hereby commend W. T. "Bill" Harris for his exemplary performance as president of the University Research Park from 1967 to 1977."

Members gave Harris a standing ovation expressing their gratitude. In a further expression of gratitude, W. T. "Bill" Harris was elected lifetime director and honorary chairman.

David Taylor, a director almost from the beginning of University Research Park and an executive of Celanese Corporation with extensive experience in performing and administering industrial research, was elected president to succeed Harris.

As the new president, David Taylor concentrated in 1977 on the study made by Walcott, Nunnally, and Beaton and on plans to improve roads and utilities serving the park. At the meeting of June 20, 1977, President Taylor recommended that University Research Park contribute $10,000 to a merit scholarship fund being established at UNCC in honor of Chancellor Colvard, who had submitted his request to retire at the end of 1978, and his wife, Martha. He reported that Mr. and Mrs. Edwin Jones, Jr. had given a challenge grant of $25,000 to launch this merit scholarship fund.[11] The recommendation was approved. The financial report at the end of 1977 showed that the park had approximately $200,000 over and above outstanding commitments. At the last meeting of the board in 1977 it was reported that the extension of Harris Boulevard from Highway 49 to Newell had been included in the DOT's work program.

Although the organization was out of debt and held modest financial reserves, it was apparent that neither President Taylor nor members of the board were satisfied with the rate of the University Research Park's development.

---

[11] By the end of 1987, the corpus of this fund was more than $1 million and four meritorious students, selected annually, were receiving full-expense scholarships.

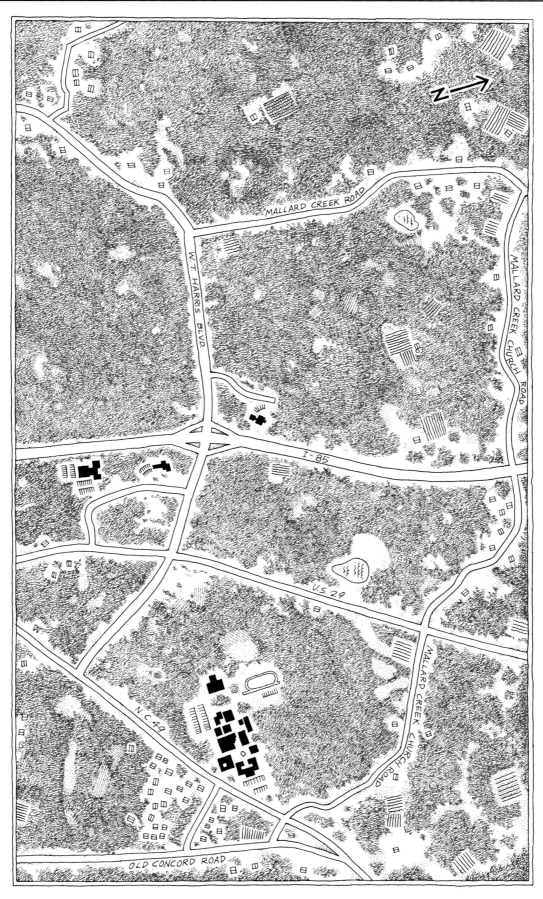

University Research Park (left of center), The University of North Carolina at Charlotte (lower center) — 1977

UNCC Continues to Grow and Commitment of Leaders Remains Strong

Notwithstanding the absence of major new developments, most, if not all, directors maintained a strong commitment to the purposes which created University Research Park. The general environment was more favorable than it had been in the beginning. Enrollment at UNCC had increased about 400 percent, from 1,715 students in 1966 to 8,504 in 1977; enrollment of graduate students had increased from 163 in 1969, when the first programs were approved, to 1,387 in 1977; Research Triangle Park in the Raleigh/Durham/Chapel Hill area was expanding; there was clear evidence of increasing reliance on education and technology in the economy; and cooperation among all governmental and institutional agencies involved in planning University City was excellent. Had these conditions not existed it would have been difficult to sustain a viable organization composed of already-busy people.

By 1977 there was encouraging news that more action was on the horizon. On November 17, 1977, President Taylor sent each director a copy of "An Appraisal of University Research Park" by Nelson Nunnally, David Patterson, and Wayne Walcott of the Department of Geography and Earth Sciences at UNCC, and asked them to study the recommendations in preparation for full discussion at the next meeting. The recommendations included some relaxation of tenant restrictions and ways of improving industry-targeting and promotion. Perhaps the most important of the recommendations was: "A full-time director position ought to be established, and the director's activities should encompass all phases of park development from policy decisions to promotional efforts."

Several scholars of the Department of Geography and Earth Sciences were involved at different critical times in relating economic theory and data analysis to the development of research parks in the United States. Walcott and Nunnally had a paper published in the American Industrial Development Council's Journal of April, 1979 entitled "Revitalizing Research Parks." They analyzed the misconceptions responsible for failures. They also discussed the importance of such factors as zoning, recruitment, and the relationship to universities.

The UNCC study stimulated other suggestions from the Charlotte Chamber of Commerce and from directors. G. Jackson Burney, University Research Park executive director and chief executive officer of the Charlotte Chamber of Commerce, and members of his staff prepared a summary of developments to date and proposed a "marketing strategy." This was sent to board members. President Taylor ended 1977 by leading an in-depth study of what actions might be taken to accelerate development of the park.

A TURNING POINT

*"Five years from now we can look forward to
having a thriving residential community there."*
—*Fred Bryant*

The year 1978 turned out to be the most exciting one to date. Planning took on new character with the use of professional development consultants and expansion of planning to include much-needed residential facilities. IBM announced it would build its long-planned facility, Phillip Morris announced it would build in nearby Cabarrus County, and the governor of the state agreed to expedite the extension of Harris Boulevard to I-77. In addition, local government agencies committed resources to encourage development in northeast Mecklenburg County.

Advice of Developers Sought

Soon after his election as president, David Taylor created an ad hoc committee composed of some officers and directors of the park, developers, and business executives to take a critical look at ways and means of stimulating more activity in achieving the park's goals. Meeting with President Taylor at the Greater Charlotte Chamber of Commerce Briefing Center on January 25, 1978, were C. C. Cameron, John Belk, G. Laux, Pat Hall, A. G. Odell, Dean W. Colvard, William J. Veeder, and G. Jackson Burney. Two members of the ad hoc committee, Thomas Belk and Edwin L. Jones, Jr., were unable to be present. Committee suggestions included: (1) renew discussions with the county commission and the city council; (2) complete Harris Boulevard to I-77; (3) develop growth in the northern part of the county as sewage and water services become available; (4) spur further residential development through the planned retail shopping center; (5) coordinate the various committees through an executive director; and (6) resolve differences of opinion as to whether emphasis should be on acquiring up to 2,000 acres or whether the size of the park should be limited to 1,000 acres.

At the meeting of directors on May 5, 1978, Fred Bryant, acting director of the Charlotte/Mecklenburg Planning Commission, and his associate, Tom Powers, along with Lee Dukes, director of the Charlotte/Mecklenburg Utility Department, reported on planning for water and

sewer facilities. They pointed out that extension of Harris Boulevard toward I-77 would make a great difference in that area. Director John A. Tate, Jr. said that he believed University Research Park could do something about getting Harris Boulevard extended.

Extension of Harris Boulevard and Residential Development Planned

On September 6, 1978, President Taylor convened the executive committee and some invited guests to consider further the plan for extending Harris Boulevard to I-77 and to launch a residential development. Present were W. A. Bowen, C. C. Cameron, Dean W. Colvard, W. H. Daugherty, Jr., Claude Q. Freeman, Sr., William S. Lee, John A. Tate, Jr., and William J. Veeder. It was agreed that University Research Park should proceed at once to acquire options on land along the corridor that was expected to contain Harris Boulevard. A motion was passed to commit $100,000 to acquire options. The thinking was that, by having control of an area suitable for single and multi-family housing, it would be possible to negotiate with developers to maintain the integrity of the area. There was tacit agreement among the bankers present that they would support the park board in these endeavors. The University Research Park treasury was nearing depletion and borrowing more funds would be required. John A. Tate, Jr. presented an action plan with a list of assigned responsibilities: land and housing — Claude Q. Freeman, Sr. and Louis Rose, Jr.; financial — W. A. Bowen; planning — John A. Tate, Jr.; road — Dean W. Colvard; utilities — Seddon "Rusty" Goode, Jr.; and presentations to official groups — David Taylor.

Three Important Stimuli

Three developments in 1978 greatly increased confidence that ten years of hard work and planning were bearing fruit in further reality and substance for the park. The first, and by far the most important, was the announcement by IBM in June that its systems communications division would build a plant and laboratory on its park property. An article in the *Charlotte Observer* on July 23, 1978, quoted City/County Planner Fred Bryant as saying that "IBM's coming may well mean the long-sought development of the northeast quadrant of Mecklenburg County... Five years from now, we can look forward to having a thriving residential community there." The article, written by M. S. Van Hecke, executive business editor, went on to note that promoters of the ten year old "University City" envisioned healthy residential development in the area. It was reported that IBM expected to employ about 1,600 people. IBM began immediately to clear the land for their first buildings. Groundbreaking ceremonies were held on September 20, 1978.

The second major development in 1978 was an announcement by Phillip Morris Company of plans to build a major manufacturing plant between University Research Park and Concord. Although this plant was to be in Cabarrus County and bore no direct relation to the research park, it represented another economic force which would encourage development of residential areas north of Charlotte.

The third development with great impact was a commitment by Governor James B. Hunt to expedite the extension of Harris Boulevard from Mallard Creek Road to I-77 south of Davidson and Lake Norman. Director John A. Tate, Jr., with assistance from others, had been studying possible routes and desirable areas for residential development. At the meeting of directors on October 27, 1978, Dean W. Colvard reported that, after conferring with President Taylor, he went to Raleigh to discuss the importance of this road with Governor Hunt. Governor Hunt agreed to expedite the extension of Harris Boulevard to I-77. The commitment included purchasing a four-lane right-of-way, the immediate construction of about four miles as four-lanes with the remainder to be two-lane construction. In making this report it was emphasized that this commitment was as firm as a political commitment could be. A follow-up meeting with Governor Hunt and representatives of the park board and other selected community leaders, along with officials of the North Carolina Department of Transportation, was recommended.

Residential Development Stressed

At the October 27th meeting President Taylor updated the board on authorization the executive committee had given John A. Tate, Jr. to form a committee to make contacts with the Charlotte/Mecklenburg Planning Commission and others to encourage attention to planning in northern Mecklenburg County. Tate reported that a housing study had been made and that special attention had been given to extending Harris Boulevard to the Sunset rather than the Reames Road area. He emphasized the compatibility of residential development in this part of the county with the goals of the park and the university.

The emphasis of the committee was upon: (1) developing an up-to-date land use plan for a large area around University Research Park; (2) extending Harris Boulevard; (3) providing water and sewer services; and (4) planning and initiating a housing plan. He said the committee's basic aim was to try to change the development environment in the area of the park.

The board approved the actions taken by the president and others acting under his direction and authorized officers to proceed with the initiatives as discussed in this meeting. The year 1978 ended with an upturn in spirit, activity, and expectations.

Resurgent Emphasis on Planning and Financing

Claude Q. Freeman, Sr. emphasized the importance of presenting to the planning authorities requests that make sense "not just for our little section, but for the whole area. If we get the road, it makes sense to extend the water to loop the system . . . we can set the tone for housing."

Freeman had been working diligently to put together a visual presentation to be used not only to convince political bodies of the importance of University Research Park to the community but also to sell it to prospective corporate or governmental residents. Norman Pease, Jr. assigned his associate, Mike Tye, to assist in this task. UNCC made the services of Dorlan Mork and the university's Learning Resources Center available. Lacking an office separate from the Charlotte Chamber of Commerce, this team had to overcome the inconvenience of working in separate facilities. Freeman's office had drawings and charts on walls and tables; the J. N. Pease Associates conference room was used for reviewing and editing film; the UNCC Learning Resources Center provided narration for the visuals. Adaptations were provided for specific audiences and prospects. This was dubbed by participants as "Claude Freeman's Dog and Pony Show." When separate and more spacious work quarters were provided, the visual and graphic presentations attained more sophistication.

At the first meeting in 1979, January 11, President Taylor welcomed Dr. E. K. Fretwell Jr. who had succeeded Dean W. Colvard following his retirement as chancellor of UNCC. The board was authorized to obtain credit as needed for the purchase of additional land to be used in the development of the park and the corridor. The financial report showed a balance of almost $200,000, but this was not thought adequate to purchase the land that would be needed for residential development. The officers were given broad authority to continue securing necessary loans and making transactions they judged to be in order. This was the first of several successive actions taken to vest power to act in smaller bodies so that response times could be shortened. Also at this meeting the president, vice presidents, treasurer, and secretary

IBM

were designated members of the executive committee. As vice president of University Research Park, Chancellor Fretwell became an active member of the executive committee. The purchase of the Ernest Haynes property through City National Bank added 15.86 acres at a total cost of $42,029, $2,650 per acre. For future park expansion, this property extended to the northeastern side of Mallard Creek.

Director J. N. Glenn, in consultation with William S. Lee, president of Duke Power Company, had made contact with the firm that managed the Forrestal Conference Center at Princeton, New Jersey and had arranged for the director to visit with Chancellor Colvard in the latter part of 1978. Further study revealed that the kind of conference center they were interested in building might be more suitable to another location. A report was also made on a visit to a hotel/conference center built by a private company in the heart of the medical center of The University of Alabama at Birmingham. Colvard agreed to continue studying this phase of a possible development for the park and pointed out that Chancellor Fretwell would soon appoint a new director of the UNCC Institute of Urban Studies who might be called upon for assistance.

The 1979 election of directors changed the board's composition in important ways. Betty Chafin and Elisa-

E. K. Fretwell Jr.

beth G. Hair were elected to represent the Charlotte City Council and the Board of County Commissioners, respectively. Mayor Edwin Knox had been elected at an earlier meeting. Richard Bevier became the first officer from the new IBM facility to represent that company. John Crosland, Jr., a real estate developer, was also elected. E. K. Fretwell Jr., C. C. Cameron, Ben T. Craig, Harry J. Nicho-

las, John A. Tate, Jr., and Seddon "Rusty" Goode, Jr. were elected vice presidents.

Planned residential development and purchasing additional land to expand the park were high priority issues in 1979. One small but needed tract of about one acre straddling Mallard Creek north of the intersection of Research Drive and Louis Rose Place was purchased for $42,000. Working through Fred Bryant, director of the City/County Planning Commission, President Taylor arranged for a committee, composed of himself and Directors Freeman, Pease, Rose, Tate, and Colvard, to review the University Research Park program for officers of the commission on March 29, 1979. A presentation was made to the Planning Commission on May 1, 1979. A thirteen-minute slide presentation prepared by Claude Q. Freeman, Sr., Norman Pease, Jr., and UNCC served as the basis for these presentations. Under the headline "Prompt Study Promised on Research Park Place" the *Charlotte Observer* published a report of that meeting the following day. Principal points of emphasis were: (1) University Research Park planned to double the park's size and encourage housing nearby; (2) the plan envisioned adding 3,000 jobs to the county, 1,000 acres to the park, and 1,000 homes in that part of the county; (3) the Planning Commission was requested to approve the concept of northward expansion of the park and the idea of a major residential development west and north of the park; (4) appropriate zoning be provided; and (5) the Planning Commission join in urging state and local governments to expedite completion of Harris Boulevard to I-77 and extension of water and sewer facilities to the area. Chairman Allen Tate promised a prompt review.

John A. Tate, Jr. and Claude Q. Freeman, Sr. made a similar report to Lee Dukes of the Charlotte/Mecklenburg Utility Department on April 6, 1979. The committee met with county commissioners on June 4, 1979.

Long Range Plan

At the April 26 meeting John A. Tate, Jr. distributed a "Proposed long-range plan for University Research Park, 1979-85." This proposal primarily dealt with residential developments along the Harris Boulevard extension. Lengthy negotiations with DOT were required to create a proper relationship between Harris Boulevard and properties which had been purchased for future residential developments.

The statistical summary of properties and employees as of early 1979, Table 4, was included in the long-range plan.

The long-range plan also contained data on tax values which provided convincing evidence of the tax revenues which University City was generating.

A specific objective of the long-range plan for residential development by the end of 1985 was to facilitate the building of 400 single family units and 400 group housing units at an average price of $60,000 each and 200 apartments at an average price of $40,000. It was estimated that land required for 1,000 units would not exceed 500 acres. The total value of these residential units, when developed, was estimated at $56,000,000. Further development of 2,000 housing units and an additional 1,000 acres of land was projected for the five years 1986-90.

It was obvious that the projected plans would require considerable expenditures by the city and the county for water and sewer facilities. With the assistance of utility engineers and city/county planners, realistic estimates for these substantial expenditures were made. Estimates indicated probable costs for sewer lines to be $3 million and water lines $2 million. Tate indicated that University Research Park was thinking in terms of a $100 million project — $40 million of construction in the park and $60 million in new housing. When translated into economic terms, this meant 3,000 new jobs, housing for 1,000 families, and $100 million on the tax books. The support of the Charlotte-Mecklenburg Planning Commission was assured by a resolution which passed on May 1, 1979:

> WHEREAS, the Charlotte-Mecklenburg Planning Commission has received from the University Research Park Corporation Board an outline of a commitment, by them, to a bold, imaginative plan to provide development impetus to the Northeast portion of the urbanizing area; and
>
> WHEREAS, the Charlotte-Mecklenburg Planning Commission does find and agree that;
>
> (1) The proposal to provide development opportunity for increased employment and housing in this area is in harmony with general policy guides and objectives established in the Comprehensive Plan, and
>
> (2) Expansion of the Research Park and the initiation of major housing opportunities for this area conform to planning programs already underway;
>
> NOW, THEREFORE, BE IT RESOLVED the Charlotte-Mecklenburg Planning Commission does declare:
>
> (1) Concurrence with the general outline of programming presented to them on May 1, 1979 by the University Research Park Corporation Board; and
>
> (2) Commitment in time and staff to provide the planning guidance necessary to detail and define the desirable location and form of the proposed development, both residential and non-residential; and
>
> (3) Support for the proposal that immediate attention be given to determining the specific location of needed utilities and the specific alignment of Harris Boulevard extended to I-77, as well as determining a funding mechanism for their timely construction; and
>
> BE IT FURTHER RESOLVED, that the Charlotte-Mecklenburg Planning Commission does assign its staff the responsibility to evolve a detailed planning process which will accomplish this commitment.
>
> RESOLVED this 1st day of May, 1979.
>
> *Signed by H. Allen Tate, Jr.*
> Chairman

Table 4

STATISTICAL SUMMARY OF PROPERTIES AND EMPLOYEES

Owner of Property	Land Acres	Building Sq. Ft.	Jobs	Est. Value of Land Buildings
Reeves Bros.	20	27,000	42	$ 998,910
Allstate	33	181,000	800	4,603,770
Collins & Aikman	130	77,500	275	3,914,330
IBM (when completed)	446	600,000	1,600	16,655,610
University Research Park	174	0	0	1,076,390
Queens Properties	268			681,800
Totals	1,071	885,500	2,717	$27,930,810

Both city and county governments were on record favoring actions which would encourage development in the northern part of Mecklenburg County. One-time expenditures to install utilities would be repaid by increased tax values and the creation of new jobs.

At the meeting on April 26, 1979, the University Research Park board approved items of the long-range plan under the headings "Action Plan to Initiate Major Housing Development" and "Specific Objectives of Residential Development by Year-End 1985." The effect of this action was far reaching. It set in motion the second major borrowing of funds from banks, the total amount exceeding the amount borrowed to purchase the land which had been sold to IBM.

Treasurer W. A. Bowen reported that six banks: North Carolina National Bank, Wachovia Bank & Trust Company, First Union National Bank, Northwestern Bank, First Citizens Bank & Trust Company, and Piedmont Bank & Trust Company, had each committed $250,000 to make purchases of land up to a total of $1.5 million. President Taylor signed a note formalizing this commitment on May 24, 1979. The interest rate was to be the maximum permitted by applicable law at the time advances were made. By the middle of June, 1979, President Taylor could announce that approximately 250 acres known as the Slayton, DeArmon, and Fox properties had been bought at approximately $5,000 per acre. It was to be held for sale to private builders who were willing to develop residential areas in accordance with the plans proposed.

As the tempo of activities was accelerating, care was taken to keep all local governmental officials informed and up-to-date. Under the leadership of John A. Tate, Jr. and assisted by President Taylor and Directors Colvard, Fretwell, and Pease, a presentation was made to the Board of County Commissioners on June 4, 1979. Commission Chairman Ed Peacock and County Manager Glen C. Blaisdell arranged the meeting.

Enter "University Place"

Chancellor E. K. Fretwell Jr. invited Dr. James W. Clay, who had been on special assignment to the chancellor, to the board meeting on August 1, 1979. Dr. Clay discussed the possibility of developing the university property

bounded by I-85, Harris Boulevard, and Highway 29 into a planned community to include a hotel and conference center and shopping and residential areas. This was the introduction to what became known later as "University Place."[12] It was also the first discussion of development of that area involving facilities other than a hotel and continuing education center.

At this meeting, executive Director G. Jackson Burney reported on further contacts with the Princeton group which had been contacted earlier about building a conference center and requested that a committee be appointed to make a feasibility study. Directors Leo E. Ells, Ben Tison, and W. F. Barnes were appointed to that committee.

W. F. Barnes reported committee recommendations resulting from their meeting on December 20, 1979. They recommended that plans be made for a dual facility involving a hotel and continuing education center and that sufficient land be set aside for that purpose. Their proposal assumed that the hotel would be built and operated by private capital and management and that the conference center would be owned and operated by UNCC. Food and lodging would be provided by the hotel. They recommended further that these plans be coordinated with the developer of University Place. At that time, they were considering the possibility of a request for the conference center being made to the Legislature in 1981. UNCC, with the assistance of an architect, proceeded to develop a preliminary plan for the conference center. Need for the hotel-conference center was further emphasized by a study made by Nelson Nunnally and Wayne Walcott in March, 1980. In their conclusion they stated that "it seems clear from the results generated by this study that there is a considerable un-met need in the UNCC/University Research Park area for conference facilities and an affiliated hotel/motel which are properly designed and conveniently situated. The facility would also meet the needs of other businesses and public organizations within the Charlotte area . . . " Under date of June 30, 1980, one director of University Research Park wrote Vice President C. C. Cameron a confidential letter offering to pledge $100,000 of personal funds to stimulate other commitments to get the "learning center" project activated.

---

[12] See Chapter VIII.

ACCELERATED ACTIVITY

"The entire northeast quadrant of the county is destined for greatness."
—Seddon Goode, Jr.

Late 1979 through 1981 was the most active development period in University Research Park's first two decades. Although no new firms were close to IBM in size, six new firms announced plans to occupy space in the park setting the tone for the park's second decade. These actions and announcements were what the directors had strived long and hard to achieve.

At the October 5, 1979 board meeting, IBM representative R. B. Bevier announced that the first 100,000 square feet of floor space of its new facility in the park had been completed and invited the board to hold its next meeting there. At that meeting in December, directors toured the IBM facility for the first time.

Electric Power Research Institute

Also in 1979 plans for one new tenant were announced. At the October board meeting director Edwin L. Jones, Jr. introduced Tom Nemzek the recently appointed president of the new J. A. Jones Construction Company subsidiary, J. A. Jones Applied Research Company. This company had been formed to build and operate a new facility under contract with Electric Power Research Institute (EPRI), an organization funded by more than 600 electric utility companies throughout the United States. EPRI is headquartered in Palo Alto, California. University Research Park was selected after a search for sites was narrowed to Research Triangle Park, Atlanta's Technology Park, and University Research Park. Competing with several national research organizations, the Jones Company won the contract to build and operate the Electric Power Research Institute Nondestructive Evaluation Center. The new facility was to be built along Harris Boulevard on property owned by Queens Properties, another Jones subsidiary. The property was zoned as part of the park. In making the announcement, Jones also spoke of the need for a motel and restaurant in the park. EPRI purchased the 9.4 acres (from the Queens Properties' portion of the park) at $20,000 per acre.

The new president, Tom Nemzek, told the directors that the new subsidiary would concentrate its efforts on "technology transfer" designed to apply results of research on equipment and procedures to field use in the shortest time possible. He indicated that they would also be involved in training programs that would insure that qualified persons perform all required inspections in power plants. He said they planned to work with universities to promote their involvement in supplying trained personnel. He assured the board that no hazardous materials would be stored or used at the facility. William S. Lee III, president of Duke Power Company and a member of the Board of Directors of EPRI, expressed that organization's pleasure that the new subsidiary would be located in Charlotte. Nemzek and Lee emphasized the importance of the hospitality and interest expressed by Charlotte's business community in site selection. The groundbreaking ceremony for the Nondestructive Evaluation Center was held on January 16, 1980. The project was moving ahead without delay.

New Economic Estimates and Developments

At the 1980 annual director's meeting, President Taylor asked Dr. James Clay of the Urban Institute of UNCC to report on economic studies relevant for employment in the park area. Dr. Clay estimated current employment at 2,000 and projected 11,000 by 1985. He also projected a payroll of $200 million annually within a decade. The year 1980 brought more good news as three firms announced plans to build in the park. Additional announcements, almost annually, during the decade would bring the number of tenants to twelve by late 1987.

Automatic Data Processing

Early in 1980 negotiations began with Automatic Data Processing South, incorporated in Delaware and headquartered in Miami, Florida. This company did extensive data processing for corporations and governmental agencies. A purchase of 9.2 acres at $22,500 per acre (a total of $207,000) was completed in May. Later this property was sold to Fairfax Investment Company for development.

Verbatim/Kodak

Also in 1980 negotiations were initiated with Verbatim Company, a leading manufacturer of floppy disks and other magnetic media for computer data storage. Governor James B. Hunt had made overtures to high-tech industries in California's Silicon Valley to consider locating in North Carolina. Verbatim decided to locate its first expansion outside California in the University Research Park. They bought 37.165 acres at $23,000 per acre (a total of $854,795) and built their first structure of 80,000 square feet. In 1983 a second building was begun. The first building was designed to allow expansion up to 300,000 square feet. They planned to employ about 300 people. In mid-1985 Verbatim was purchased by Eastman Kodak Company. In 1986 it was announced that Verbatim's corporate headquarters would relocate from Sunnyvale, California to University Research Park. With the completion of this transfer, Charlotte was to become Verbatim's headquarters for worldwide manufacturing and marketing.

On July 14, 1987, Richard Bourns, president of Verbatim, announced that part of their facilities would be converted into a high-tech manufacturing plant for Eastman Kodak to produce newly developed optical information storage discs. This added activity was expected to create 50 to 100 new jobs and require more than $10 million in expenditures for new equipment. Optical discs, based on laser technology, represented a major advancement in data storage capability. The announcement stated that "a single 14-inch disc could hold all of the data on a stack of papers 92 stories high." This operation, scheduled to be activated in 1989, was described as a state-of-the-art, laser based, white laboratory coat operation functioning in a sterile environment to prevent contamination. In an editorial dated July 15, 1987, the *Charlotte Observer* referred to this announcement as "yet another opportunity for Charlotte to put its name before the world in association with a highly advanced technology."

In late 1987, Verbatim/Kodak purchased an additional 15 acres of land for future expansion.

Union Oil of California

The Union Chemicals Division of Union Oil of California started negotiations in 1980 for 5.3 acres (at $32,892 per acre) to locate a 25,000 square foot building. This center, in place and dedicated on October 6, 1982, was estimated to cost $2.6 million. This technical services laboratory tests chemical products and adhesives as a support service for Union Oil's petrochemical group which serves paint, paper, fabric finishing, and other industries. In the facility, chemists, engineers, and lab technicians — spe-

cialists in polymer chemistry and physical testing — engage in formula development, evaluation, experimentation, and simulation of manufacturing processes. They provide a range of technical support, from applications research through trial runs of manufacturing.

Dow Jones — *Wall Street Journal*

The Dow Jones Company acquired 8.712 acres in October, 1981 at $37,500 per acre (a total of $326,700) to build one of its seventeen national sites for printing the *Wall Street Journal*. This daily publication has a national circulation of about two million subscribers. The $11 million University Research Park plant receives satellite transmissions of financial material and prints newspapers for distribution to the Carolinas, Virginia, a part of Tennessee, and Georgia.

Fairfax Properties

As the number and diversity of companies in the park increased, the officers and directors realized office space might be needed for individuals or firms doing business with park residents. Consequently, Fairfax Properties bought 30.22 acres of prime property in late 1981 for an office building. The price was $45,000 per acre (a total of $1,359,900). However, demands for additional office space at IBM had grown to such extent that this firm, already located in the park, negotiated a contract with Fairfax Properties to lease the entire building for administrative services. Fairfax Properties also bought 9.2 acres from Automatic Data Processing, built a second office building and also rented it to IBM. They also bought adjoining property vacated by Reeves Brothers, Inc.

Southern Bell

In January, 1983 Southern Bell bought 26.63 acres at $40,000 per acre (a total of $1,065,200) to build a multi-state switching center. Their 350,000 square foot building was constructed at a cost of approximately $30 million. The new digital switching machines, manufactured by Northern Telecom, incorporate the latest in telecommunications switching technology, including such custom calling services as three-way calling, call forwarding, call waiting, and speed calling.

American Telephone & Telegraph Communications

AT&T Communications is a subsidiary of American Telephone & Telegraph Company. In December, 1984 AT&T purchased a tract of 28.3 acres at $46,254 per acre. Queens Properties provided 5.3 acres; the remaining 23 acres were part of the University Plantation tract owned by University Research Park. The cost of the 215,000 square foot building was estimated to be $20 million. This data service center eliminated the need to contract with Southern Bell and independent telephone companies for billing services. The complex was expected to operate on a 24-hour schedule. About 100 AT&T employees were to be transferred to Charlotte and about 700 were to be employed locally.

Electronic Data Systems Corporation (EDS)

On March 1, 1985, Pizzagalli Investment Company bought 8.108 acres at the intersection of Research Drive and David Taylor Drive for $57,500 per acre (a total of $466,210). A building of 100,000 square feet costing $5 million and completed in November 1985 was constructed and leased (later sold) to EDS, a subsidiary of General Motors. EDS also bought adjacent lots and gave University Research Park a three year contract to buy back those lots at the purchase price plus 10 percent per annum.

EDS, the electronics arm of General Motors Corporation, was based in Dallas. Their first operation was designed to employ 325 to 350 workers and to perform two functions: serve as a computer center for 750 credit units in the eastern United States and as an information processing center for General Motors' components parts division. In June, 1987 EDS announced the location of a new facility which will occupy 12,862 square feet in the Mallard Creek Center, an office park located in the University Research Park and developed by Charter Properties, one mile from their other operations. University Research Park President Goode characterized this operation as another "addition to a growing data processing concentration within the park."

University Memorial Hospital

In the late 1960s and early 1970s, the Mecklenburg/Union Health and Hospital Council commissioned a study of the area's future hospital needs. A recommendation to the council for a new hospital in the Randolph Road area of Charlotte generated opposition, particularly from citizens living in the northern sections of the city. There was strong sentiment that future medical facilities should not be concentrated in one area and that additional facilities were needed in northern Mecklenburg County. During the 1970s there were changes in the health planning organizations but the lack of hospital facilities in the northern part of the county resulted in the addition of hospital beds in a facility in Huntersville.

As plans for a new hospital moved closer to reality in the early 1980s, Mecklenburg County still owned a portion of the Green Acres property adjoining UNCC on the east opposite the site being considered for the mixed-use development which would eventually become University Place. Because of the mutual advantages of building a new hospital on property owned by the county and locating it to serve the university and the northern part of the county, the university and county commissioners agreed on the University City location.

In 1985, the Hospital Authority opened a 130-bed University Memorial Hospital with a wing to accommodate doctors offices. This state-of-the-art hospital was expected to help meet the needs of residents of Cabarrus, Iredell, and northern Mecklenburg Counties. According to the Hospital Authority the new facility "is committed to health care that is close to the people, highly specialized, economical, efficient, and individualized."

Home Savings of America

The nation's second largest savings and loan organization, Home Savings of America, based in Irwindale, California, began negotiations early in 1987 for a center in the eastern United States. The 98-year old company's main business was residential mortgages and its assets at the end of 1986 were 27.5 billion. It was said to be the largest generator of adjustable rate mortgages in the United States.

Later in the year, Home Savings optioned approximately 60 acres in the University Research Park at $73,000 per acre. When this purchase was to be finalized it was expected that the center would process all mortgages originating east of the Rocky Mountains. "It would accept loan payments, send out tax and insurance payments from escrow funds, and answer inquiries from mortgage holders."[13] Home Savings planned to begin construction of 350,000 square feet of space in early 1988. A similar center at Irwindale, California employed about 1,200 people. This plan when fully operational could employ 3,000 and have 1,000,000 square feet of space.

University Plantation

A very important acquisition of land adjoining University Research Park occurred in 1983. A tract of 170 acres known as the Barnhardt property was placed in trust with the park to sell. University Research Park made a down payment of $275,000 and entered into an agreement for distribution of sales proceeds and for complete purchase at a specified time. The sale agreement provided for an additional payment of $15,000 per acre at the time of resale plus a percentage of the resale price in excess of $30,000 per acre. Parts of this tract were sold to AT&T, and Home Savings.

Charter Properties

Late in 1985 Charter Properties bought 19.5 acres at $60,000 per acre and optioned an additional 50 acres. On this property they built a 75,000 square foot office building for rent. Any use must conform to University Research Park zoning. The lease of 12,862 square feet to EDS, previously mentioned, represented a good beginning for this property to serve the University Research Park's purposes.

---

[13] From news release in *Charlotte Observer*, May 6, 1987, by M.S. Van Hecke quoting Senior Vice President Don Brackenbush.

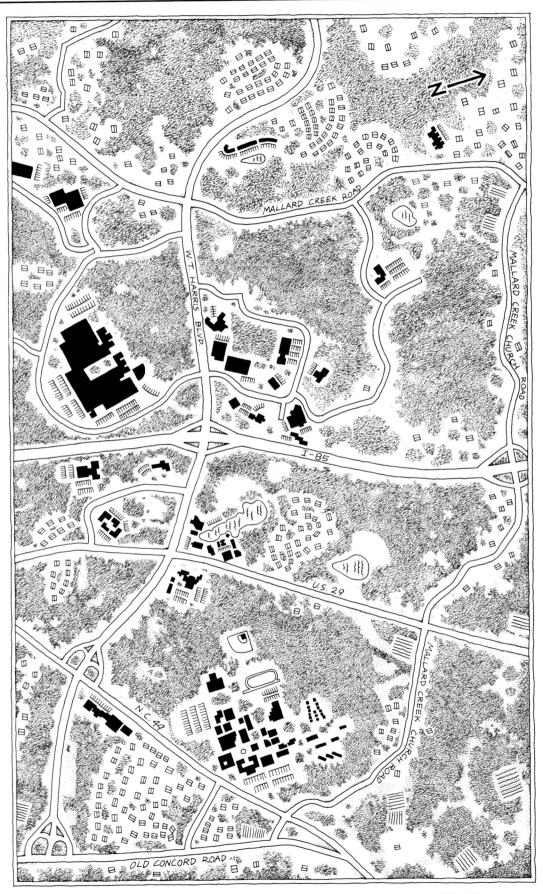

University Research Park, University Place, University Memorial Hospital, and The University of North Carolina at Charlotte — 1987

Nearby Developments

Although not located in the park or committed to research service and administration, some developments in the vicinity of University Research Park have had major economic impacts.

On March 31, 1978, Phillip Morris Company, a leading company in cigarettes, beer, and food, announced its purchase of 2,100 acres between University Research Park and Concord for a cigarette manufacturing plant of considerable size. Their manufacturing operations began in 1983. The plant, with 1.8 million square feet of covered space (the equivalent of 60 football fields) was one-half mile long. Its total cost was $295 million. Approximately 250 acres of the property were landscaped. By 1986 the payroll included 1,260 employees; 460 salaried and 800 paid by the hour. They manufactured 4.7 billion cigarettes in 1985 and estimate an increase in production to 60 billion by 1988.

Also in the vicinity of University Research Park, The Charlotte Motor Speedway was growing each year, generating economic activity which benefits nearby enterprises and adds to the demand for more residential development, commercial and retail space, and hotel rooms. This organization attracts hundreds of thousands of race fans to the area and provides an enormous stimulus to retail sales. It employs many people not employable by residents of the park. Its operations are of such quality and magnitude that it captures national and international attention.

Dating from the inception of University Research Park, a major deterrent to development was the lack of choice residential areas and the relative scarcity of amenities in north Charlotte. To encourage planned residential development, the park borrowed $1.5 million from local banks and bought approximately 250 acres of land on either side of the projected extension of Harris Boulevard north of Mallard Creek Road in 1979. The property, known as the DeArmon and Slayton tracts, was held for sale to developers who agreed to build attractive homes for middle and upper-income families. This property was purchased in 1979. It was sold at cost to John Crosland Company to build 82 homes in an area named Norcroft, a development of single-family traditional homes costing an average of about $118,000. A second tract was sold to Carmel Land Company to build 50 homes in an area named Sweetwater. The average cost per home was about $175,000, with four homes selling for $250,000 or more.

In late 1986, Home Builders Association of Charlotte sponsored a HomeArama featuring twelve houses in the Mallard Trace development. Each home, built by a different developer, was open for display for several days. The prices ranged from $119,000 to $140,000 for homes of 2,000 to 2,500 square feet.

On October 13, 1986, *Business Journal* reported that builders believed there was a market in the vicinity of University City capable of absorbing 1,500 new homes and that plans were underway for builders to commit $160 million in the area. At that time published brochures identified more than twenty developments expected to total more than the number projected in *Business Journal*. The scarcity of choice housing that represented the greatest deficiency in the University City area was suddenly being overcome. Sales records also continued to encourage development.

In addition to choice homes, new community facilities and amenities were appearing. An elementary school on Mallard Creek Road was scheduled for completion in 1988; a branch of the public library to serve University Place was in the planning stages; churches of several denominations had been built; day care facilities were being opened; and the Crosland shopping area on Highway 49 was adding retail outlets. The last leg of Harris Boulevard connecting Highway 49 and I-77 south of Davidson was open for traffic September 25, 1986.

All of this, together with the new vitality generated by University Place, transformed the northeast side of the county into one of the most dynamic economic growth areas of the region.

Home Savings of America

E.P.R.I. — Electric Power Research Institute

Verbatim

Union Oil of California

Dow Jones

Southern Bell

AT&T — American Telephone and Telegraph Communications

EDS — Electronic Data Systems Corporation

University Memorial Hospital

UNIVERSITY PLACE

"University Place and the selection of the Carleys as developers is the most exciting announcement I have had the pleasure of making in my eight years as governor of North Carolina."
—James B. Hunt, Governor

One of the most innovative actions affecting the quality of life in University City was the launching of a metropolitan service center, the highly successful development, University Place. Whereas the idea for developing the park originated among business leaders in the Charlotte Chamber of Commerce and was developed in cooperation with UNCC, University Place was the brain child of two university geographers.

By 1979 several converging forces were destined to bring added vitality to University City. Among them were: (1) adoption by the park board of a "Proposed Long-Range Plan for University Research Park, 1979-85," proposed by John A. Tate, Jr.; (2) passage by the Charlotte/Mecklenburg Planning Commission of a resolution, described in Chapter VI, to encourage residential development in the area; (3) action by University Research Park directors to provide funding to purchase and hold land adjoining the park for future housing plans; and (4) studies by Douglas M. Orr, Jr. and James W. Clay exploring development of a satellite urban center. These studies were brought to the attention of park directors by Chancellor/Director E. K. Fretwell Jr. on August 10, 1979 (see Chapter VI).

By the late 1970s, Charlotte's pattern of urban growth had become a community issue. Consensus had been reached among many segments of the community that more forceful action was needed to counterbalance the rapid development that was occurring unabated in the south and southeast quadrants of the county. In an editorial entitled "Magnet North" in the *Charlotte Observer* on October 28, 1978, Jack Claiborne wrote, "a study of park

potential by UNCC geographers showed that residential development nearby would make it even more attractive to industry." The unbalanced growth was not only increasing traffic congestion and overloading the water and sewer infrastructure in one direction, but it appeared that the central city would eventually be shunted to the geographic periphery of the community.

Actions taken by the Charlotte/Mecklenburg Planning Commission prompted their planner, Steve Griffin, to confer with Clay and Orr to solicit assistance in moving ahead with a planning effort in the University Research Park area. At the time Clay was a professor of geography and Orr, also a geographer, was vice chancellor for student affairs at the university. Both had worked with Planning Commission staff on a number of projects in the past. The three agreed that retail development was lacking. Fortunately, strip development had been prevented in the immediate area of the university by zoning. However, the owner of the property zoned for needed retail development on Highway 49 had been slow to develop the designated area. It was clear that economic and locational forces had changed since the original zoning of University City. The three also agreed that a more desirable form of future development would be clustered growth focusing on a mixed-use planned community similar to the metropolitan service centers introduced in the Charlotte/Mecklenburg 1995 Comprehensive Development Plan. The concept of satellite population centers also had been discussed earlier by Clay, Orr, and Alfred Stuart in the *Charlotte-Mecklenburg Atlas*. These discussions set the stage for bold new action.

Utilizing schematics of planned communities elsewhere in the world, as well as demographic data about growth patterns in the Charlotte and university areas, a slide presentation about a planned community for northeast Mecklenburg was assembled. One of the first presentations was to Chancellor E. K. Fretwell Jr. who had arrived in Charlotte a few months earlier as the university's second chancellor and who served as a vice president and director of the park. Fretwell recognized the unique opportunity that existed. He supported the idea of this additional involvement of the university in addressing the problem of Charlotte's lopsided growth toward the southeast.

Clay, Orr, and Fretwell assembled a small working task force of university officials to begin immediate planning. Invited to join the group were David Taylor, chairman of The Foundation of UNCC and University Research Park, Vice Chancellor for Business Affairs Leo E. Ells, and Chancellor Emeritus Dean W. Colvard. Beginning in the summer of 1979 the group met periodically to chart action needed on various fronts: land-use planning, site selection, financial considerations, and political contacts. It

Douglas M. Orr, Jr.

University Place Emerges

In response to the Planning Commission request for assistance and ideas, Clay and Orr began to provide the leadership necessary for a myriad of projects designed to direct a portion of the community's growth to the university area. The purpose of the effort was to further enhance aesthetics and livability in the University City area. Timing for such an effort seemed ideal. Given the kind of population growth that IBM, the research park, and the university were likely to generate, there appeared to be a window of opportunity for a new plan.

During the spring of 1979, Clay and Orr drafted the general planning precepts for a mixed-use center in the vicinity of the university and the park. Their work drew upon dual concepts. One was the concept of the metropolitan service center (later called urban development centers in the updated 2005 Comprehensive Development Plan for Charlotte-Mecklenburg). The second was the concept of new towns — planned communities based on classic walled medieval towns and popularized in Europe since the turn of the century.

James W. Clay

was clear that a carefully planned public/private approach, including university and government officials as well as private enterprise, were keys to success. Chancellor Fretwell then directed Clay to spend a portion of the 1979 summer months conducting demographic, land-use, and infrastructure studies of the area.

Site Recommended for Town Center

Key developments took place at the task force meeting of August 28, 1979. Orr suggested that a tract of 240 acres of land owned by the university and bordered by I-85, Harris Boulevard, and Highway 29, seemed ideally located for a mixed-use center. This was part of the land formerly owned by Mecklenburg County and given by the county, along with additional acreage, to the state for the development of UNCC. There had been discussion among research park directors from time to time about the possibility of building a hotel and continuing education center in this area. UNCC had been amenable to this possibility but had tentatively reserved the remainder of the tract for future unspecified development of the university. While the site was contiguous with the campus of the university it was somewhat remote from the campus core which fronted on Highway 49. But it was well-situated for a mixed-use town center, highly accessible to both the university and University Research Park, and fronting major transportation arteries. Orr and Clay made a convincing case that a town center would be an ideal complement to both the university and the park. It was agreed that should this land be used for non-university purposes other land should be acquired to accommodate future growth of UNCC.

Urban Institute Role

Also during the task force meeting of August 28, Chancellor Fretwell suggested that the town center project might be an appropriate undertaking for the Urban Institute. At the time, the university was conducting a national search for a director of the Urban Institute. There was consensus that the town center project would add a new dimension to the Urban Institute's mission. Fretwell and Orr agreed that Clay was the ideal candidate to become director of the institute. In November Chancellor Fretwell announced his appointment, charging him with using its resources to coordinate the planning for the town center project. Already underway by Chancellor Fretwell were plans to restructure the university's top administration and create a new Division of Research and Public Service to include the Urban Institute. The new division was to be headed by Orr. The reorganization, which took place a few months later, positioned Orr and Clay to play key roles in planning the town center project.

Task Force Responsibilities

By the fall of 1979, it was clear that major tasks lay ahead. Market and need assessments were necessary. A master plan for the site was needed. Basic to using the tract of land under consideration was securing the approval for selling or leasing the designated site to a developer for construction of the town center.

In the work of the task force, Clay and Orr were responsible for land-use planning and community coordination. Fretwell, Taylor, and Ells were responsible for working with The Foundation of UNCC to assemble acreage which the foundation could convey to the university in exchange for the 240-acre site, thereby putting the town site in the hands of an organization which could negotiate with a developer. Approvals for the exchange, as well as related legal questions, had to be cleared through the Council of State composed of top elected state officials and chaired by the Governor. There was also the necessity of obtaining the approval of Mecklenburg County Commissioners to remove the reversion clause requiring this property to revert to Mecklenburg County if it was not used for university purposes. Because of his long-time acquaintance with county and state officials former Chancellor Colvard agreed to assist in obtaining the necessary clearances with governmental leaders.

Planning Goals for University Place Project

At this point overall goals were developed to guide the project and communicate to the various constituencies the purpose of the effort. Project goals outlined by the task force were to:

1. Provide major public and commercial services for the northeastern quadrant of Charlotte/Mecklenburg.
2. Redress the historic growth imbalance in Mecklenburg County.
3. Ensure orderly and planned growth for the area around the university as well as the northeastern part of the county in general.
4. Stimulate further economic development for the county's northeastern quadrant and the University Research Park.
5. Serve the UNCC campus community.
6. Effectively tie into the community highway and transit system.
7. Achieve a high degree of self-containment and the advantages that accrue — reduction of journey to work, enhanced sense of community.
8. Provide for a diverse mix of functions (retail, office, educational, medical, cultural, housing, etc.) and resident population.
9. Capitalize on the several unique advantages of site and development circumstances to produce a new town that can be a model for the nation.

Background and Pre-Planning Studies

In late fall 1979, Clay had completed a survey of employers in the University Research Park-university-Cabarrus County corridor to determine existing basic employment and projected employment for 1980-85. The results were significant. While the existing basic employment (excluding service center employment such as education, retail, etc.) was 2,108, the planned employment and unannounced new basic jobs were projected to increase the basic employment base to 11,708 by 1985. Using a standard multiplier the projected non-basic employment and accompanying total residential population could reach 58,540 by 1985! The data were extremely important because to be fully successful, it was believed that at least 50 percent of the people who work in a planned community should also live there — the so-called "self-containment" principle.

Since the new town project was in keeping with the university's urban mission, faculty expertise was called upon to assist in the planning process. Twelve faculty task forces were assembled to conduct feasibility studies including such topics as housing, retailing, transportation, and public services. These studies helped provide the basis for the subsequent town center land-use plan.

Community Support Solicited

By the summer of 1980, Clay and Orr were making presentations to community and government organizations regarding plans for a new mixed-use town center between University Research Park and the university. The presentations generated curiosity and interest but many were skeptical that the market for such an effort would not be in place until at least the turn of the century. Developers were particularly sensitive to the lack of a large existing population base to justify major retail development which in turn depended upon an adequate population base. Consequently a "Catch 22" condition existed whereby no critical element was large enough to cause a breakthrough. Much like leaders who persisted during the early years of the park's development, Clay and Orr continued to try to generate interest, hoping that the community would capture the vision.

Finally on September 18, 1980, the *Charlotte Observer* ran a story headlined "UNCC Planning Small Town for 3,000 People," stating that a metro center being planned by the university might be one of five such satellite centers proposed in the earlier 1995 Comprehensive Plan.

Not surprisingly, residents in the university area began to express concern about the implications of the new town plan. They were especially vocal about possible downzoning of their property. As a result of expressions of both skepticism and alarm, Clay and Orr devoted considerable time for almost three years talking to individuals and addressing civic groups, clubs, and churches

about how the new town plans should stimulate growth and enhance livability and property values throughout the area. No stones were left unturned to see that individuals and groups throughout the community, from neighbors to elected officials, developed a sense of ownership of the project.

Leo E. Ells

University Metro Town Center Endowment, Inc.

In the meantime, Fretwell, Ells, Taylor, and Colvard were working on the land exchange. After a series of contacts and briefings with each of the county commissioners, the reversion clause was waived on August 9, 1980.

The Foundation of UNCC played an important role in making it possible for university and community interests to move forward with plans for the new town center. With the help of Claude Q. Freeman, Sr., who had been actively involved in University Research Park negotiations since 1976, it purchased acreage needed for future expansion of the university. By combining this land with a portion of the tract formerly known as the Pharr Estate which the foundation already owned it was possible to make the exchange on an acre-for-acre basis. However, since the 240-acre site was to be used for a commercial enterprise, it was necessary to protect the tax exempt status of the foundation in the land transaction process. To this end, David Taylor as chairman of the foundation board appointed a committee composed of Robert Lassiter, Jr., C. D. Spangler, Jr., Leo E. Ells, Seddon "Rusty" Goode, Jr., Claude Freeman, Sr., and J. Norman Pease, Jr., to study and recommend the possible need for a separate corporation to handle the project. The committee recommended that a separate organization should be created. Attorney Robert W. King, Jr. of Moore and Van Allen composed the Articles of Incorporation and Bylaws of a subsidiary nonprofit corporation which was named the University Metro Town Center Endowment, Inc. (see Appendix B.3.). Its single member was The Foundation of UNCC . This organization was designed to handle transactions between the developer, to be chosen, and The Foundation of UNCC.

By the end of 1980, the necessary approval for the land exchange had been gained from the university Board of Trustees, UNC System Board of Governors, and finally the Council of State on December 9, 1980. The latter approval came with the strong support of Governor James B. Hunt, Jr. and Chief Budget Officer John Williams.

With these approvals secured and the 240 acres transferred to the University Metro Town Center Endowment, Inc. the project was ready for the next major move. Once the subsidiary corporation owned the land it could be sold or leased to a developer. Attorney Robert Lassiter headed the new organization and other members included Chancellor Fretwell; Vice Chancellor Ells; David Whitlock, Vice President of Wachovia Bank and Trust Company; Charles Myerly, Executive Director, UNCC Foundation; William White, Charter Properties, Inc.; Ralph Carestio, Jr., Senior Vice President, NCNB; and Eugene B. Graham, Vice President, First Union National Bank.

Meanwhile, local elected and appointed officials continued their strong support of development of northeast Mecklenburg County as important to balancing the community's growth, and the new town project in particular. A sixteen member task force, chaired by Charlotte/Mecklenburg Planning Commission Chair Peggy Culbertson, was appointed by the Charlotte City Council and the Board of County Commissioners to address growth strategies for the northeastern quadrant. Resolutions were passed by the Charlotte City Council, the Board of County Commissioners, the Charlotte/Mecklenburg Planning Commission, and the Board of Education, supporting the research park/university area development and the new town project itself. Likewise, in July 1981, the Charlotte Chamber of Commerce and the UNCC Board of Trustees passed supporting resolutions.

Visits to Other Planned Communities

With the process well underway for completing the land exchange, and with feasibility studies from the faculty task forces and the earlier Urban Institute survey clearly indicating a need for a mixed-use development, Clay and Orr set their sights on developing a master plan for the 240-acre site.

A series of visits to planned communities in the United States and Europe was scheduled. The first trip, in the summer of 1981, was to Harbison, South Carolina, a planned community outside Columbia. The visit was particularly useful because Harbison President Lester Gross served also as president of the prestigious International New Town Association. Trips were also made to well-known planned communities outside Washington, D.C.: Reston, Virginia and Columbia, Maryland. Both effectively utilized water as a centerpiece for development.

Because historically Europe has led in new town development, Clay and Orr visited planned communities in the Netherlands, Belgium, Scotland, and England. They also attended a European symposium on new towns. From the European visit they gained an appreciation for "people places" in mixed-use settings that give cities street life and activity throughout the day. Europe's atmospheric squares, plazas, and gathering points, some hundreds of years old, still work well. They attended the 1983 International New Town conference in Barcelona, Spain, and were particularly impressed with Barcelona's "Las Ramblas," a legendary people place where the whole world seems to walk by.

While the European new towns are largely public sector undertakings and in some cases the housing structures are fairly plain by American standards, there was much to be learned by the Europeans' success at creating people centered places. Excellent public transit gives pedestrians priority over vehicles throughout the communities. The use of water, sometimes in modest but effective ways, was significant. Active street level store fronts give the streets a sense of life and activity, especially since residential units and offices were often located over shops. And, great attention was invariably given to greenways and recreation. All of these features were carefully noted as they designed a master plan for the project in Charlotte.

Meanwhile, in fall 1981 the task force decided that a permanent name was needed for the site. Various terms such as "Town Center," "New Town," and "University Metro Town" had been used up to this point. It was David Taylor who suggested "University Place" as an appropriate name to relate the town center to the university environment. The group agreed and from that time on the town center was known as "University Place," distinguishing it from the larger surrounding geographic region known as "University City."

International New Town Symposium

By late 1981, it was apparent that a bold move was necessary to draw community attention to University Place. The task force was convinced that a unique opportunity existed. Clay and Orr decided to host a symposium at the university on planned communities and mixed-use developments from an international perspective. The symposium would focus on the University Place project as a case study which might be developed in private partnership, as well as cite examples from elsewhere. Contacts made in Europe, nationally-known developers, planners, and academicians from the United States were invited to participate. James Rouse, developer of Columbia, Maryland and other nationally-known projects, agreed to be the keynote speaker.

The symposium, which took place January 21-22, 1982, represented a major turning point in the history of the project. Media began giving much more attention to the immediate potential of University Place. Keynote speaker James Rouse successfully stimulated the community's vision of what was possible in the University Research Park-university area. He captured the attention of his audience with a stirring quotation from Daniel Burnham: "Make no little plans, they have no magic to stir the blood and probably themselves will not be realized. Make big plans: aim high in hope and work, remembering that a noble, logical diagram once recorded will never die, but long after we are gone will be a living thing, asserting itself with evergrowing insistency." Rouse predicted that the demographics from the earlier economic employment base study might turn out to be conservative.

One of the featured speakers for the symposium was David Carley, president of Carley Capital Group of Madison, Wisconsin. He made a presentation on "Putting Large Mixed-Use Development Deals Together." Carley's presentation, with his special flair for public speaking, was one of the highlights of the conference. Of special significance were discussions over dinner as to his view of University Place and the potential that it offered. Carley made a lasting impression on his hosts and the seeds were planted for his later direct involvement with University Place.

Master Plan Developed

As a result of the new town visits and the symposium, some concrete ideas for a master plan were taking shape. It was determined that a professional planning firm should be retained to incorporate the ideas generated thus far. On April 1, 1982, the front page of the *Charlotte Observer* announced: "UNCC gets top planner for New City as David Wallace of Philadelphia, an internationally known architect, designer and educator, has agreed to develop the master plan for University Place, the heart of a 50,000 population University City." Wallace and his firm, Wallace, Roberts, and Todd, were regarded as bold designers with credits that included Baltimore's Inner Harbor and Charles Center, Norfolk's Waterside, and Amelia Island Plantation off the Florida coast.

The planning firm held a planning charette at the university on May 3, 1982. A cross section of the community leadership was invited to attend. The charette not only generated good ideas for the University Place master plan but further cemented a sense of ownership on the part of community leaders from the public and private sectors. Follow-up trips by Clay and Orr to the consultant's offices in Philadelphia led to a final plan which was approved by the University Metro Town Center Endowment, Inc. Board on August 5, 1982.

Also during the late summer of 1982, the Charlotte/Mecklenburg Planning Commission, Charlotte City Council, and Board of County Commissioners approved the University Place plan. Like most mixed-use master plans, it was a first edition which would be revised several times in the future. However it did establish the basic framework, with mixed-use development a major characteristic. The plan established performance standards and made specific recommendations for phased development of the site. The project was now ready to enter into a significant new phase: the selection of a developer for University Place.

Carley Capital Group Announced as Developer

In late 1982, the University Metro Town Center Endowment, Inc. received proposals from real estate developers. After a national solicitation and a series of prospect interviews and meetings, Carley Capital Group was selected unanimously as developer and on December 23, 1982, a contract was signed. The public announcement took place at a press conference on January 18, 1983, on the university campus. Among those present were Governor James B. Hunt, UNC President William C. Friday, County Commission Chairman Fountain Odom, Charlotte Mayor Eddie Knox, UNCC Trustee Chairman Thomas Belk, and David and James Carley. Governor Hunt called the appointment of Carley Capital Group for development of University Place "the most exciting announcement" he had the pleasure of making in his eight years as governor of North Carolina. A January 19th *Charlotte Observer* editorial expressed the sentiment of the community by stating:

"One day, Charlotteans may look back on Tuesday's events at UNC-Charlotte and note that it was there that Charlotte and Mecklenburg County turned an important corner in their growth and development. Tuesday's long-awaited announcement about a developer for University Place as a $300 million town center on Charlotte's northeast fringe has that kind of bold, historic potential. It means that all the elements needed to make University Place the magnet that reorients Charlotte's development pattern from southeast to northeast now appear to be in place.

In choosing David Carley, the UNCC Foundation, owners of the 240-acre University Place site, have selected a developer who seems to understand and be excited by the opportunities available at University Place. A man with stunning credentials in both education and industry — a Ph.D. in political science, former dean of the Wisconsin Medical College, former president of the National Association of Public Television Stations, former president of Inland Steel Development Corporation — he talks enthusiastically about the enriching educational, industrial and residential cross-currents that are possible there.

He brings the resources and prestige to put University Place in the same league with Dilworth and Myers Park as high quality suburban communities. When promoters of Dilworth wanted to expand that neighborhood in 1910, they hired the Olmsted brothers from the first rank of national landscape architects. When Myers Park was started, its promoters engaged the eminent John Nolen. UNCC's appointment of Dr. David Carley has the potential to create that same quality for University Place."

The Master Plan Revised and Finalized

In early spring of 1983, the Carley Capital Group contracted the services of the UNCC's Urban Institute and its director, James W. Clay, to direct the early development of University Place. Carley also contracted the services of a local architectural firm, Odell Associates, and a general contractor, Metric Constructors, for the development of the needed infrastructure and Phase I.

Working with the architects, significant additions and modifications were made. While maintaining the program uses as they were, University Place's master plan was revised to reflect two major axes: an elongated north-south axis along a 10 acre lake (modeled after San Antonio's Riverwalk) and an east-west pedestrian corridor (after Barcelona's Las Ramblas). The entire geographic focus of the project would be "reverse frontage," toward the lake, rather than the more traditional highway orientation.

The design framework, general concepts, and 14 programmatic and character themes were described in the report Clay and Orr drafted, "University Place — Design Concept and Themes." In this paper, its axes were described as follows:

"University Place is to be a well planned mixed-use development which will have a variety of uses; its parts will be functionally linked and attractively designed to give an overall 'village-like atmosphere.' Hopefully, it will be perceived as a 'special place' by those who live, work, and visit. The development of University Place is expected to contribute substantially to a strong sense of community for the University City area and to enhance its image as an important research and education center.

University Place is designed around two major axes — an elongated 10 acre north-south lake and an east-west pedestrian corridor. The lake will provide a major focal point for the project and will be highly visible from vantage points both inside and outside the project. Landmark design features at each end of the lake will help focus the view down the lake axis. A waterspout in the lake will accentuate the water image. The winding lake edge has been designed in meticulous detail. Much of the southern half of the lake will be a 'hard edge' — improvements featuring small wharfs, and other lakefront amenities —

in keeping with its planned 'urban' character. The shoreline will be lined with shops, restaurants, viewing areas, outdoor cafes, and other festively designed facilities. University Place will focus on street level activity. The northern half of the lake will have a softer and more passive character compatible with its residential use. The water theme will extend beyond the lake into other parts of the project to strengthen the theme. An attractive walkway, encircling the lake, will provide pedestrian amenity. The lakewalk will be connected to a project-wide pathway system which, in turn, will be connected to the adjacent county Greenway Park System.

The second axis, the east-west pedestrian corridor will extend the width of University Place to align with an expected UNCC pedestrian walkway and transit connection. The corridor, like Barcelona's world famous "Las Ramblas" corridor, is to be lined with a collage of shops, flower vendors, trees, and pedestrian gathering points. The pedestrian corridor will focus retail activities with people in a linear pattern. The corridor is to be planned with attention to detail. It will be attractively landscaped and paved with brick and textured materials. Other appropriate efforts will be made to contribute to a festive environment. At the same time, the corridor will provide convenient access for the automobile. The retail activity along the corridor will function as a convenience shopping center which will look and feel like a European village center. An attractive bridge will connect the convenience retail corridor with the major retail complex."

Odell Associates responded to these concepts and themes by a meticulous redesign of the master plan and the infrastructure for Phase I. Odell also designed the award winning heart of University Place, "Shoppes at University Place," and later the highly acclaimed Hilton Hotel.

To ensure that these themes were effectively carried out, a Design Review Committee was established to review and critique all infrastructure developments and new buildings, and was comprised of the following individuals: Planning Commission Director Martin Cramton, UNCC Architecture Dean Charles Hight, Architecture Professor Robert Anderson, Land Design President Brad David, along with Clay and Orr.

In the fall of 1983, Rich Galling, a Carley employee, was transferred from Carley's Milwaukee office to join Clay and to serve as project manager of University Place. Galling resigned in February, 1985 and Clay took a two-year leave of absence from UNCC to work full time for the Carley Capital Group to continue the oversight of University Place.

Construction Begins for University Place

On March 20, 1984, thirteen months after the Carley Group was selected as developer, a groundbreaking ceremony took place, attended by Governor Hunt, and construction began. In August of that year, the first building, the Montessori School, was opened. And on September 28, 1985, University Place celebrated with its Grand Opening, attended by approximately 20,000 people, as its Walden Court, New Shoppes at University Place and Lakeshore Village opened their doors. Thereafter, project openings were continuous — Welwyn Cluster Homes, Audubon Park Townhouses, University Place Offices, Lakefront Shoppes, and the Hilton Hotel. By fall of 1987, almost $100 million had been invested, almost one-fourth of the anticipated built-out cost.

While Odell Associates was to have the lead role in the design of University Place, many other designers contributed to the quality of the complex. David Furman designed Lakeshore Village, Walden Court, the Montessori School and Audubon Park; William Little and Associates designed the Oasis Temple, United Carolina Bank and First Union National Bank; Reg Narmour designed the Welwyn Cluster Homes; Jenkins and Peer contributed their talent to Lakefront Shoppes; Atkinson-Dyer, the theatre complex; and Gantt-Huberman, the One University Place office building.

By 1987, University Place was the town center for the emerging University City. Neither University Place nor University City was ever conceived as a separate corporate entity. It represented a carefully planned satellite urban center of a growing city, Charlotte. With the announcement of a regional shopping complex to be developed by the Hahn Group, University City was fulfilling its promise. Visitors from throughout the United States and many foreign countries were visiting University Place and the surrounding area to study not only the unique land-use design but the public-private partnership process that successfully melded a research park, a university, and a mixed-use town center in a concerted planning and development effort. When the continuing education and conference center is built as planned, University Place will represent a model of private enterprise-public education cooperation in providing lifelong learning conducted by the university and the business world as partners.

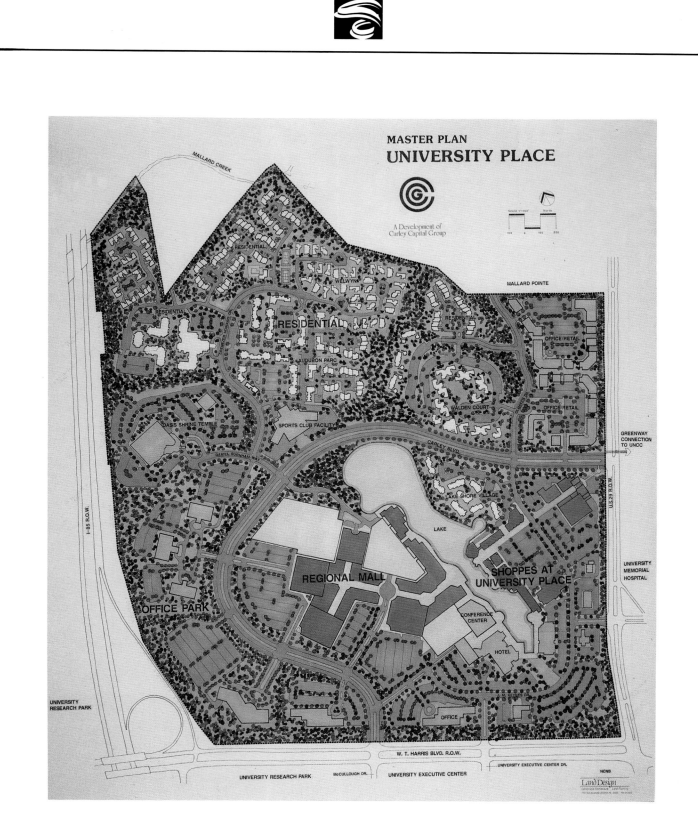

University Place master plan

Hilton Hotel on the lake

Shoppes at University Place

University Place at night

University Place Cinema

Slug's Restaurant and Lakeshore Village

University City celebration at University Place

REORGANIZATION AND A HOME OFFICE

During its first fifteen years, the University Research Park had no home office, address, or, for several years, no letterhead. The Charlotte Chamber of Commerce, where the idea of the park was born, provided secretarial services without remuneration for the first four years. Financial records were kept by one of the banks and by the park treasurer, who was a bank representative. Prior to the sale of land to IBM, the park had no income other than $51,000 generated by memberships and a few corporate gifts. There were no paid employees. Research park business was conducted by officers, directors, and committees on a voluntary basis.

When land purchases or sales were made, realtors collected specified commissions. Payments were made to attorneys for legal services and to others for some professional planning functions. When funds became available through the sale of land, the directors voted small grants to the Chamber of Commerce to partially offset operations costs. For a two year period beginning in 1976, the park and the Chamber of Commerce shared the employment costs of a full-time industry recruiter on a 50/50 basis.

Changes in Management and Facilities

Soon after he assumed office in 1977, President David Taylor set in motion several studies of research parks. On the basis of information compiled from a study made by the Urban Institute at UNCC and other recommendations, Taylor proposed, and the board approved, a series of structural and procedural modifications. The massive construction program launched by IBM in 1978, the several new tenants that had bought property and begun building soon thereafter, and the recommendation of special studies reinforced the need for a separate office and the commitment of more personnel to the operation of the research park. After conferring with the president of the Chamber of Commerce, it was agreed that the joint employment of an industry recruiter would be discontinued.

Separate Office and Operating President

President Taylor and Vice President Goode determined that Goode, who was serving as chairman of First Charlotte Corporation, would be able to devote half of his time as the chief administrative officer of the park. At the meeting of the board in 1981, Goode was elected president and Taylor chairman. The charter and bylaws were amended to provide for an operations committee and a finance committee. The amended bylaws specified that the chairman of the corporation would be chairman of the finance committee. Elected to serve with Taylor on the finance committee were C. C. Cameron, Ben T. Craig, William H. Dougherty, Harold Hoak, Seddon Goode, Jr., Harry J. Nicholas, and John A. Tate, Jr. The new bylaws also specified that the president would serve as chairman of the operations committee. Additional members were David Burkhalter, C. C. Cameron, E. K. Fretwell Jr., William S. Lee, III, John A. Tate, Jr., and David Taylor. Under the new plan, the Executive Committee would cease to exist. UNCC and the Chamber of Commerce would continue to be represented by vice presidents. It was pointed out that "In no way does the proposed organization diminish the powers or authority of University Research Park's main Board." It seemed obvious, however, that if the streamlining described was achieved, board members not on one of the two committees would have much less month-to-month involvement. Goode provided office space in the First Charlotte Corporation suite on the twenty-fourth floor of First Union Plaza.

Accounting Moved to UNCC

In late 1980, University Research Park Treasurer W. A. Bowen, vice president of Wachovia Bank and Trust Company, accepted the presidency of a bank in Tulsa, Oklahoma. Following his departure and with the approval of Chancellor E. K. Fretwell Jr., the financial affairs of the park were transferred to Financial Services at UNCC. University Research Park Director Leo E. Ells was vice chancellor for business affairs at UNCC. His accounting staff could provide professional oversight for fiscal matters previously provided by the banks. It seemed obvious to all concerned that the volume of financial transactions to be handled was on the verge of substantial growth, and this arrangement, strengthened by annual audits by an outside accounting firm, would provide checks and balances on the growing volume of financial transactions.

President Becomes Full-Time

The steady increase in activity convinced Chairman Taylor and President Goode that a separate and independent office and a full-time executive staff were desirable. A suite of offices was rented and furnished on the nineteenth floor of the First Union Plaza and President Goode was employed as chief executive officer with a support staff.

"The Dog and Pony Show"

To promote the park, visual and audio-visual materials were developed and continuously revised. These promotional materials became known internally as Claude Freeman's "Dog and Pony Show." When Freeman succeeded General Paul Younts as a director and member of the Real Estate Committee of the research park in July 1971, he encouraged the development of promotional material that "made sense." During his first years as director, leaflets and brochures were developed by special committees and sent to major corporations throughout the country. By late 1980, Mary Ray Denton and Dorlan Mork of the UNCC Learning Resources Center and Norman Pease, Jr. and his associates were putting the finishing touches on the audio-visual presentation entitled "The Future is Now," complete with recorded music and narration by Governor James Hunt, County Commission Chairman Liz Hair, and Chancellor E. K. Fretwell Jr.

After Seddon "Rusty" Goode, Jr. became president and the University Research Park had its own suite of offices, more resources were devoted to audio-visual presentations. The walls of the offices were covered with colorful maps of existing and potential developments. Adaptations were made for presentation to specific corporations. In preparation for one of his trips to Japan, President Goode employed George Van Allen to work with Fujiko Kellen of Kellen International to prepare his presentation and to translate the audio portion into the Japanese language. Freeman continued to work with the central office staff to make communication more effective by updating the graphics.

Other Changes

The new form of organization streamlined the decision-making process so it could handle, with much greater dispatch, a rapidly growing volume of business, but it also brought about other changes. It was now possible to hold catered luncheons for visitors and prospects in the research park offices. This represented a great leap forward in available physical facilities. It also represented a very substantial increase in annual office operating expenditures. An increase in land sales during this particular period made it possible for the organization to operate with a great deal more professionalism and a more adequate staff than in the past. Prior to 1980 the annual operating budgets, excluding interest paid on borrowed money and expenses involved in land transactions, were usually less than $30,000.

Another development demonstrating the desirability of the new organization and office arrangements followed the retirement of C. C. Cameron as chairman of First Union Corporation. He had been elected vice chairman of the research park and vice chairman of The Foundation of UNCC. David Taylor had announced his intention to resign as chairman of these two organizations and it was anticipated that Cameron would succeed him in these capacities. First Union Corporation was to provide him an office following his retirement but it turned out that his office could be arranged in connection with the park offices, making it more convenient for all concerned. As these changes were occurring, Governor James Martin appointed Cameron chief financial officer for the State of North Carolina, a position which he did not expect to hold indefinitely.

A related development was the movement of the office of The Foundation of UNCC to the nineteenth floor of the First Union Plaza. This provided a setting in which Cameron could discharge his responsibilities as chairman of the Foundation from offices in close proximity. It also provided common conference facilities which could serve several related purposes.

Members of University Research Park Corporation Decline

With the merger or liquidation of some of the 29 original member corporations (listed in Chapter III), the number of park members was reduced. The enlarged and constantly changing Board of Directors served as a means of involving additional community leaders in the increasing tempo of activities.

OFFICERS AND DIRECTORS

*"The unusual thing about the Charlotte business community —
is they are willing and continue to be willing to
encourage progress in the park in spite of the risk."*
—Claude Q. Freeman, Sr.

The University Research Park has been fortunate throughout its existence in having strong leadership in the Charlotte community guiding its destiny. Lists of officers, board members, and member representatives are shown in Tables 5 and 6.

From its birth in the Charlotte Chamber of Commerce in 1966 through its first twenty years, twenty presidents or chairmen[14] of the chamber have served on the University Research Park Board of Directors. Each person serving in this high office has been chosen on the basis of demonstrated leadership ability, thereby assuring built-in strength. W. T. Harris was president of the chamber when the park was organized and was president of University Research Park for its first ten years. David Taylor, also a former Chamber of Commerce president, succeeded Harris and served as president of the park until the organization of the board was changed in 1980, at which time Seddon Goode, Jr. became president and David Taylor became chairman. C. C. Cameron was elected chairman in 1986 with the understanding that Taylor, as vice chairman, would direct the organization until Cameron relinquished his duties as the state's top financial officer.

Four of the first directors elected (W. T. "Bill" Harris,

C. C. Cameron

Harry J. Nicholas, John A. Tate, Jr., and Dean W. Colvard) served on the board throughout the first twenty years. David Taylor, Edwin L. Jones, Jr., and J. Norman Pease, Jr. were elected only a few months from the inception of the park and served throughout the two decades. Jones' representation was somewhat unique in that his company owned a large tract of the dedicated land. Others who served more than ten years include A. G. Odell, Jr., Claude Q. Freeman, Sr., Ted H. Ousley, and Seddon "Rusty" Goode, Jr.

Twenty senior officers of local banks have represented their companies on the board for various periods of time during the first twenty years. Each financial institution committing funds has been represented on the board from the time of its first commitment.

All corporations contributing to the founding of University Research Park have been represented continuously on the board. Collins & Aikman Corporation, the first resident, has had representation on the board almost from the board's beginning.

The chancellor of UNCC has been actively involved in the planning and operation of the Park from the beginning. His responsibility for nominating some of the directors has been exercised in close cooperation with the Chamber of Commerce and the chairman of the nominating committee to assure that persons with special contributions to make are not overlooked. The charter and by-laws have been amended from time to time to enlarge

---

Beginning in 1976, the title of the top elected official was designated "chairman," the chief administrative officer was designated as "president."

the Board of Directors. Well in advance of the retirement of the first UNCC chancellor, the Vice Chancellor for Business Affairs, Leo E. Ells, became a director. This assured a continuity of UNCC representation while a new chancellor was being installed. Other members of the UNCC faculty and staff added during the latter part of the twenty year period included, in addition to Chancellor E. K. Fretwell Jr., Vice Chancellor Douglas M. Orr, Jr., and the Director of the Urban Institute James W. Clay.

Other directors have included mayors, city council members, county commissioners, and legislators. The list of officers and directors includes 125 of Charlotte's leading people. With the exception of real estate commissions, legal fees, and payments to staffs, services have been rendered without compensation. University Research Park is indeed a creation of enlightened community leadership and cooperation between town and gown.

Table 5
OFFICERS OF UNIVERSITY RESEARCH PARK 1966-1986

YEAR	CHAIRMAN	PRESIDENT	VICE PRESIDENT	SECRETARY	TREASURER	ASSISTANT SECRETARY	ASSISTANT SEC./TREAS.	ASSISTANT TREASURER
1966		J. W. Grier, Jr.	James Y. Preston	Francis I. Parker	Francis I. Parker		James Y. Preston	
1967		W. T. Harris	J. Scott Cramer Graeme Keith John A. Tate, Jr.	Carl Horn	B. L. Ray			Harry J. Nicholas
1968		W. T. Harris	J. Scott Cramer Graeme Keith John A. Tate, Jr.	Carl Horn	B. L. Ray			
1969		W. T. Harris	J. Scott Cramer Graeme Keith John A. Tate, Jr.	Carl Horn	B. L. Ray			
1970		W. T. Harris	J. Scott Cramer Graeme Keith	E. T. Anderson/ Emery Inman	Patrick N. Calhoun	William M. Ficklen		
1971		W. T. Harris	W. A. Bowen Dean W. Colvard Graeme Keith	Emery Inman	Patrick N. Calhoun	William M. Ficklen		
1972		W. T. Harris	W. A. Bowen Dean W. Colvard Graeme Keith	Emery Inman	Patrick N. Calhoun	William M. Ficklen		
1973		W. T. Harris	W. A. Bowen Dean W. Colvard	Emery Inman	Patrick N. Calhoun	William M. Ficklen		
1974		W. T. Harris	W. A. Bowen Dean W. Colvard	Emery Inman	Patrick N. Calhoun	William M. Ficklen/ Charles Crawford		
1975		W. T. Harris	W. A. Bowen Dean W. Colvard	Emery Inman	J. W. Claud	G. Jackson Burney		
1976		W. T. Harris	W. A. Bowen Dean W. Colvard	Emery Inman	J. W. Claud			
1977	W. T. Harris (Honorary Lifetime)	David Taylor	Dean W. Colvard	John A. Tate, Jr. Harry J. Nicholas	Robert Kitterman			
1978		David Taylor	Dean W. Colvard Harry J. Nicholas	John A. Tate, Jr.	Robert Kitterman			
1979		David Taylor	C. C. Cameron Ben T. Craig E. K. Fretwell Jr. Seddon Goode, Jr. Harry J. Nicholas John A. Tate, Jr.	W. A. Bowen	William Dougherty			
# 1980	David Taylor	Seddon Goode, Jr.	C. C. Cameron E. K. Fretwell Jr. Bland Worley	John A. Tate, Jr.	John A. Tate, Jr.			
1981	David Taylor	Seddon Goode, Jr.	C. C. Cameron E. K. Fretwell Jr. Bland Worley	John A. Tate, Jr.	John A. Tate, Jr.			
1982	David Taylor	Seddon Goode, Jr.	C. C. Cameron E. K. Fretwell Jr. Wallace J. Jorgenson	John A. Tate, Jr.	John A. Tate, Jr.			
1983	David Taylor	Seddon Goode, Jr.	C. C. Cameron Larry Dagenhart E. K. Fretwell Jr.	John A. Tate, Jr.	John A. Tate, Jr.			
1984	David Taylor	Seddon Goode, Jr.	C. C. Cameron E. K. Fretwell Jr. Harold G. Hoak	Judith R. Hamilton	Francis B. Kemp			
1985	David Taylor	Seddon Goode, Jr.	E. K. Fretwell Jr. J. Gary Morgan Leroy Robinson	J. Gary Morgan	Francis B. Kemp	Robert W. King, Jr. A. Grant Whitney, Jr.		
1986	C. C. Cameron David Taylor*	Seddon Goode, Jr.	E. K. Fretwell Jr. Francis B. Kemp*** J. Gary Morgan**	J. Gary Morgan**	Francis B. Kemp***	Carolyn T. Hawkins A. Grant Whitney, Jr.		

Operations Committee:
David Taylor, Chairman   Seddon Goode, Jr.
David Burkhalter   William S. Lee III
C. C. Cameron   John A. Tate, Jr.
E. K. Fretwell Jr.

Finance Committee:
David Taylor, Chairman   Harold G. Hoak
C. C. Cameron   Harry J. Nicholas
Ben T. Craig   John A. Tate, Jr.

* David Taylor was elected vice chairman to serve until C. C. Cameron relinquishes his duties as chief financial officer for the State of North Carolina
** J. Gary Morgan was designated vice president and secretary
*** Francis B. Kemp was designated vice president and treasurer

Table 6

DIRECTORS, OFFICERS, AND MEMBERS FOR THE FIRST TWENTY YEARS

NAME	COMPANY AFFILIATION	DIRECTOR	OFFICER	MEMBER[15]
Ackerman, F. D.	Southern Bell			x
Allen, James A.	Celanese Corp.	x		x
Anderson, E. T.		x	x	
Barnes, W. Faison		x		
Barnhardt, William M.	Southern Webbing Mills	x		
Barr, Walter		x		
Belk, Thomas M.	Chamber of Commerce, Belk Stores Services	x		x
Bevier, R. B.	IBM	x		x
Bodycott, Eugene	Odell Associates	x		
Bourns, Richard T.	Verbatim	x		
Bowen, W. A.	Wachovia	x	x	x
Broadrick, George H.	First Citizens			x
Bryant, Donald G.	Chamber of Commerce, Harry & Bryant	x		
Burkhalter, David A.	Belk Stores Services	x		x
Burney, G. Jackson	Chamber of Commerce		x	
Calhoun, Patrick N.	Chamber of Commerce, NCNB	x	x	x
Cameron, C. C.	FUNC	x	x	x
Cannon, James G.	American Credit Co.	x		x
Chaffman, James A.	IBM	x		x
Claud, J. W.	NCNB	x	x	x
Clay, James W.	UNCC	x		
Colvard, Dean W.	UNCC	x	x	
Copeland, E. H. Jr.	Odell Associates	x		x
Craig, Ben T.	FUNC	x	x	x
Cramer, J. Scott	Wachovia	x	x	x
Crawford, Charles	Chamber of Commerce		x	
Crosland, John Jr.	John Crosland Co.	x		x
Crutchfield, Charles H.	Chamber of Commerce, WBTV	x		
Dagenhart, Larry J.	Chamber of Commerce, Smith, Helms et al	x	x	
Davidson, Don	Chamber of Commerce, Washburn Graphics, Inc.	x		
Denton, Donald	Chamber of Commerce, Collier, Cobb & Assoc.	x		
Dickson, Stuart	Ruddick Corp.	x		
Dietrich, Robert	Celanese	x		x
Dougherty, William H.	NCNB	x	x	x
Drummond, Jere A.	Southern Bell	x		x
Duncan, Buell H.	Piedmont Natural Gas	x		x
DuPuy, Carla	County Commission	x		
Ells, Leo E.	UNCC	x		
Evans, R. O.	Concrete Supply	x		x
Ficklen, William M.	Chamber of Commerce		x	
Frederick, Leon C.	Collins & Aikman	x		x
Freeman, Claude Q. Sr.	Freeman, McClintock et al	x		x
Fretwell, E. K. Jr.	UNCC	x	x	
Frisch, Michael	Collins & Aikman	x		x
Gantt, Harvey B.	Mayor, Charlotte	x		
Glenn, James N.	FUNB	x		x
Goode, Seddon Jr.	URP	x	x	
Grace, Charles L.	Cummins	x		
Gray, Carroll	Chamber of Commerce	x		
Greenspan, Frank	Reeves Bros.	x		x
Grier, Joseph W. Jr.	Grier, Parker et al	x	x	x
Hair, Elisabeth G.	Sunbelt Communications	x		
Hamilton, Judith R.	URP		x	
Haney, T. S. (or J. T.)	Concrete Supply			x
Harris, James J.	James J. Harris & Co.			x
Harris, W. T.	Chamber of Commerce, Harris-Teeter Co.	x	x	x
Hawkins, Carolyn T.	URP		x	
Hicks, Charles S.	Odell Associates	x		x
Higginbottom, John T.	AT&T	x		
Hoak, Harold G.	Wachovia	x	x	x
Hodges, Luther H. Jr.	Chamber of Commerce, NCNB	x		x
Horn, Carl Jr.	Duke Power Company	x	x	x
Hynes, James E. S.	Chamber of Commerce	x		
Inman, Emery	Northwestern Bank	x	x	x
Jones, D. W.	Chamber of Commerce, Duke Power Company	x	x	x

---

[15] The 29 member corporations are listed in Chapter III. Different executives have represented their companies in different years.

NAME	COMPANY AFFILIATION	DIRECTOR	OFFICER	MEMBER[15]
Jones, Edwin L. Jr.	J. A. Jones Construction	x		x
Jorgenson, Wallace J.	Chamber of Commerce, WBTV	x	x	
Keffer, John F.		x		
Keith, Graeme	FUNB & BarclaysAmerican	x	x	x
Kemp, Francis B.	NCNB, Chamber of Comm.	x		x
Kendrick, Hal	Collins & Aikman	x		x
King, Robert W. Jr.	Moore & Van Allen		x	
King, W. E. Jr.		x		
Kirby, Al C.	Vinson Realty			x
Kitterman, Robert	FUNB	x	x	x
Knox, H. Edward	Mayor, Charlotte	x		
Latimer, Edwin P.	Chamber of Commerce, American Credit	x	x	x
Laughey, Al	Collins & Aikman	x		x
Laux, Gar	Arnold Palmer Cadillac	x		
Lee, William S. III	Chamber of Commerce, Duke Power Company	x		x
Lewis, John D.	Arthur Andersen	x		
Lockwood, Barbara	County Commission	x		
Maxheim, John H.	Piedmont Natural Gas	x		x
McQuilkin, Frank	Collins & Aikman	x		x
Moore, Dwight B.	Duke Power Company	x		x
Moore, Joseph D.	Reeves Bros.	x		x
Morgan, J. Gary	URP		x	
Nemzek, Thomas A.	EPRI	x		
Nicholas, Harry J.	First Citizens	x	x	x
Nurkin, Harry A.	Memorial Hosp.	x		
Odell, A. G. Jr.	Odell Associates	x		x
Odom, T. L.	County Commission, Attorney	x		
Orr, Douglas M. Jr.	UNCC	x		
Ousley, Theodore H.	Allstate	x		
Parker, Francis I.	Parker, Poe et al	x	x	x
Pease, J. Norman Jr.	J. N. Pease Assoc.	x		x
Phelps, J. Bailey	Fiber Industries			x
Pickard, J. David	Piedmont Natural Gas	x		x
Porter, Richard M.	Queens Properties	x		
Preston, James Y.	Attorney	x	x	
Rash, Betty Chafin	City Council	x		
Ray, B. L.	Exxon	x	x	
Ray, Tom	County Commission	x		
Robinson, Leroy	Chamber of Commerce, Belk Stores Services	x		x
Rose, Louis L. Jr.	Southern Real Estate	x		x
Rose, Louis L. Sr.	Southern Real Estate	x		x
Ryan, John J.	Southern Bell	x		x
Schoch, Hampton		x		
Sessoms, W. M.		x		
Skinner, B. Franklin	Southern Bell	x		x
Sloan, J. D.	Duke Power Company	x		x
Snyder, Robert D.	UNCC	x		
Spangler, C. D. Jr.	Spangler Construction	x		x
Street, E. R.	McDevitt & Street			x
Street, James A.	Triangle Research Inst.	x		
Tate, John A. Jr.	NCNB	x	x	x
Taylor, David	Chamber of Commerce, Celanese Corp.	x	x	x
Temple, John	IBM	x		x
Terpak, Ronald J.	IBM	x		x
Thomas, Alan	Southern Bell	x		x
Thompson, Sydnor	Parker, Poe et al			x
Tison, Ben III	NCNB	x		x
Trosch, Minette Conrad	City Council	x		
Vinson, Ed	Vinson Realty	x		x
Walsh, Stephen R.	Walsh Properties	x		
White, Jim	NCNB	x		x
Whitney, A. Grant Jr.	Grier, Parker et al		x	x
Worley, Bland W.	Chamber of Commerce, American Credit Co.	x	x	x
Wyatt, Jerry H.	Reeves Bros.	x		x
Younts, Paul	Younts Realty	x		x

UNIVERSITY RESEARCH PARK AND UNIVERSITY CITY — 1987

"In many ways University City is something of an experiment. The combination of a university, a research park, and a town center seems to be without parallel anywhere."
—James W. Clay and Douglas M. Orr, Jr.

In 1967 the first University Research Park brochure boldly stated: "University Research Park, when fully developed, has the potential of generating an investment in the community of $200 million and creating more than 10,000 new jobs." Twenty years later reality exceeded projections. By 1987, University City, the 20-square mile area surrounding the park and the university, was home to more than 60,000 people. It was estimated that more than 13,000 worked in the area. There were more than two dozen housing developments, several shopping complexes, new office buildings, a hospital, plus banks, theaters, restaurants, and a new elementary school. In 1987, University City was the county's boom town. It was estimated that new investment in the area's seven year period since 1980 was approaching $4 billion and the tax value of real estate had multiplied severalfold.

University Research Park corporations alone had constructed almost four million square feet of floor space, at an estimated cost exceeding $300 million. Park employees numbered more than 7,000. Another 3,200 were employed by UNCC, the university medical complex, and nearby Phillip Morris. Using a standard multiplier of 1.5 to estimate secondary employment (support and related services) resulting from this base number there were projected to be an additional 15,300 jobs in the community. The magnitude of the park's economic impact on the community stemmed from endless sources. To cite one example, in 1985 IBM alone pumped $400 million into the local economy through payrolls, gifts to charity, education and public service, and purchases.

University City

While The University of North Carolina at Charlotte and University Research Park were University City's pioneer institutions, by 1987 University City was rapidly becoming the diverse commercial, educational, medical, and residential community envisioned twenty years earlier. The four contiguous centerpiece components — the

park, the university, University Place, and University Memorial Medical Center — were surrounded by burgeoning development. Newspapers from the *New York Times* to West German dailies had called attention to the area. The American Association of State Colleges and Universities awarded the university its Theodore Mitau Award for outstanding institutional innovation. The reviewers of seventy-nine nominations for the award found the university's role in the development of University City to be an impressive example of successful cooperation with both private enterprise and government.

A University City plan, approved by City Council and the Board of County Commissioners in 1983, provided a guiding framework for development of the area. Called the UNCC District Plan, it covered approximately 20 square miles and was the first of a series of small area plans developed in the county. It recognized the importance of the employment base provided by the park and called for its expansion. The plan reaffirmed the importance of the area beyond its role as an employment and educational center. Developed by the Planning Commission and reviewed extensively by citizens, business, and education leaders in the University City area, it laid the foundation for the development of quality residential areas and service entities to complement the park and the university. It also called for the development of a gateway area at the intersection of North Tryon Street, Highway 29, and Highway 49 as an entrance to University City.

According to the UNCC District Plan and earlier plans developed by the Mecklenburg County Parks and Recreation Department, "the best planned part of the county's greenway park system" will eventually run through the University City area. The linear park will include more than 130 acres in University City. About thirty acres of the greenway system will link the university and University Place with walkways, running paths, and a fitness trail. Property in University Place has been dedicated by the developers to extend the greenway into the heart of the town center and University Research Park is developing its portion which will include almost 50 acres. The final section will link residential areas west of the park (in the area of Harris Boulevard and Mallard Creek Road) with the park, University Place, and the university.

Accessibility to the University City area improved over the twenty year period. With the completion of I-77 in the late 1970s and Harris Boulevard in 1986, the park is located on one of North Carolina's five interstates and a second, I-77, is several minutes away. A third, I-40 is accessible in twenty-five minutes. With the completion of another limited access highway, the Billy Graham Expressway, Charlotte's new airport facility, completed in 1982, is fifteen minutes from the park. And downtown Charlotte is less than fifteen minutes away. In 1988 construction will begin to widen Newell-Hickory Grove Road which would become a continuation of the southern portion of Harris Boulevard. Completion of this road will provide better access to east and south Charlotte.

University Place had become the centerpiece of the University City area. More than $75 million has been spent on construction and when development is complete, the 250-acre complex will have four million square feet of buildings and represent an investment of more than $400 million. Lakeside development in University Place already included one of Charlotte's premier restaurants, a new 93,000 square foot, four-story office building, a Hilton Hotel, and lakeshore condominiums. Along the nearby pedestrian axis were more restaurants, shops, theatres, banks, and services. Three residential communities, featuring apartments and luxury single family homes, were located a short distance from the village center. Eventually these communities would be linked to one another and to the retail core by a planned pathway system. An additional entrance to the university, off Harris Boulevard, will be constructed in 1988. Eventually this will bring new university development to the doorstep of University Place.

University City's medical complex was growing. The $16 million, 130-bed hospital facility, opened in 1985, was serving as a magnet for other technical and health-related activities. The complex had two large specialty clinics and more than thirty-five primary care physicians were located in the complex.

More than thirty-five single-family residential subdivisions had been constructed in University City since 1980. In 1987 there were more than 5,500 single-family and 3,500 multi-family units in the area and twenty developers, already active in University City in late 1987, had indicated that they planned to build 12,000 new units during the next three to five years. A new university chancellor's home was to be built in 1988. The Foundation of UNCC was assisting the university to meet this long outstanding need. Property was purchased off Mallard Creek

Church Road, opposite the AT&T entrance to the park, for the chancellor's residence. The home was to be located in Colvard Park, an up-scale subdivision being developed according to design standards written by the dean of the UNCC College of Architecture, Charles Hight.

University City's first new public school was to open in January, 1988 adjacent to Colvard Park on Mallard Creek Road. The need for both junior and senior high schools were being studied.

To the north of University City a new industrial corridor was developing. More traditional industries complementing park high-tech tenants were locating in the Highway 29/I-85 corridor in neighboring Cabarrus County. Phillip Morris, located in the corridor, employed approximately 1,400 in 1987. Also located on more than 2,000 acres north of the University City area was the twenty-seven year-old Charlotte Motor Speedway, the second largest seating event in the nation, with grandstand seating capacity exceeding 100,000. It was one of the most attended raceways in the country, with more than 700,000 visitors annually at eight events. The Charlotte Convention and Visitors Bureau estimated that the speedway contributed over $96 million to the state's economy in 1987.

The Park's First Twenty Years: Sources of Strength

Economic conditions fluctuated dramatically during University Research Park's first twenty years. Uncommon vision, faith in the future, and daring leadership were required to initiate and sustain the organization through the ups and downs of economic cycles over the twenty year period. Even with strong leadership there were periods when progress was slow and when the future seemed uncertain.

Strength of the organization stemmed from several factors: (1) the idea of a research park was soundly conceived and accepted by the Charlotte Chamber of Commerce; (2) University Research Park was able to develop an effective affiliation with Collins & Aikman and J. A. Jones Company (through its subsidiary, Queens Properties) which resulted in the dedication of their contiguous land holdings to the park; (3) leaders had an unrelenting commitment to the proposition that education and discovery would become increasingly important in economic growth; (4) appropriate documents were carefully developed by competent attorneys; (5) major banks displayed faith in the future and acted on their convictions by providing loans to the park to purchase land and operate prior to the generation of any income; (6) there was concurrent and cooperative planning for the development of UNCC, economic growth of the community, and improvement in the quality of life; (7) appropriate participation was invited and received from city, county, and state governmental agencies in the sound planning of University City, University Research Park, and UNCC.

The University of North Carolina at Charlotte

The University of North Carolina at Charlotte

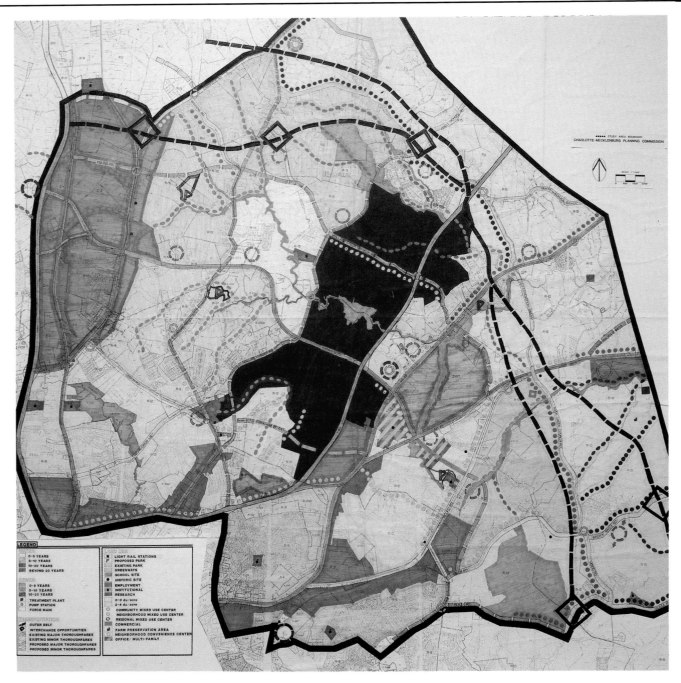

UNCC District Plan

University City

One University Place

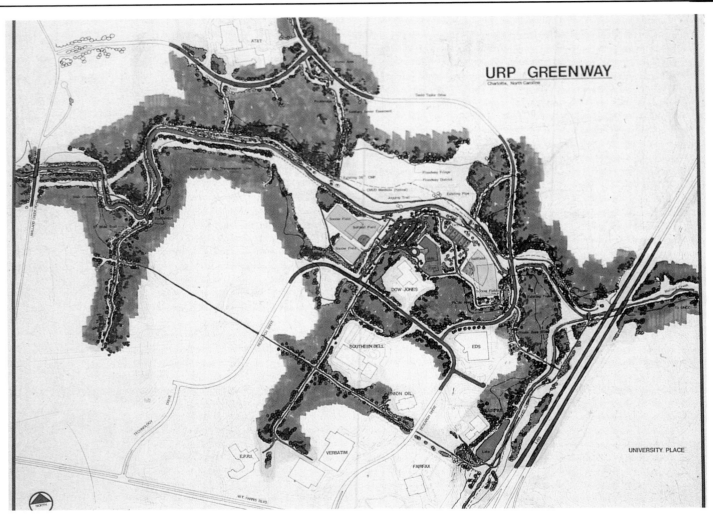

University Research Park Greenway

Lake at University Place

UNCC's Growth

The University of North Carolina at Charlotte was the flagship of development in northeastern Mecklenburg County. From an enrollment of 1,800 commuting students when University Research Park was organized late in 1966, there was growth ranging from two to thirty-five percent annually during the twenty year period. By 1987 there was dormitory space for 4,000 students with one hundred percent occupancy and total enrollment had grown to more than 12,000. The first air conditioned dormitories at a public college or university in North Carolina were built at UNCC in 1968. More than 1,800 of the students, about the same number as total enrollment in 1967, were taking graduate studies in fifteen approved programs. Full-time faculty had increased from about one hundred in 1967 to more than five hundred in 1986 with more than four hundred in addition drawn from the community to serve as part-time faculty. The administrative and operative staff numbered about 1,500. Library holdings had grown from forty thousand to four hundred thousand volumes.

In addition to the Theodore Mitau Award previously mentioned, UNCC has received wide acclaim for its academic programs. All of its professional programs have received full national accreditation. This is regarded as an important achievement for an institution that has been granting baccalaureate degrees for fewer than 25 years. *U.S. News and World Report* named UNCC one of the South's best comprehensive universities in two consecutive reports. The same periodical also listed the university as one of the two best buys among comprehensive universities of the South. *Money* magazine also ranked UNCC as one of the nation's top ten values in higher education. Numerous outstanding individual achievements by students have received attention. A good example is the UNCC accounting student who ranked number one among all those taking the CPA examination in 1987.

The annual operating budget for UNCC increased from $2.6 million in 1966-67 to $73.5 million in 1986-87. More than half of the total budget went to payrolls and fringe benefits. About half of the total annual operating expenditures were made up of student fees and service enterprises such as dormitories, dining halls, parking facilities, bookstores, vending machines, and others which derived their income from sales and services. The State of North Carolina was appropriating only about half of the operating budgets. In the twenty year period from 1966 to 1986, UNCC spent more than $60 million for buildings. One fourth of this building expenditure was generated by the university through revenue bonds to be repaid by fees for services and sales of food and supplies.

The University and the Community

UNCC's planning, in cooperation with the community, gained in breadth and sophistication. Through the Urban Institute, the International Studies Center, The University Business Incubator Center, the Office of Continuing Education and Extension, The Center for Business and Economic Research, the six colleges, thirty departments, and the 100,000 watt public radio station, WFAE, there was increasing interaction with the community. A professor of history became a principal spokesman for historic preservation; a vice chancellor and director of the Urban Institute were the principal scholars and visionaries stimulating the creation of University Place; professors of political science served on the Planning Commission and the Mecklenburg County Board of Elections; an Urban Institute administrator became the executive director of The University Business Incubator Center to help create new industries; all professional programs received full accreditation; in cooperation with North Carolina State University and The University of North Carolina at Chapel Hill respectively, doctoral programs were offered in engineering and teacher education; contract research grants, supporting studies in almost all departments, increased each year and totaled almost $4 million in 1987; the chairman of the Board of Trustees and chancellor chaired the University City leaders in consideration of improvements in quality of life and improved economic development of the whole area; and faculty members served on the Board of Trustees of Johnson C. Smith University and numerous other organizations.

UNCC's Urban Institute was established at the university in 1970 to give direction to the institution's emerging role as an urban university. It has played an important role in linking university and community planning and economic development activities. The Institute was created as an urban version of well tested agricultural research and extension programs. In 1987 the Institute had a $1 million-plus annual budget, a dozen prospering applied research and public service programs, and a track record of serving the city and the region. The Institute is the secretariat for the University City Group composed of representatives of the park, the university, University Place, and others interested in the future of the area. It coordinated the preplanning phase of University Place and has conducted economic development studies for the park. The model used by the university as it worked with community personnel to plan University Place was being adapted by the president of Johnson C. Smith University, Dr. Robert L. Albright, with assistance from the Urban Institute, to redevelop the area surrounding that university. In addition to economic development and planning, the Urban Institute had community-oriented applied research and public service programs in transportation, waste management, low income neighborhood improvement, leadership training, local government assistance, and market analysis. The Urban Institute maintained a computerized geographically based data bank and has published two dozen economic atlases and profiles including joint projects with the Department of Geography and Earth Sciences for a Charlotte-Mecklenburg atlas, *Charlotte: Trends and Patterns of a Dynamic City* and a forthcoming atlas, *Land of the South,* to be published by Oxmoor Press.

The terms "urban university" and "way-out-there" had very different connotations than those of 1967. A trip from UNCC or the park to the center of Charlotte or the towns of Concord and Kannapolis required about the same time as a trip from the southpark area to the uptown area. With 15,000 alumni living in Charlotte, UNCC had surpassed all other universities and colleges in alumni residing in the area. More than half of the alumni graduated in Arts and Sciences; more than 5,000 had degrees in Accounting and Business Administration; almost 4,000 in Education and Allied Professions; more than 2,000 in engineering; about 1,500 in Nursing; and almost 500 in Architecture. Many graduates were employed by firms operating in the park.

The University and the Park

As had been anticipated when University Research Park was launched interactions among personnel of UNCC and firms located in the park have increased as research programs and graduate studies at UNCC have expanded. Specialists from IBM and other firms have been involved in sharing their expertise in classrooms in mathematics, statistics, computer science, engineering, and other areas. Research projects underwritten by some of the resident companies have involved faculty. Through UNCC's cooperative student placement programs, undergraduate students have gained industrial experience while continuing their studies. Many employees of firms in the park have used the facilities of UNCC's library. IBM has provided UNCC with many units of computing equipment. A partial gift by Collins & Aikman of their building on North Tryon Street facilitated the establishment of The University Business Incubator Center.

In addition to educational and cultural programs available on campus, employees in the research park benefited from university-sponsored continuing education courses designed expressly for them. Each year more than one hundred short courses and seminars in engineering, information science, and management were conducted at plant sites and on campus by the university's

Office of Continuing Education and Extension. This arrangement gives reality to the idea of life-long learning and benefits employees in the park and at the university. Employees are able to keep up-to-date professionally with courses which are very accessible and the university faculty keep abreast of new developments "in the field" as they interact with professionals dealing with everyday challenges.

With 2,000 students and 80 faculty, UNCC's College of Engineering was the second largest program in the state. In 1987 the college hired a full-time director of engineering research and industrial development to increase the university's capability in this area. In addition to microelectronics and precision manufacturing labs, the college will have sophisticated labs for optical devices, computers, transportation, and materials development research by 1989.

In the early 1980s UNCC became one of six institutions to form the Microelectronics Center of North Carolina (MCNC). The statewide network was funded by the General Assembly to conduct educational programs and research in technologies related to semiconductor materials, fabrication processes, integrated circuit design, and computer science. UNCC, Duke, North Carolina State, North Carolina A&T, UNC-Chapel Hill, and the Research Triangle Institute were collaborating with MCNC, located in Research Triangle Park. Approximately 15 UNCC engineering faculty and more than 20 graduate and 50 undergraduate students were involved in microelectronics at UNCC.

In 1987 mutually reinforcing relationships between the university and the park led to funding for an Applied Research Center on the UNCC campus. Through the efforts of University Research Park, UNCC, and Central Piedmont Community College, an agreement was reached on a plan to provide applied research capability and training for park resident Kodak/Verbatim. Legislative leaders were persuaded that the UNCC/CPCC/University Research Park-Kodak/Verbatim arrangement will serve as a prototype to enhance economic development in the state. The Applied Research Center, an $8 million facility to be built on the university campus, would house major new university laboratories. CPCC received $2.5 million for equipment for optical disc manufacturing and training; UNCC received $1 million for equipment; and $3 million was committed over a two year period for program development and training. The new laboratory would be a place where the Colleges of Engineering and Business, applied natural and social sciences and the Urban Institute would work more effectively with business and industry to engage in applied research, technology transfer, and joint enterprises related to the park.

The University Business Incubator Center

Described as "a space for success," The University Business Incubator Center opened in 1986. Administered by the Urban Institute and a board of thirty prominent leaders in the business community and at UNCC, by 1987, seven small emerging corporations were housed in a building formerly occupied by Collins & Aikman on North Tryon Street. The facility was acquired through a gift-purchase arrangement by The Foundation of UNCC. These "incubator" companies had the benefits of low rent, shared overhead expenses, and access to a wide range of management and professional skills provided by members of the board and UNCC specialists. These budding companies were high-tech oriented. The University Business Incubator Center was a response to the belief expressed by founders of Research Triangle Park and University Research Park, viz., research generates new industries.

University Research Park Gifts to UNCC

From its inception UNCC has grown at a rate never before experienced by officials in state government or the university system. From the beginning funds from special sources have been necessary to assure a high level of university performance. University Research Park has responded to UNCC's special needs at critical times. University Research Park grants to UNCC in its first twenty years totaled almost $350,000.

The first was a grant of $100,000 in 1971 to help establish a development office to provide leadership in securing private gifts for support of academic programs. An additional grant of $6,000 was made to support the formation of the Athletic Foundation to assist in launching intercollegiate competition in basketball and other sports.

In 1977 The Foundation of UNCC received a challenge grant of $25,000 from a private source to establish an endowment to support merit scholarships named in honor of the retiring chancellor and his wife. The park contributed $10,000. Ten years after the challenge grant was made other gifts had increased this fund to more than a million dollars, enabling the full support of fifteen or more gifted students each year.

When UNCC applied for a public radio station, the park made $50,000 available to purchase transmitting equipment for the 100,000 watt station, which became WFAE. Smaller grants have been made to support creation of WFAE's "Thistle and Shamrock," which airs weekly on 123 stations across the country. The program, which is broadcast by American Public Radio, draws national attention to the station, the university, the state, and Charlotte.

The College of Engineering was confronted with a critical space need which threatened its accreditation at a time when state funds were not available through the Board of Governors and the state. University Research Park made a grant of $150,000 to the college. The grant was supplemented by a private gift and transfer of state funds to build the Civil Engineering wing.

When UNCC was authorized as the fourth campus of what was then The Consolidated University of North Carolina, it was without many of the facilities which had already been provided to other campuses through state appropriations. Among other inadequacies, there was no home for the chancellor. A very modest state appropriation was secured for a temporary home, but as the University grew the need for a more adequate home for entertaining students, faculty, and university guests became increasingly apparent. A continuing high rate of growth necessitated giving top priority for UNCC capital projects to other essential buildings. The temporary home had been occupied for almost twenty years. University Research Park once again responded to a UNCC need and committed $150,000 to expedite purchase of a residence which the university system and the state had not seen fit to provide.

In addition to the grants mentioned, other funding of special studies by the Urban Institute and the Department of Geography and Earth Sciences served the park and the community well.

The Foundation of UNCC

Although the primary purpose of The Foundation of UNCC is to support academic excellence in the university, indirectly it has played an important role in the development of University City. One of the earliest investments of the foundation was the purchase of the Pharr estate, a tract of 72 acres on Highway 49. This purchase was made, with the expectation of appreciation in value, to assure future use of that property by UNCC. When Harris Boulevard was planned, The Foundation of UNCC, Mecklenburg County, UNCC, and University Research Park agreed to give the right-of-way for a divided boulevard from Highway 49 to Mallard Creek Road to encourage the state to build the road. Once again, the foundation played a major role in clearing the way for University Place to be built at a strategic location.

As noted earlier, University Metro Town Center Endowment, Inc. was created to handle the negotiations with a developer for University Place. When this transaction was completed, the foundation received $3.4 million, enabling UNCC to take further steps in developing academic excellence. The foundation was also reimbursed by the developer for purchases of land for the university to replace acreage occupied by University Place. With the support of a trust fund, the university has also developed Van Landingham Glen, an outstanding rhododendron garden, which is open to the public.

University Research Park Residents — 1987

As of 1987 there were a dozen University Research Park residents and commitments from others. Table 7 lists residents of the park and statistics pertaining to their operations.

As was the case in the Research Triangle Park, the University Research Park had relatively little activity during its first ten years. When IBM launched its building program in 1978 things began to happen. The magnitude of the IBM operation is illustrated by noting that they employ more than half of the 7,000 people working in the park and that their campus of fifteen buildings contained more square footage than all buildings on the UNCC campus.

Table 7

1987 RESIDENTS, DATES ESTABLISHED, ACREAGE, SQUARE FOOTAGE, AND NUMBER OF EMPLOYEES

COMPANY	YEAR ACTIVATED	ACRES PURCHASED	SQUARE FOOTAGE	EMPLOYEES 1986
Collins & Aikman[a]	1967	114.0	77,000	300
Allstate Insurance[b]	1971	33.0	185,000	415
IBM[c] (bought)	1970	428.1	2,500,000	5,000
(activated)	1978			
Electric Power Research Institute[d]	1979	9.4	67,000	50
Verbatim	1980	37.2	200,000	320
Union Oil of California	1981	5.3	25,000	26
Dow Jones	1981	8.7	39,500	25
Fairfax Properties[e]	1981	60.4	325,000	Rented to IBM
Southern Bell	1983	26.6	350,000	
AT&T[f]	1984	28.3	215,000	800
EDS (Pizzagalli)	1985	8.1	100,000	125
Charter Properties	1986	19.5	no building	
		778.6	4,083,500	7,061

[a] Collins & Aikman originally had a tract of approximately 160 acres, now own 114 acres (bought from Pendeltons).

[b] Allstate bought from Collins & Aikman.

[c] IBM bought more adjoining property outside University Research Park, approximately 1,200 acres.

[d] EPRI bought from Jones property.

[e] Includes 21 acres, originally bought from Jones, a building purchased from Reeves Brothers, and 9.2 acres and a building purchased from Automatic Data Processing.

[f] AT&T bought 5.26 acres of their property from Jones.

Financial Resources

During the first four years of its operation University Research Park generated a total of $51,000 from 29 memberships ($1,000 each) and contributions of $22,000 as shown in Chapter III, Table 2. The cash flow required to purchase land and pay for improvements was borrowed from four banks. Real estate was pledged as security. By 1970 indebtedness to banks and original landowners was approaching $1 million.

When the land sale to IBM was consummated in 1970 the park paid all of its indebtedness and had almost $1 million in reserve. But it owned no property. A purchase of 150 acres (land already zoned as a part of the park) from Queens Properties put the park back into business. It owned 150 acres free of debt and had funds to expend for other purposes.

In April of 1969 the directors of the park again authorized borrowing from six banks to purchase land suitable for residential development to be sold later to developers. North Carolina National Bank, Wachovia Bank & Trust Company, First Union National Bank, Northwestern Bank, First Citizens Bank & Trust Company, and Piedmont Bank & Trust Company committed loans up to $250,000 each, for a total of $1.5 million. Land purchased under this plan was sold at cost to developers to initiate residential development.

When the loans for residential development were repaid, additional loans were made to expand park acreage and to extend streets and utilities. Fortunately for the park, values of the improved land were accelerating. At the end of the twenty year period the auditors' report showed members equity, in addition to the $51,000 originally contributed by members, of more than $3 million. Practically all of the income generated by the park during its first twenty years came from the sale of sites in the park.

At the end of the first two decades the total capital input was $51,000 in memberships and contributions. Collins and Aikman Corporation and Queens Properties were still the owners of 368 acres of undeveloped land within the park. The park owned 306 acres and had options on an additional 250 acres. The cash flow had been provided by major banks with faith in the future of University Research Park.

Benefits to State and Community

There is no single measure for the success of Research Triangle Park or University Research Park. One measure of contributions to the community is the increase in tax values. Given University City's success it was not surprising that the City of Charlotte proposed annexation of an area including University Research Park in 1985. Although the city had reaped substantial tax benefits, Mecklenburg County's benefits had been greater because the park was outside the city limits. Based on tax appraisals for 1987, the value of land and improvements owned by residents in the park exceeded $250 million and yielded an estimated $1.5 million in tax revenue. This does not include inventory and other taxes. The park paid the county more than $20,000 in taxes on the property it owned in 1986. The tax base of University Place alone was more than $90 million. It should be noted that capital intensive industries generally contribute more to the tax base than they require in services. Park tenants fall into this category. Officials of University Research Park agreed that annexation should occur in 1994. The General Assembly of 1987 enacted legislation stating that "As of June 30, 1994, the corporate limits of the City of Charlotte shall be extended to include therein" the area described as University Research Park. Reference has also been made to the diverse and hefty contributions of one company, IBM, for support of education, culture, and community welfare.

When Governor Luther Hodges was promoting Research Triangle Park in the 1950s and the Chamber of Commerce proposed University Research Park ten years later, a major stated purpose was to improve North Carolina's low rank in per capita income. While it is not easy to relate the changes which have occurred on a cause and effect basis, some of the statistics are impressive. When the Research Triangle was launched in 1956, North Carolina ranked forty-third among the states in average per capita income. This was only seventy-one percent of the national average. This figure increased to seventy-eight percent in 1966, eighty-four percent in 1976, and eighty-five percent in 1986. By 1986 the state's rank was thirty-sixth. North Carolina's reputation as a progressive state has, beyond question, been greatly enhanced by the success of Research Triangle Park and the Triangle Research Institute associated with it. University Research Park has added to that image in recent years and has introduced new sources of economic strength to the region around Charlotte.

The model of education beyond the high school in the Charlotte area is somewhat unique in the state as well as in the nation. High quality offerings in community colleges and carefully monitored linkages of those colleges with a university provide opportunities for training people with widely varying interests, abilities, and ages. Failures and dropouts are reduced by encouraging and supporting enrollments in community colleges with transfers to a university after abilities have been improved and vocational interests have been evaluated. The enrollment profile at UNCC is unlike that of most universities. Due to the high percentage of transfer students, about sixty percent of the instruction is at the junior level and above. Students are admitted to community colleges without college board examinations. They have a wide choice of vocational subjects. After completing two years at the community college, if they choose to pursue an academic degree they are eligible for admission to UNCC. Studies have shown that students with proven motivation and established confidence in their own abilities perform as well as those admitted to UNCC as freshmen on the basis of examinations. This kind of linkage between the community college and the university encourages team efforts in responding to the needs of industry as described in the case of UNCC/CPCC and Verbatim/Kodak. As the university expands its research and graduate programs, training and retraining are available in Charlotte which cover very wide spectrums of subjects and students.

University City and its many components, including University Research Park, have become an integral part of the Charlotte community. Its future is bright not only because of the concerned stewardship and planning that went into the creation of University City over the past twenty years, but also because that working relationship continues strong. The tripartite partnership of private enterprise, government, and educational institutions has University City for proof of its effectiveness. The importance of a continued spirit of common purpose regarding zoning petitions, residential site planning, commercial mix, and infrastructure investment have been well demonstrated and bodes well for the future of the area. The park and the university are not ends unto themselves, but rather means for achieving the desirable ends of higher income and enriched quality of life for the people of North Carolina.

APPENDIX A

UNIVERSITY RESEARCH PARK
SYNOPSIS
RESEARCH ZONING DISTRICTS

PURPOSE

The purpose of the Research District Zoning (RE-1 and RE-2) is to provide a campus-type atmosphere for the park's tenants. The standards established for these districts are designed to promote sound, permanent research installations. In addition, the RE-2 District is oriented toward research development and high technology manufacturing operations. Development within these districts should be characterized by spacious and extensively landscaped settings with emphasis on aesthetic and environmental considerations.

PERMITTED USES

While there are a number of conventional miscellaneous uses which are permitted in the research districts such as parks, farms, recreation centers, country clubs, and day care centers, there are in actuality only a few specifically stated uses that have a significant effect on what is occurring in the research districts. While these are few in number, they permit a substantial range of activities within their general category alignment. These uses include:

1. Proto-type production facilities and pilot plants.
2. Pharmaceutical preparations and production facilities.
3. Production facilities for electronic computing and communications equipment and related devices.
4. Optical, dental, and medical laboratories.
5. Applied and basic research laboratories.
6. Graphics research and production facilities.
7. Offices, business, professional and corporate.
8. Uses similar to those listed above.

Obviously, the last use indicated is a general one, intended to indicate that within the constraints of the research zoning ordinance, any uses in the general area of those listed would be considered for these research districts.

AREA, YARD, AND HEIGHT REGULATIONS

The research districts are deliberately established to provide large tract requirements and a spacious concept of site development. To accomplish this the following standards apply to uses in the research districts:

1. Minimum lot area — 4 acres.
2. Minimum lot width — 400 feet (lots having any part of their frontage on the circular portion of a cul-de-sac may use 200 feet as the minimum lot width).
3. Minimum side and rear yards for lots of 4 to 10 acres — 35 feet; for lots greater than 10 acres — 50 feet.
4. Minimum setback for lots of 4 to 10 acres — 100 feet; for lots greater than 10 acres — 150 feet.
5. Maximum height is 40 feet (except that height may be increased if minimum side and rear yards are increased by 1 foot for each 2 feet in building height over 40 feet).
6. Minimum unobstructed open space — 70%.

DEVELOPMENT STANDARDS

In order to insure further the attainment of the objectives of the ordinance, a number of development standards have been established for the research districts. These standards are as follows:

1. Outside storage of any materials, supplies, or products shall not be permitted in the research district.
2. All utility distribution lines must be placed underground in the research districts.
3. A gate or security station may be located in a required yard or setback.
4. Several environmental performance standards apply to uses in the RE-1 District. These include a review of noise, odors, glare, exterior illumination, vibration, smoke, dust, gases and radioactive waste materials. The requirements of each of these should be examined more specifically in order to determine if any problems would exist. Again, it should be emphasized that these standards apply only in the RE-1 District.
5. Signs are permitted in all research districts but are controlled as to size and number.
6. Development of any use in a research district must conform to conventional parking and loading standards and, in addition, parking of motor vehicles will not be permitted in any required setback nor within 20 feet of any interior lot line. Parking areas must be paved with dust-free, all-weather surfaces and must be properly drained and landscaped. Spaces within the required setback must be not used as maneuvering space for the parking of vehicles except that driveways providing access to the parking area may be installed across a setback area. Underground parking structures are permitted.

For a more detailed and specific application of these requirements to a given situation, further discussion is suggested with either the University Research Park office or the Zoning Administration for Charlotte/Mecklenburg. A complete copy of the Zoning Regulations regarding the research districts will be furnished upon request.

APPENDIX B-1

These documents consist of:
1. Articles of Incorporation of Park Development, Inc. filed with the Secretary of State of North Carolina, November 28, 1966
2. Articles of Amendment of Park Development, Inc. filed January 24, 1967, changing the name to University Research Park, Inc. and making certain other changes
3. Articles of Amendment of Articles of Incorporation of University Research Park, Inc. filed February 28, 1967, adding Article IX dealing with distribution of assets on liquidation, and
4. Articles of Amendment and Restated Charter of University Research Park, Inc. filed June 17, 1981.

(as submitted by the Honorable Thad Eure, Secretary of State, North Carolina as the total documentation of Articles of Incorporation and Charter — October 10, 1986)

ARTICLES OF INCORPORATION
OF
PARK DEVELOPMENT, INC.

THIS IS TO CERTIFY that we, the undersigned, being persons of full age, do hereby make and acknowledge these Articles of Incorporation for the purpose of forming a nonprofit corporation under and by virtue of the provisions of Chapter 55A of the General Statutes of North Carolina, and to that end we do hereby set forth:

ARTICLE I
The name of the corporation is PARK DEVELOPMENT, INC.

ARTICLE II
The period of duration of the corporation shall be unlimited.

ARTICLE III
The purposes for which the corporation is organized are:
A. To foster and stimulate the physical, economic, cultural, educational and social growth and development of Charlotte and Mecklenburg County, North Carolina, for the benefit generally of the citizens thereof, by devoting funds, properties, and resources to the attraction of business, governmental, cultural, scientific, and educational enterprises to locate facilities in the City and County.
B. To acquire, develop and dispose of (by sale, lease, gift or otherwise) real property in Mecklenburg County, North Carolina, for the purpose of establishing and maintaining a research park area or areas for location by businesses, corporations, firms, governmental agencies, cultural, scientific, and educational institutions, and other entities desiring locations for the construction of plants and facilities suitable to the conducting of research and development.
C. To make gifts of money or property to such religious, charitable, or eleemosynary organizations located or operating in Mecklenburg County, North Carolina, as shall in the judgment of the directors be engaged in work conducive to the aims of this corporation.
D. To cooperate with other individuals, corporations, firms or associations, whether they are charitable or profit making in nature, that are engaged in programs concerned with attracting businesses, firms, corporations, government agencies, cultural, scientific, and educational institutions, and other entities to locate plant and research facilities in Charlotte and Mecklenburg County; and to that end to enter into partnership and joint venture arrangements and to acquire stock or other interests in corporations seeking to achieve those purposes.

In furtherance of the foregoing purposes, the corporation shall have and exercise any, all, and every power which a nonprofit corporation organized under the provisions of the North Carolina Nonprofit Corporation Act may be authorized to exercise but not any other power.

ARTICLE IV
The corporation shall be a nonprofit, nonstock charitable corporation. The corporation shall have no members. No part of the net earnings or funds of the corporation shall inure to the benefit of any private shareholder, member or individual, and no part of the activities of the corporation shall be the carrying on of propaganda or otherwise attempting to influence legislation, nor shall the corporation intervene in any political campaign on behalf of any candidate for public office. Although no part of the earnings or income of the corporation shall inure to the primary benefit of its directors, officers or employees, either directly or indirectly, individually or collectively, the corporation may pay compensation in a reasonable amount to its directors, officers, and employees for services rendered by them.

ARTICLE V
The number of persons constituting the initial Board of Directors of the corporation shall be three (3). Thereafter, the number of Directors, the manner of their election and the manner of filling a vacancy on the Board of Directors created by reason of the death, resignation or removal of a Director shall be determined by the bylaws of the corporation. In no event shall the number of Directors be less than three (3).

The names and addresses of the persons who are to serve as Directors until their successors have been elected and have qualified are as follows:

NAME	ADDRESS
Joseph W. Grier, Jr.	1869 Queens Road West, Charlotte, N. C.
Francis I. Parker	630 Museum Drive, Charlotte, N. C.
James Y. Preston	1995 Ferncliff Road, Charlotte, N. C.

ARTICLE VI
The initial bylaws of the corporation shall be adopted by the Board of Directors by majority vote. The power to alter or amend the bylaws shall be determined by the initial bylaws.

ARTICLE VII
The address of the initial registered office of the corporation is in care of Francis I. Parker, Law building, 724 East Trade Street, Charlotte, North Carolina, and the name of the initial registered agent at such address is Francis I. Parker.

ARTICLE VIII
The names and addresses of the incorporators are as follows:

NAME	ADDRESS
Joseph W. Grier, Jr.	1869 Queens Road West, Charlotte, N.C.
Francis I. Parker	630 Museum Drive, Charlotte, N. C.
James Y. Preston	1995 Ferncliff Road, Charlotte, N. C.

IN WITNESS WHEREOF, we have hereunto set our hands and seals, this 28th day of November, 1966.

Signed by Joseph W. Grier, Jr.
Signed by Francis I. Parker
Signed by James Y. Preston

ARTICLES OF AMENDMENT
OF
ARTICLES OF INCORPORATION
OF
PARK DEVELOPMENT, INC.

Park Development, Inc., a nonprofit corporation organized under the laws of the State of North Carolina, does hereby amend its Articles of Incorporation in the manners hereinafter enumerated and, pursuant to Chapter 55A of the General Statutes of North Carolina, does set forth the following:

1. The name of the corporation is Park Development, Inc.
2. The amendments to the Articles of Incorporation which have been adopted and which shall hereafter be effective are the following:
    A. That Article I of the Articles of Incorporation be amended by deleting said Article in its entirety and inserting in lieu thereof the following:

    The name of the Corporation is University Research Park, Incorporated.
    B. That Article IV of the Articles of Incorporation be amended by deleting therefrom the second sentence thereof which reads, "The Corporation shall have no members,"

and inserting in lieu thereof the following:
The Corporation shall have members.
3. The Corporation has no members having voting rights. The amendments herein set forth were adopted at a meeting of the Board of Directors of the Corporation held on January 5, 1967, at which meeting the amendments received a vote of a majority of the Directors in office.

IN WITNESS WHEREOF, the Corporation has caused these Articles of Amendment to be executed by its President and attested by its Secretary or its Assistant Secretary, on the 5th day of January, 1967.

PARK DEVELOPMENT, INC.
signed by W. T. Harris
President

Attest:
signed by Harry Nicholas
Assistant Secretary

ARTICLES OF AMENDMENT
OF
ARTICLES OF INCORPORATION
OF
UNIVERSITY RESEARCH PARK, INCORPORATED
(formerly Park Development, Inc.)

University Research Park, Incorporated (formerly Park Development, Inc.), a nonprofit corporation organized under the laws of the State of North Carolina, does hereby amend its Articles of Incorporation in the manner hereinafter enumerated and, pursuant to Chapter 55A of the General Statutes of North Carolina, does set forth the following:

1. The name of the Corporation is University Research Park, Incorporated (the name of the Corporation was formerly Park Development, Inc.).
2. The Amendment to the Articles of Incorporation which has been adopted and which shall hereafter be effected is the following:

That a new Article be inserted in the Articles of Incorporation, denominated Article IX, reading as follows:

"Upon liquidation of the Corporation, all of the net assets thereof shall be distributed to the Foundation of The University of North Carolina at Charlotte and or to and among such other institutions of higher education as shall be determined by the Board of Directors. Provided, no distribution shall be made to any institution unless such institution

qualifies for exemption as an organization described in Section 501(c)(3) of the Internal Revenue Code as presently in force and effect."

3. The Corporation has no members having voting rights in regard to amendments of the Articles of Incorporation. The amendment herein set forth was adopted by the Board of Directors of the Corporation on February 23, 1967, by vote of a majority of the Directors in office.

IN WITNESS WHEREOF, the Corporation has caused these Articles of Amendment to be executed by its President and attested by its Secretary or its Assistant Secretary on the 23rd day of February, 1967.

UNIVERSITY RESEARCH PARK, INCORPORATED
signed by W. T. Harris
President

Attest:
signed by Harry Nicholas
Assistant Secretary

ARTICLES OF AMENDMENT AND RESTATED CHARTER
OF
UNIVERSITY RESEARCH PARK, INCORPORATED

University Research Park, Incorporated, a nonprofit corporation organized under Chapter 55A of the General Statutes of North Carolina and qualified as a tax-exempt organization under Section 501(c)(6) of the Internal Revenue Code, does hereby amend and integrate its Articles of Incorporation pursuant to Sections 55A-35 and 55A-37.1(e) of the General Statutes of North Carolina so that as amended and integrated said Articles shall read, in their entirety, as follows:

ARTICLE I

The name of the corporation is UNIVERSITY RESEARCH PARK, INCORPORATED.

ARTICLE II

The period of duration of the corporation shall be unlimited.

ARTICLE III

The purposes for which the corporation is organized are:

A. To foster and stimulate the physical, economic, and social growth and development of Charlotte and Mecklenburg County, North Carolina, for the benefit generally of the citizens thereof, by devoting funds, properties, and resources to the attraction of business, governmental, and business enterprises to locate facilities in the City and County.

B. To acquire, develop and dispose of (by sale, lease, gift, or otherwise) real property in Mecklenburg County, North Carolina, for the purpose of establishing and maintaining a research park area or areas for location by businesses, corporations, firms, governmental agencies, and other entities desiring locations for the construction of plants and facilities suitable to or compatible with the conduct of research and product development.

C. To make gifts of money or property to such religious, charitable, or eleemosynary organizations located or operating in Mecklenburg County, North Carolina, as shall in the judgment of the directors be engaged in work conducive to the aims of this corporation.

D. To cooperate with other individuals, corporations, firms or associations, whether they are charitable or profit making in nature, that are engaged in programs concerned with attracting businesses, firms, corporations, governmental agencies, and other entities to locate plant and research facilities in Charlotte and Mecklenburg County; and to that end to enter into partnership and joint venture arrangements and to acquire stock or other interests in corporations seeking to achieve those purposes.

E. In carrying out the objects enumerated in paragraphs A through D, the members and Directors of the corporation from time to time shall have broad authority and discretion to use the funds and property belonging to the corporation in such manner as shall to them seem most conducive to those ends and to the physical, economic, and social development of Charlotte and Mecklenburg County and to the benefit of the citizens generally of Charlotte and Mecklenburg County.

F. Notwithstanding any other provision of these Articles of Incorporation, of the bylaws of the corporation, or of any action taken by the Board of Directors or the members hereof, no part of the net earnings or funds of the corporation shall inure to the benefit of any private shareholder, member, or individual, and no part of the activities of the corporation shall be the carrying on of propaganda or otherwise attempting to influence legislation; nor shall the corporation intervene in any political campaign on behalf of any candidate for public office.

G. In furtherance of the foregoing purposes, the corporation shall have and exercise any, all, and every power which a nonprofit corporation organized under the provisions of the North Carolina Nonprofit Corporation Act may be authorized to exercise but not any other power.

ARTICLE IV

The corporation shall be a nonprofit, nonstock charitable corporation. The corporation shall have members with the qualifications and rights of its members to be as set forth in the bylaws of the corporation. Although no part of the earnings or income of the corporation shall inure to the primary benefit of its directors, officers, or employees, either directly or indirectly, individually or collectively, the corporation may pay compensation in a reasonable amount to its directors, officers, and employees for services rendered by them.

ARTICLE V

The number of Directors, the manner of their election, the manner of filling a vacancy on the Board of Directors, and the powers of the Board shall be as set forth in the bylaws of the corporation.

ARTICLE VI

The address of the registered office of the corporation is 2400 First Union Tower, Charlotte, North Carolina, and the registered agent at such address is Seddon Goode. (Mecklenburg County).

ARTICLE VII

Upon liquidation of the corporation, all of the net assets thereof shall be distributed to the Foundation of The University of North Carolina at Charlotte; provided that if such Foundation is no longer in operation, such assets shall be distributed to The University of North Carolina at Charlotte; and if such University is no longer in operation, such assets shall be distributed to and among such other institutions of higher education as shall be determined by the Board of Directors; provided, however, that no distribution shall be made to any institution unless such institution qualifies for exemption as an organization described in Section 501(c)(3) of the Internal Revenue Code as presently in force and effect.

The members of the corporation have no voting rights in regards to amendments of the Articles of Incorporation. The foregoing amendment and integration of the Articles of Incorporation was adopted by the Board of Directors of the corporation on April 16, 1981, by vote of a majority of the Directors then in office.

IN WITNESS WHEREOF, the corporation has caused these Amended and Integrated Articles of Incorporation to be executed by its President and attested by its Secretary or its Assistant Secretary on the 9th day of June, 1981.

UNIVERSITY RESEARCH PARK, INCORPORATED
signed by Seddon Goode, Jr.
President

ATTEST:
signed by Robert W. King, Jr.
Assistant Secretary

APPENDIX B-2

BYLAWS

The bylaws of URP, as originally adopted, provided for no less than three (3) and no more than twenty-one (21) directors with specified numbers to be nominated by the Charlotte Chamber of Commerce, the chancellor of UNCC, and by the membership in the annual meeting. Amendments to increase the number of directors as new constituencies were added and to specify the number to be nominated by UNCC, the Chamber of Commerce, and the floor have been made on several occasions. Other minor changes were made. By action taken in March 1980 no less than three (3) and no more than thirty-five (35) directors were authorized. Twelve (12) were to be nominated by the Charlotte Chamber of Commerce, twelve (12) by the chancellor of UNCC, and eleven (11) from the floor at the annual meeting. A major amendment (adopted April 16, 1981) provided for an "Operations Committee" and changed the processes for conducting business.

The primary responsibility of members is to elect directors from nominations submitted by the Chamber of Commerce, the chancellor of UNCC, and by the members. The numbers to be nominated by each are specified in the bylaws.

The primary responsibilities of directors are:
(1) to elect, appoint, or dismiss officers and committee members,
(2) to amend, add to, or repeal the Articles of Incorporation and bylaws,
(3) to establish the Operations committee, the Finance Committee, or other committees deemed appropriate.

The Operations Committee is given primary responsibility for conducting the business of the corporation. The Finance Committee has primary responsibility for borrowing money, selecting depository banks, selecting auditors, and advising the Board of Directors and the Operations Committee on financial matters. The president is given primary administrative responsibility.

BYLAWS OF
UNIVERSITY RESEARCH PARK, INCORPORATED
Charlotte, North Carolina
(Integrated as of March 26, 1981)

ARTICLE I

Objectives and Purposes.

SECTION 1: The objects for which this Corporation is formed are as follows:

A. To foster and stimulate the physical, economic, and social growth and development of Charlotte and Mecklenburg County, North Carolina, for the benefit generally of the citizens thereof, by devoting funds, properties and resources to the attraction of business, governmental, and business-related enterprises to locate facilities in the City and County.

B. To acquire, develop, and dispose of (by sale, lease, gift, or otherwise) real property in Mecklenburg County, North Carolina, for the purpose of establishing and maintaining a research park area or areas for location by business, corporations, firms, governmental agencies, and other entities desiring locations for the construction of plants and facilities suitable to the conducting of research and product development.

C. To make gifts of money or property to such religious, charitable, or eleemosynary organizations located or operating in Mecklenburg County, North Carolina, as shall in the judgment of the directors be engaged in work conducive to the aims of this corporation.

D. To cooperate with other individuals, corporations, firms or associations, whether they are charitable or profit making in nature, that are engaged in programs concerned with attracting businesses, firms, corporations, government agencies and other entities to locate plant and research facilities in Charlotte and Mecklenburg County; and to that end to enter into partnership and joint venture arrangements and to acquire stock or other in-

terests in corporations seeking to achieve those purposes.

In furtherance of the foregoing purposes, the corporation shall have and exercise any, all and every power which a nonprofit corporation organized under the provisions of the North Carolina Nonprofit Corporation Act may be authorized to exercise but not any other power.

SECTION 2: In carrying out the objects enumerated in Section 1, the members and Directors of the Corporation from time to time shall have broad authority and discretion to use the funds and property belonging to the Corporation in such manner as shall to them seem most conducive to those ends and to the physical, economic, and social development of Charlotte and Mecklenburg County and to the benefit of the citizens generally of Charlotte and Mecklenburg County.

SECTION 3: Notwithstanding any other provision of these bylaws, of the Articles of Incorporation of the Corporation, or of any action taken by the Board of Directors or the members hereof, no part of the net earnings or funds of the Corporation shall inure to the benefit of any private shareholder, member or individual, and no part of the activities of the Corporation shall be the carrying on of propaganda or otherwise attempting to influence legislation; nor shall the Corporation intervene in any political campaign on behalf of any candidate for public office.

ARTICLE II

Members.

SECTION 1: Admission to membership. Individuals, firms, or corporations may be admitted to membership in this Corporation upon a vote of a majority of the members of the Board of Directors, or of a majority of the members of the Executive Committee o the Board of Directors if an Executive Committee shall have been established, and upon the payment by such individual, firm or corporation of the then established membership fee.

SECTION 2: Membership fee. The fee to be paid for membership in this Corporation shall be One Thousand Dollars ($1,000) and in no event may any one individual, firm, or corporation have more than one membership.

SECTION 3: Capital contribution. Upon becoming a member of the Corporation and making the initial contribution thereto, a member shall be entitled to a certificate from the officers of the Corporation evidencing his membership. Any member may make an additional capital contribution to the Corporation at any time, but no such additional contribution shall entitle him to additional membership.

SECTION 4: Transfer of membership. Membership or any interest in this Corporation shall not be assignable by any member nor shall membership or any interest in this Corporation pass to any personal representative, heir, or beneficiary of any deceased member.

ARTICLE III
Meetings of Members and Election of Directors.

SECTION 1: Annual meeting. The annual meeting of the members of the Corporation shall be held in the City of Charlotte, North Carolina, at such place as may from time to time be designated by the Board of Directors, at a time as designated by the Board of Directors in the notice of the meeting, on the first Wednesday of February, in each year, for the purpose of electing Directors and for the transaction of such other business as may be properly brought before the meeting.

SECTION 2: Special Meetings. Special meetings of the members may be held upon call of the President or Secretary or of a majority of the Board of Directors at such place within or without the State of North Carolina, as may be stated in the notice thereof and at such time and for such purpose as may be stated in the notice.

SECTION 3: Notice of meetings. Notice of the time, place, and the purpose of each meeting of the members, signed by the President or a Vice President or a Secretary or an Assistant Secretary shall be delivered either personally or by mail to each member of record entitled to vote at such meeting not less than ten (10) days before the meeting; provided that no notice of adjourned meetings need be given. If mailed, the notice shall be directed to each member entitled to notice at his address as it appears on the membership book of the Corporation unless he shall have filed with the Secretary a written request that notices intended for him be mailed to some other address, in which case, it shall be mailed to the address designated in such request. Such further notice shall be given as may be required by law. Meetings may be held without notice if all members entitled to vote thereat are present in person or by proxy or if notice of the time, place, and purpose of such meeting is waived by telegram, radiogram, cablegram or other writing, either before or after the holding thereof, by all members not present and entitled to vote at such meeting.

SECTION 4: Quorum. A quorum at all meetings of the members shall consist of a majority of the members of the Corporation represented in person or by proxy; if there be no such quorum, a majority of

the members present or represented may adjourn the meeting from time to time to a further date without further notice other than the announcement at such meeting, and when a quorum shall be present upon such adjourned date, any business may be transacted which might have been transacted at the meeting as originally called.

SECTION 5: Conduct of meetings. Meetings of the members shall be presided over by the President, or, if he is not present, by a Vice President, or, if none of the Vice Presidents are present, by a Chairman to be chosen at the meeting. The Secretary or an Assistant Secretary of the Corporation or, in their absence, a person chosen at the meeting, shall act as Secretary of the meeting.

SECTION 6: Voting. Each member of the Corporation shall, at every meeting of the members, be entitled to one (1) vote in person or by proxy.

SECTION 7: Proxies. No proxy shall be deemed operative unless and until signed by or on behalf of the member and filed with the Corporation. In the absence of limitations to the contrary contained in the proxy, the same shall extend to all meetings of the members and shall remain in force eleven (11) months from its date, and no longer.

ARTICLE IV
Directors.

SECTION 1: Number, qualification, and term of office. The number of Directors of the Corporation shall be not less than three nor more than thirty-five (35). Each Director shall hold office until his death, resignation, retirement, removal, or disqualification, or until his successor is elected and qualified.

SECTION 2: Election of Directors. The Directors in office at the adoption of these bylaws shall continue in office until the first annual meeting of the members. Thereafter, Directors of the Corporation shall be elected annually at the annual meeting of members, commencing with the annual meeting of March 1980, from and after which date there shall be thirty-five (35) directors. Directors shall be elected by the members in the following manner: Twelve (12) Directors shall be elected from nomination made by the executive committee of the Charlotte Chamber of Commerce. In each year, prior to the first Wednesday of February, the Chairman of the Board of Directors of the Charlotte Chamber of Commerce shall certify to the secretary of the corporation the nominees for directors made by the executive committee of the Charlotte Chamber of Commerce for the coming year.
Twelve (12) Directors shall be elected from nominations made by the Chancellor of The University of North Carolina at Charlotte. In each year, prior to the first Wednesday in February, the Chancellor of The University of North Carolina at Charlotte shall certify to the secretary of the Corporation the nominees for Directors made by him for the coming year.
Eleven (11) Directors shall be elected by the members from nominations made from the floor at the meeting.

SECTION 3: Vacancies. Whenever any vacancy shall have occurred in the Board of Directors by reason of death, resignation, removal from office, or otherwise, it may be filled by the votes of a majority of the Directors then in office at any meeting and the person so elected shall be a Director until his successor is elected.

SECTION 4:   Meetings. The meetings of the Board of Directors shall be held at such place or places within or without the State of North Carolina as may from time to time be determined by a majority of the Board. Regular meetings of the Board shall be held at such time and place as shall from time to time be determined by resolution of the Board of Directors. Special meetings may be held at any time upon the call of the President or Vice President or of not less than a majority of the Directors then in office.

SECTION 5:   Notice of meetings. Written notice of the time and place, and, in the case of special meetings, the purpose, of every meeting of the Board shall be duly served on or sent, mailed, or telegraphed to each Director not less than ten (10) days before the meeting, except that a regular meeting of the Board may be held without notice immediately after the annual meeting of the members at the same place as such meeting was held for the purpose of electing or appointing officers for the ensuing year; provided, that no notice of adjourned meetings need be given. Meetings may be held at any time without notice if all the Directors are present or if those not present waive notice of the time, place, and purpose of such meeting by telegram, radiogram, cablegram, or other writing, either before or after the holding thereof.

SECTION 6:   Quorum of Directors. A majority of the Directors shall constitute a quorum for the transaction of business, and the action of a majority of the Directors present at any meeting at which a quorum is present shall be the action of the Board of Directors; provided, that if the Directors shall, severally and/or collectively, consent in writing to any action to be taken by the Corporation, such action shall be as valid corporate action as though it had been authorized at a meeting of the Directors. If at any meeting of the Board there shall be less than a quorum present, a majority of those present may adjourn the meeting from time to time until a quorum shall have been obtained.

SECTION 7:   Removal from office. Any member of the Board of Directors who fails to attend more than three (3) consecutive regular or special meetings of the Board of Directors shall be considered as being automatically removed from membership upon the Board of Directors, unless the remaining members of the Board, by the affirmative vote of a majority thereof, determine that the absences of said Director were reasonable under the circumstances, in which event the absences shall be deemed waived.

SECTION 8:   Powers of the Board. The Board of Directors shall have power and authority to carry on the affairs of the Corporation and in doing so may elect or appoint all necessary officers or committees; may employ all such employees as shall be requisite for the conduct of the affairs of the Corporation; may fix the compensation of such persons; may prescribe the duties of such persons; may dismiss any appointive officer or agent without previous notice. The Board of Directors may, in the absence of an officer, delegate his powers and duties to any other officer or director for the time being.

SECTION 9:   Power to make bylaws. The Board of Directors shall have power to make and alter any bylaw or bylaws.

SECTION 10:   Executive and other committees. The Board of Directors may, by resolution passed by a majority of the whole Board, designate two or more of their number to constitute an Executive or any other committee, who, to the extent provided in said resolution, shall have and exercise the authority of the Board of Directors in the management of the business of the Corporation between the meetings of the Board.

ARTICLE V
(probably recommended by Executive Committee March 12, 1981)
Operations Committee.

SECTION 1:   Appointment and qualification. The Board of Directors shall appoint an Operations Committee consisting of seven persons, each of whom shall serve at the pleasure of the Board of Directors. No member of the Operations Committee need be a member or officer of the Corporation or a member of the Board of Directors. One member of the Operations Committee shall be appointed by the Board of Directors to serve as Chairman.

SECTION 2:   Meetings. The meetings of the Operations Committee shall be held at such place or places within or without the State of North Carolina as may from time to time be determined by the Chairman of the committee. Regular meetings of the Board shall be held at such time and place as shall from time to time be determined by resolution of the Operations Committee. Special meetings may be held at any time upon the call of the Chairman of the committee.

SECTION 3:   Notice of meetings. No notice shall be required for regular meetings of the Operations Committee. Notice of the purpose, time, and place of every special meeting of the Operations Committee shall be duly served on or sent, mailed, telegraphed, telephoned, or personally communicated to each committee member not less than five (5) days before the meeting.

SECTION 4:   Quorum. A majority of the Operations Committee shall constitute a quorum for the transaction of business, and the action of a majority of the committee members present at any meeting at which a quorum is present shall be the action of the Operations Committee; provided, that if all members of the committee shall, severally and/or collectively, consent in writing to any action to be taken by the Corporation, such action shall be as valid as though it had been authorized at a meeting of the Operations Committee. If at any meeting of the Operations Committee there shall be less than a quorum present, a majority of those present may adjourn the meeting from time to time until a quorum shall have been obtained.

SECTION 5:   Powers of the Committee. The Operations Committee shall have full power and authority to carry on the business of the Corporation with respect to the acquisition, ownership, financing, development and disposition of real property. Such power and authority shall include, without limitation, the power and authority on behalf of the Corporation to approve contracts for purchase and sale of real property; leases of real property to or from others; applications and petitions to public authorities for rezoning, variances, subdivision approvals, and the like for the benefit of real property in which the Corporation has an interest; contracts for the design and construction of improvements to or on real property of the Corporation; borrowing of money to finance acquisition development or improvement of real property of the Corporation; to order tests, surveys, inspections and investigations of the real property of the Corporation, including marketing and feasibility studies; and to authorize one or more officers of the Corporation to execute documents of every kind and description, including contracts, deeds, leases, notes, and mortgages, for carrying out the decisions of the Committee.

ARTICLE VI
Officers.

SECTION 1: Election or appointment. The Board of Directors as soon as may be after the annual election of the Directors in each year shall elect from their number a President of the Corporation, and shall also elect a Vice President, a Secretary, and a Treasurer; and may from time to time select one or more Vice Presidents, Assistant Secretaries, and Assistant Treasurers. The same person may hold any two offices except those of President and Secretary. The Board may also appoint such other officers and agents as they may deem necessary for the transaction of the affairs of the Corporation.

SECTION 2: Qualifications. No officer, other than the President need be a member of the Corporation or a member of the Board of Directors.

SECTION 3: Term of office. The term of office of all officers shall be one year or until their respective successors are chosen but any officer may be removed from office at any meeting of the Board of Directors by the affirmative vote of a majority of the Directors then in office, whenever in their judgment the interests of the Corporation will be served thereby provided the Board of Directors shall have power to fill any vacancies in any offices occurring from whatever reason.

SECTION 4: Powers and duties. The officers of the Corporation shall respectively have such powers and perform such duties in the management of the property and affairs of the Corporation, subject to the control of the Directors, as generally pertains to their respective offices, as well as such additional powers and duties as may from time to time be conferred by the Board of Directors.

SECTION 5: General powers as to negotiable paper. The Board of Directors may, from time to time, prescribe the manner of the making, signature, or endorsement of bills of exchange, notes, drafts, checks, acceptances, obligations, and other negotiable paper or other instruments for the payment of money and designate the officer or officers, agent or agents who shall, from time to time, be authorized to make, sign or endorse the same on behalf of the Corporation.

ARTICLE VII
Fiscal Year, Seal.

SECTION 1: Fiscal year. The fiscal year of the Corporation shall commence on the 1st day of November and end on the 31st day of October.

SECTION 2: Corporate Seal. The Board of Directors shall provide a suitable corporate seal for use by the Corporation.

ARTICLE VIII
Amendments.

SECTION 1: The bylaws of the Corporation may be amended, added to, or repealed, or other or new bylaws may be adopted in lieu thereof by the affirmative vote of a majority of the Board of Directors of the Corporation.

ARTICLE IX
Liquidation.

SECTION 1: Upon liquidation of the Corporation, all of the net assets thereof shall be distributed to the Foundation of The University of North Carolina at Charlotte and/or to and among such other institutions of higher education as shall be determined by the Board of Directors. Provided, no distribution shall be made to any institution unless contributions to such institution will qualify for a charitable deduction under the Internal Revenue Code.

Integrated as of December 28, 1976.

BYLAWS OF
UNIVERSITY RESEARCH PARK, INCORPORATED
Charlotte, North Carolina
(As approved at the annual meeting on April 16, 1981)

ARTICLE I
Offices.

SECTION 1. Principal office. The principal office of the Corporation shall be located in Charlotte, North Carolina.

SECTION 2. Registered office. The registered office of the Corporation required by law to be maintained in the state of North Carolina may be, but need not be, identical with the principal office in the state of North Carolina. The address of the registered office may be changed from time to time by the Board of Directors.

ARTICLE II
Members.

SECTION 1. Admission to membership. Individuals, firms, or corporations may be admitted to membership in this Corporation upon a vote of a majority of the members of the Board of Directors and upon the payment by such individual, firm, or corporation of the then established membership fee.

SECTION 2. Membership fee. The fee to be paid for membership in this Corporation shall be One Thousand Dollars ($1,000). In no event may any one individual, firm or corporation have more than one membership. The amount of the membership fee may be increased or decreased by the Board of Directors or by the Operations Committee.

SECTION 3. Capital contribution. Upon becoming a member of the Corporation and making the initial contribution thereto, a member shall be entitled to a certificate from the officers of the Corporation evidencing his membership. Any member may make an additional capital contribution to the Corporation at any time, but no such additional contribu-

SECTION 4. tion shall entitle him to additional membership. Transfer of membership. Membership or any interest in this Corporation shall not be assignable by any member nor shall membership or any interest in this Corporation pass to any personal representative, heir, or beneficiary of any deceased member. The membership or any interest shall expire upon the death or dissolution of the member and no person or entity shall be entitled to any refund with respect to said membership or interest.

ARTICLE III
Meetings of members.

SECTION 1. Annual meeting. The annual meeting of the members of the Corporation shall be held in the city of Charlotte, North Carolina, at such time and place as may be designated each year by the Operations Committee in the notice of the meeting, for the purpose of electing Directors and for the transaction of such other business as may be properly brought before the meeting.

SECTION 2. Special meetings. Special meetings of the members may be held upon call of the President or Secretary or of a majority of the Board of Directors at such place within or without the state of North Carolina, as may be stated in the notice thereof and at such time and for such purpose as may be stated in the notice.

SECTION 3. Notice of meetings. Notice of the time, place and the purpose of each meeting of the members, signed by the President, a Vice President, the Secretary or an Assistant Secretary shall be given by any usual means of communication to each member of record entitled to vote at such meeting not less than ten (10) days before the meeting; provided that no notice of adjourned meetings need be given. If mailed, the notice shall be directed to each member entitled to notice at his address as it appears on the membership book of the Corporation unless he shall have filed with the Secretary a written request that notices intended for him be mailed to some other address, in which case it shall be mailed to the address designated in such request. Such further notice shall be given as may be required by law. Meetings may be held without notice if all members entitled to vote thereat are present in person or by proxy or if notice of the time, place, and purpose of such meeting is waived by any usual means of communication, either before or after the holding thereof, by all members not present and entitled to vote at such meeting.

SECTION 4. Quorum. A quorum at all meetings of the members shall consist of a majority of the members of the Corporation represented in person or by proxy; if there be no such quorum, a majority of the members present or represented may adjourn the meeting from time to time to a further date without further notice other than the announcement at such meeting, and when a quorum shall be present upon such adjourned date, any business may be transacted which might have been transacted at the meeting as originally called.

SECTION 5. Conduct of meetings. Meetings of the members shall be presided over by the Chairman of the Board of Directors, or, if he is not present, by the President, or, if neither of them is present, by a Chairman to be chosen at the meeting. The Secretary or an Assistant Secretary of the Corporation or, in their absence, a person chosen at the meeting, shall act as Secretary of the meeting.

SECTION 6. Voting. Each member of the Corporation shall, at every meeting of the members, be entitled one (1) vote in person or by proxy. The voting rights of members shall be limited to the right to elect Directors of the Corporation in accordance with Article IV hereof.

SECTION 7. Proxies. No proxy shall be deemed operative unless and until signed by or on behalf of the member and filed with the Corporation. In the absence of limitations to the contrary contained in the proxy, the same shall extend to all meetings of the members and shall remain in force eleven (11) months from its date, and no longer.

ARTICLE IV
Directors.

SECTION 1. Number, qualification, and term of office. The number of Directors of the Corporation shall be thirty-five (35). Each director shall hold office until his death, resignation, retirement, removal, or disqualification, or until his successor is elected and qualified. Directors need not be residents of the state of North Carolina or members of the Corporation.

SECTION 2. Election of directors. Directors of the Corporation shall be elected annually at the annual meeting of members. Directors shall be elected by the members in the following manner:
Twelve Directors shall be elected from nominations made by the Executive Committee of the Charlotte Chamber of Commerce. In each year, ten days prior to the annual meeting of members, the Chairman of the Board of Directors of the Charlotte Chamber of Commerce shall certify to the Secretary of the Corporation the nominees for directors made by the Executive Committee of the Charlotte Chamber of Commerce for the coming year.
Twelve Directors shall be elected from nominations made by the Chancellor of The University of North Carolina at Charlotte. In each year, ten days prior to the annual meeting of members, the Chancellor of The University of North Carolina at Charlotte shall certify to the Secretary of the Corporation the nominees for directors made by him for the coming year.
Eleven Directors shall be elected by members from nominations made from the floor at the meeting.

SECTION 3. Vacancies. Whenever any vacancy shall have occurred in the Board of Directors by reason of death, resignation, removal from office, or otherwise, it may be filled by the votes of a majority of the Directors then in office at any meeting and the person so elected shall be a Director until his successor is elected.

SECTION 4. Meetings. Regular meetings of the Board of Directors shall be held at such times and places, within or without the state of North Carolina, as may from time to time be determined by a majority of the Board, except that a regular meeting of the Board may be held without notice immediately after the annual meeting of the members and at the same place as such meeting for the purpose of electing or appointing officers for the ensuing year. Special meetings of the Board may be called by the Chairman of the Board of Directors, the President, the Secretary or by a majority of the Board of Directors at such place within or without the state of North Carolina, as may be stated in the notice thereof and at such time and for such

SECTION 5. purpose as may be stated in the notice.

Election of chairman. At the meeting of the Board of Directors held immediately after the annual meeting of members, the Directors shall elect from their number a Chairman of the Board who shall serve until his successor shall have been duly elected and qualified.

SECTION 6. Notice of meetings. Notice of the time and place, and, in the case of special meetings, the purpose, of every meeting of the Board shall be given to each Director by any usual means of communication not less than ten (10) days before the meeting; provided, that no notice of adjourned meetings need be given. Meetings may be held at any time without notice if all the Directors are present or if those not present waive notice of the time, place and purpose of such meeting by any usual means of communication either before or after the holding thereof.

SECTION 7. Quorum of directors. A majority of the Directors shall constitute a quorum for the transaction of business, and the action of a majority of the Directors present at any meeting at which a quorum is present shall be the action of the Board of Directors; provided, that if all of the Directors shall consent in writing to any action to be taken by the Corporation, such action shall be as valid corporate action as though it had been authorized at a meeting of the Directors. If at any meeting of the Board there shall be less than a quorum present, a majority of those present may adjourn the meeting from time to time until a quorum shall have been obtained.

SECTION 8. Powers of the Board. The Board of Directors shall have overall responsibility for the management of the affairs of the Corporation. The Board shall elect or appoint and may dismiss all necessary officers and committee members. The Board shall also have the power to amend, add to, or repeal the Articles of Incorporation and the bylaws and to make such other fundamental changes respecting the Corporation as are permitted by law. In addition to the Operations Committee and the Finance Committee hereinafter provided for, the Board of Directors may establish such other committees as it deems appropriate for the furtherance and accomplishment of the purposes of the Corporation.

ARTICLE V
Operations Committee.

SECTION 1: Appointment and qualification. The Board of Directors shall appoint an Operations Committee consisting of not more than seven and not fewer than four persons, each of whom shall serve at the pleasure of the Board of Directors. No member of the Operations Committee need be a member or officer of the Corporation or a member of the Board of Directors. The President of the Corporation shall serve as Chairman of the Committee.

SECTION 2. Vacancies. Whenever any vacancy shall have occurred in the Operations Committee by reason of death, resignation, removal from office, or otherwise, it may be filled by the votes of a majority of the Committee members then in office at any meeting and the person so elected shall be a Committee member until his successor is elected.

SECTION 3. Meetings. The Committee, by resolution, may fix the time and place for regular meetings. If the Committee does not set regular meetings, or in addition to regular meetings, the Chairman may call, and fix the time and place of, special meetings of the Committee.

SECTION 4. Notice of meetings. No notice shall be required for regular meetings of the Operations Committee. Notice of the purpose, time, and place of every special meeting of the Operations Committee shall be given to each Committee member by any usual means of communication not less than five (5) days before the meeting.

SECTION 5. Quorum. A majority of the Operations Committee shall constitute a quorum for the transaction of business, and the action of a majority of the Committee members present at any meeting at which a quorum is present shall be the action of the Operations Committee; provided, that if all members of the Committee shall consent in writing to any action to be taken by the Committee, such action shall be as valid as though it had been authorized at a meeting of the Operations Committee. If at any meeting of the Operations Committee there shall be less than a quorum present, a majority of those present may adjourn the meeting from time to time until a quorum shall have been obtained.

SECTION 6. Powers of the Committee. The Operations Committee shall have full power and authority of the Board of Directors (a) with respect to the Corporation's acquisition, ownership, development, and disposition of real property, and (b) with respect to all other activities of the Corporation which are not otherwise assigned by the Board of Directors or by these bylaws. The Committee's power and authority in real estate matters shall include, without limitation, the power and authority on behalf of the Corporation, (i) to approve: contracts for the purchase and sale of real property; leases of real property to or from others; applications and petitions to public authorities for rezoning, variances, subdivision approvals and the like; contracts for the design and construction of improvements to property; purchase money mortgages; (ii) to order tests, surveys, inspections and investigations real property, including marketing and feasibility studies; and (iii) to authorize one or more officers of the Corporation to execute documents of every kind and description, including contracts, deeds, leases, notes, and mortgages, for carrying out the decisions of the Committee. The Operations Committee is also authorized to select and employ such agents, professionals, and other consultants as it deems necessary or appropriate. The Committee shall determine whether, and the amount, to compensate all employees and nonemployees for services rendered to the Corporation.

SECTION 7. Committee records. A member of the Committee shall be designated as Secretary of the Committee. The Secretary shall keep minutes of Committee meetings and a record of all Committee activities.

ARTICLE VI
Finance Committee.

SECTION 1. Appointment and qualification. The Board of Directors shall appoint a Finance Committee consisting of not more than seven and not fewer than four members, each of whom shall serve at the pleasure of the Board of Directors. No member of the Finance Committee need be a member or officer of the Corporation or a member of the Board of Directors. The Chairman of the Board of Directors shall serve as Chairman of the Committee.

SECTION 2. Vacancies. Whenever any vacancy shall have occurred in the Finance Committee by reason of death, resignation, removal from office, or otherwise, it may be filled by the votes of a majority of the Committee members then in office at any meeting and the person so elected shall be a Committee member until his successor is elected.

SECTION 3. Meetings. The Committee, by resolution, may fix the time and place for regular meetings. If the Committee does not set regular meetings, or in addition to regular meetings, the Chairman may call, and fix the time and place of, special meetings of the Committee.

SECTION 4. Notice of meetings. No notice shall be required for regular meetings of the Finance Committee. Notice of the purpose, time, and place of every special meeting of the Finance Committee shall be given to each Committee member by any usual means of communication not less than five (5) days before the meeting.

SECTION 5. Quorum. A majority of the Finance Committee shall constitute a quorum for the transaction of business, and the action of a majority of the Committee members present at any meeting at which a quorum is present shall be the action of the Finance Committee; provided, that if all members of the Committee shall consent in writing to any action to be taken by the Committee, such action shall be as valid as though it had been authorized at a meeting of the Finance Committee. If at any meeting of the Finance Committee there shall be less than a quorum present, a majority of those present may adjourn the meeting from time to time until a quorum shall have been obtained.

SECTION 6. Powers of the Committee. The Finance Committee shall review the financial condition of the Corporation on a regular basis, at least quarterly, and shall give its recommendations and advice concerning such condition to the Board of Directors and the Operations Committee. The Committee shall have primary responsibility with respect to (a) the borrowing of money to finance the acquisitions, development or improvement of property and the terms and conditions of such borrowings, (provided, however, that the Operations Committee shall have the authority to obligate the Corporation on indebtedness secured by purchase money mortgages), (b) the selection of depository banks, and (c) the selection of auditors.

SECTION 7. Committee records. A member of the Committee shall be designated as Secretary of the Committee. The Secretary shall keep minutes of Committee meetings and a record of all Committee activities.

ARTICLE VII
Officers.

SECTION 1. Officers of the Corporation. The officers of the Corporation shall consist of a President, a Secretary, a Treasurer and such Vice Presidents, Assistant Secretaries, Assistant Treasurers, and other officers as the Board of Directors may from time to time elect. The same person may at the same time hold any two of the above-named offices except the offices of President and Secretary or President and Assistant Secretary. No officer, other than the President, need be a member of the Corporation or of the Board of Directors.

SECTION 2. Election and term. Except as noted below, the officers of the Corporation shall be elected by the Board of Directors and each officer shall hold office until his death, resignation, retirement, removal, or disqualification, or until his successor is elected and qualified. The Operations Committee

may appoint one or more Assistant Secretaries to serve at the pleasure of the Committee.

SECTION 3. Compensation of officers. The compensation of all officers of the Corporation shall be fixed by the Operations Committee and no officer shall serve the Corporation in any other capacity and receive compensation therefore unless such additional compensation be authorized by the Operations Committee.

SECTION 4. Removal of officers and agents. Any officer or agent elected or appointed by the Board of Directors may be removed by the Board of Directors whenever in its judgment the best interests of the Corporation will be served thereby, but such removal shall be without prejudice to the contract rights, if any, of the person so removed.

SECTION 5. Bonds. The Board of Directors may by resolution require any officer, agent, or employee of the Corporation to give bond to the Corporation, with sufficient sureties, conditioned upon the faithful performance of the duties of his respective office or position, and to comply with such other conditions as may from time to time be required by the Board of Directors.

SECTION 6. President. The President shall be the principal executive officer of the Corporation and, subject to the control of the Operations Committee and the Board of Directors, shall in general supervise and control all of the business and affairs of the Corporation. He shall, when present, preside at all meetings of the members.
He shall sign, with the Secretary, an Assistant Secretary, or any other proper officer of the Corporation thereunto authorized by the Board of Directors, any deeds, mortgages, bonds, contracts, or other instruments which the Operations Committee or the Board of Directors has authorized to be executed, except in cases where the signing and execution thereof shall be expressly delegated by the Operations Committee or by the Board of Directors to some other officer or agent of the Corporation, or shall be required by law to be otherwise signed or executed; and in general shall perform all duties incident to the office of President and such other duties as may be prescribed by the Operations Committee or by the Board of Directors from time to time.

SECTION 7. Vice Presidents. In the absence of the President or in the event of his death, inability or refusal to act, the Vice Presidents in the order of their length of service as Vice Presidents, unless otherwise determined by the Operations Committee or the Board of Directors, shall perform the duties of the President, and when so acting shall have all the powers of and be subject to all the restrictions upon the President. Any Vice President shall perform such other duties as from time to time be assigned to him by the President, the Operations Committee or the Board of Directors.

SECTION 8. Secretary. The Secretary shall: (a) attend all meetings of the members and of the Board of Directors, keep the minutes of such meetings in one or more books provided for that purpose and perform like duties for the standing committees when required, and, unless otherwise directed by the Operations Committee, shall (b) see that all notices are duly given in accordance with the provisions of these bylaws or as required by law; and (c) be custodian of the corporate records and of the seal of the Corporation and see that the seal of the Corporation is affixed to all documents the execution of which on behalf of the Corporation under its seal is duly

SECTION 9.

authorized. In general the Secretary shall perform all duties incident to the office of secretary and such other duties as from time to time may be assigned to him by the Operations Committee, the Board of Directors, or by the President, under whose supervision he shall be.

Assistant Secretaries. In the absence of the Secretary or in the event of his death, inability or refusal to act, the Assistant Secretaries in the order of their length of service as Assistant Secretary, unless otherwise determined by the Operations Committee or the Board of Directors, shall perform the duties of the Secretary, and when so acting shall have all the powers of and be subject to all the restrictions upon the Secretary. They shall perform such other duties as may be assigned to them by the Secretary, the President, the Operations Committee, or by the Board of Directors.

SECTION 10.

Treasurer. The Treasurer shall: (a) have charge and custody of and be responsible for all funds and securities of the Corporation; receive and give receipts for money due and payable to the Corporation from any source whatsoever, and deposit all such moneys in the name of the Corporation in such depositories as shall be selected by the Corporation; and (b) in general perform all of the duties incident to the office to treasurer and such other duties as from time to time may be assigned to him by the President, the Operations Committee, or the Board of Directors. The Treasurer shall prepare, or cause to be prepared, a true statement of the Corporation's assets and liabilities as of the close of each fiscal year, all in reasonable detail.

SECTION 11.

Assistant Treasurers. In the absence of the Treasurer or in the event of his death, inability or refusal to act, the Assistant Treasurers in the order of their length of service as Assistant Treasurer, unless otherwise determined by the Operations Committee or the Board of Directors, shall perform the duties of the Treasurer, and when so acting shall have all the powers of and be subject to all the restrictions upon the Treasurer. They shall perform such other duties as may be assigned to them by the Treasurer, by the President, by the Operations Committee, or by the Board of Directors.

ARTICLE VIII
Contracts, Loan, Checks, and Deposits.

SECTION 1.

Contracts. The Board of Directors or the Operations Committee may authorize any officer or officers, agent or agents, to enter into any contract or execute and deliver any instrument in the name of and on behalf of the Corporation, and such authority may be general or confined to specific instances.

SECTION 2.

Loans. No loans shall be contracted on behalf of the Corporation and no evidences of indebtedness shall be issued in its name unless authorized by a resolution of the Finance Committee or the Board of Directors. Such authority may be general or confined to specific instances. This Section shall not apply to purchase money obligations which may be authorized by resolution of the Operations Committee.

SECTION 3.

Checks and drafts. All checks, drafts, or other orders for the payment of money, issued in the name of the Corporation, shall be signed by such officer or officers, agent or agents of the Corporation and in such manner as shall from time to time be determined by resolution of the Operations Committee or the Board of Directors.

ARTICLE IX
Fiscal Year, Seal.

SECTION 1.

Fiscal year. The fiscal year of the Corporation shall commence on the 1st day of November and end on the 31st day of October.

SECTION 2.

Corporate seal. The Board of Directors shall provide a suitable corporate seal for use by the Corporation.

ARTICLE X
Amendments.

SECTION 1.

The Articles of Incorporation and the bylaws of the Corporation may be amended, added to or repealed, or other or new charter and bylaw provisions may be adopted in lieu thereof by the affirmative vote of a majority of the Board of Directors of the Corporation.

APPENDIX B-3
ARTICLES OF INCORPORATION
OF
UNIVERSITY METRO TOWN CENTER ENDOWMENT, INC.

I, the undersigned, being a person of full age, do make and acknowledge these Articles of Incorporation for the purpose of forming a nonprofit corporation under the laws of the state of North Carolina, as contained in Chapter 55A of the General Statutes of North Carolina, entitled "Nonprofit Corporation Act."

ARTICLE I

The name of the corporation shall be UNIVERSITY METRO TOWN CENTER ENDOWMENT, INC.

ARTICLE II

The period of duration of the corporation shall be perpetual.

ARTICLE III

A. The corporation is organized, solely for educational and charitable purposes, and its exclusive beneficiary shall be The University of North Carolina at Charlotte (the "University"). The corporation shall be that type of organization described in section 502(b)(2) of the Internal Revenue Code substantially all the work of which is performed without compensation.

B. In furtherance of the purposes hereinabove described, the corporation shall have the following powers:

1. To acquire real property in the vicinity of the University for the development of a comprehensively designed, agreeable, and appropriate community which would be a source of goods, services, jobs, entertainment, and housing for personal living, working, and studying in the University area, such community to be developed in consultation with the University.

2. To carry out such development by entering into such contractual arrangements with one or more private developers as its directors deem to be in the best interests of the University.

3. To engage in any and all lawful activities incidental to the accomplishment of the foregoing purposes, except as restricted herein.

ARTICLE IV

The Foundation of The University of North Carolina at Charlotte, Inc. (the "Foundation") shall be the sole member of the corporation. The corporation shall have no capital stock, but it is expected that the Foundation will transfer real and personal property to the corporation from time to time as contributions to its capital.

ARTICLE V

The governing body of the corporation shall be a Board of Directors. The number of directors, the manner of their selection, and their term of office shall be fixed by the bylaws of the corporation. The initial Board of Directors shall have eight members and shall be composed of the following persons who shall serve until their successors have been selected and qualified:

NAME	ADDRESS
Ralph M. Carestio	3820 River Ridge Road
	Charlotte, N.C. 28211
Leo E. Ells	2300 McLean Road
	Charlotte, N.C. 28213
E. K. Fretwell Jr.	3066 Stonybrook Road
	Charlotte, N.C. 28205
Eugene B. Graham, III	3929 Rhodes Avenue
	Charlotte, N.C. 28210
Robert Lassiter, Jr.	726 Hempstead Place
	Charlotte, N.C. 28207
Charles S. Myerly	4800 Sentinel Post Road
	Charlotte, N.C. 28211
William A. White, Jr.	1515 Scotland Avenue
	Charlotte, N.C. 28207
David W. Whitlock	3326 Dunaire Drive
	Charlotte, N.C. 28205

ARTICLE VI

The address of the initial registered office of the corporation in North Carolina is 200 South Tryon Street, Mecklenburg County, Charlotte, North Carolina, 28202; and the name of the initial registered agent at such address is Robert Lassiter, Jr.

ARTICLE VII

All of the net earnings of the corporation shall be distributed to the University and no part of such net earnings shall inure to the benefit of the corporation's sole member or of any private individual. No part of the activities of the corporation shall be the carrying on of propaganda or otherwise attempting to influence legislation, nor shall the corporation intervene in any political campaign on behalf of any candidate for public office.

ARTICLE VIII

The officers and directors of the corporation shall serve without compensation.

ARTICLE IX

Upon liquidation of the corporation, all of the net assets thereof shall be distributed to The University of North Carolina at Charlotte; provided that if said University is no longer in operation such assets shall be distributed to and among such other institutions of higher education as shall be selected by the Board of Directors of the corporation from among such institutions located in North Carolina which are either (i) agencies or instrumentalities of the state of North Carolina or any political subdivision thereof, or (ii) institutions which qualify for exemption as an organization described in section 501 (c)(3) of the Internal Revenue Code as presently in force and effect.

ARTICLE X

Upon completion of the organization of this corporation, the Board of Directors will adopt such bylaws as they deem advisable setting forth regulations for the governance of the corporation.

ARTICLE XI

The name and address of the incorporator is:

NAME	ADDRESS
Robert W. King, Jr.	3000 NCNB Plaza
	Charlotte, N.C. 28280

IN WITNESS WHEREOF, I have hereunto set my hand and seal this the 25th day of June, 1981.

Signed by Robert W. King, Jr.

APPENDIX B-4

BYLAWS OF
UNIVERSITY METRO TOWN CENTER ENDOWMENT, INC.

ARTICLE I
Offices.

SECTION 1: Principal office. The principal office of the Corporation shall be located in Charlotte, North Carolina.

SECTION 2: Registered office. The registered office of the Corporation required by law to be maintained in the state of North Carolina may be, but need not be, identical with the principal office in the state of North Carolina. The address of the registered office may be changed from time to time by the Board of Directors.

SECTION 3: Transfer of membership. Membership or any interest in this Corporation shall not be assignable.

ARTICLE II
Members.

SECTION 1: Membership. The Foundation of The University of North Carolina at Charlotte ("UNCCF") shall be the sole member of the Corporation.

SECTION 2: Capital contributions. UNCCF may make capital contributions to the Corporation in cash or in kind in such amounts and at such times as it deems appropriate.

SECTION 3: Transfer of membership. Membership or any interest in this Corporation shall not be assignable.

ARTICLE III
Directors.

SECTION 1: Number, qualification, and term of office. The number of Directors of the Corporation shall be eight (8). Each director shall hold office until his death, resignation, retirement, removal, or disqualification, or until his successor is elected and qualified. Directors need not be residents of the state of North Carolina or members of the Corporation.

SECTION 2: Appointment of Directors. Directors of the Corporation shall be appointed annually by UNCCF.

SECTION 3: Vacancies. Whenever any vacancy shall have occurred in the Board of Directors by reason of death, resignation, or otherwise it may be filled by the votes of a majority of the directors then in office at any meeting and the person so elected shall be a director until his successor is appointed by UNCCF.

SECTION 4: Meetings. Regular meetings of the Board of Directors shall be held at such times and places, within or without the state of North Carolina, as may from time to time be determined by a majority of the Board. Special meetings of the Board may be called by the Chairman of the Board of Directors, the President, the Secretary, or by a majority of the Board of Directors at such place within or without the state of North Carolina, as may be stated in the Notice thereof and at such time and for such purpose as may be stated in the Notice.

SECTION 5: Election of Chairman. The Directors shall elect from their number a Chairman of the Board who shall serve until his successor shall have been duly elected and qualified.

SECTION 6: Notice of meetings. Notice of the time and place, and, in the case of special meetings, the purpose, of every meeting of the Board shall be given to each Director by any usual means of communication not less than ten (10) days before the meeting; provided, that no notice of adjourned meetings need be given. Meetings may be held at any time without notice if all the Directors are present or if those not present waive notice of the time, place, and purpose of such meeting by any usual means of communication either before or after the holding thereof.

SECTION 7: Quorum of Directors. A majority of the Directors shall constitute a quorum for the transaction of business, and the action of a majority of the Directors present at any meeting at which a quorum is present shall be the action of the Board of Directors; provided, that if all of the Directors shall consent in writing to any action to be taken by the Corporation, such action shall be valid corporate action as though it had been authorized at a meeting of the Directors. If at any meeting of the Board there shall be less than a quorum present, a majority of those present may adjourn the meeting from time to time until a quorum shall have been obtained.

SECTION 8: Powers of the Board. The Board of Directors shall have overall responsibility for the management of the affairs of the Corporation. The Board shall elect all corporate officers.

ARTICLE IV
Officers.

SECTION 1: Officers of the Corporation. The officers of the Corporation shall consist of a President, a Secretary, a Treasurer, and such Vice Presidents, Assistant Secretaries, Assistant Treasurers, and other officers as the Board of Directors may from time to time elect. The same person may at the same time hold any two of the above-named offices except the offices of President and Secretary or President and Assistant Secretary. No officer, other than the President, need be a member of the Board of Directors.

SECTION 2: Election and term. The officers of the Corporation shall be elected by the Board of Directors and each officer shall hold office until his death, resignation, retirement, removal, or disqualification, or until his successor is elected and qualified.

SECTION 3: Removal of officers and agents. Any officer or agent elected or appointed by the Board of Directors may be removed by the Board of Directors whenever in its judgment the best interests of the Corporation will be served thereby.

SECTION 4: Powers and duties. The officers of the Corporation shall respectively have such powers and perform such duties in the management of the property and affairs of the Corporation, subject to the control of the Directors, as generally pertains to their respective offices, as well as such additional powers and duties as may from time to time be conferred by the Board of Directors.

ARTICLE V
Contracts, Loans, Checks, and Deposits.

SECTION 1: Contracts. The Board of Directors may authorize any officer or officers, agent or agents, to enter into any contract or execute and deliver any instrument in the name of and on behalf of the Corporation, and such authority may be general or confined to specific instances.

SECTION 2: Loans. No loans shall be contracted on behalf of the Corporation and no evidences of indebtedness shall be issued in its name unless authorized by a resolution of the Board of Directors. Such authority may be general or confined to specific instances.

SECTION 3: Checks and drafts. All checks, drafts, or other orders for the payment of money, issued in the name of the Corporation, shall be signed by such officer or officers, agent or agents of the Corporation and in such manner as shall from time to time be determined by resolution of the Board of Directors.

ARTICLE VI
Fiscal Year, Seal.

SECTION 1: Fiscal year. The fiscal year of the Corporation shall commence on the 1st day of January and end on the 31st day of December.

SECTION 2: Corporate seal. The Board of Directors shall provide a suitable corporate seal for use by the Corporation.

ARTICLE VII
Amendments.

SECTION 1: The Articles of Incorporation and the bylaws of the Corporation may be amended, added to, or repealed only by UNCCF.

APPENDIX C

EXCERPTS FROM AN INTERVIEW WITH W. T. HARRIS, DECEMBER 20, 1979 BY DEAN W. COLVARD

(C) Mr. Harris, you were president of the Chamber of Commerce at the time the University Research Park was first considered and you served as president of the University Research Park for the first ten years. What was the thinking in the minds of the people that caused you to start talking about the park?

(H) We had people who were interested in the Charlotte area to put up research places of business. We just simply did not have a place such as the Research Triangle and such as they had in Atlanta, Georgia and some places like this and, therefore, we missed some pretty good companies. We had to face up to the fact that if we wanted to increase the level of the take-home pay of the people of this community that we had to move away from the total warehouse distribution type of business and get more research and people with more education. We also felt pretty strongly that if we could bring quite a few people in here with PhDs, it would help the university to develop and between the two that this would be a worthwhile project. As you will remember, we had no water and sewer in that particular area. In fact the university was about to dry up.

(C) Who else would have been involved in discussing that matter back in the mid '60s?

(H) The major people who were involved at that time were the manager of the Chamber of Commerce, Charlie Crawford, and Bill Ficklen, an interested industrial man in the Chamber of Commerce. Bill was the most enthusiastic human being I ever met. He just never believed that anything couldn't be done. He got all fired up about this because he was the person who faced the people as they came into this community and showed them around, along with other people. In the meantime, he and I encouraged General Paul Younts, who was in the real estate business, to buy some options on some property on Highway 29 and where I-85 was being built at that point in time.

(C) That was the very beginning of the land purchase?

(H) That's right. He went out and bought an option on a couple hundred acres. He, in turn, had sold an option to Collins and Aikman based upon guaranteeing that he could get water and sewer to them. He had deposited $100,000 in escrow at First Union National Bank to guarantee that water and sewer would be put to their property line.

(C) Did he actually put up an escrow account of his own?

(H) Yes, he did — his money. That was the beginning of the University Research Park — with Collins and Aikman. I was president of the chamber in '66 and this was on my program of work. Paul Lucas[1] of Duke Power Company was chairman of the program of work for me that year. He and the committee that he headed wrote all of these things up. For instance, the concept of the University City was written up at the same time. We did not do very much the year of '66 because I personally had so much to do with the chamber that I just could not take all of the time that was required to move the research park. Then my friend, Pat Calhoun, from NCNB was made president of the chamber. Pat was one of my favorite people in this community because he was a "do it now guy." He didn't believe in playing around. Red Jones of Duke Power Company was also involved. Red, in turn, had a heart problem so we moved Pat in as president of the chamber in '67. Pat came to me and asked if I would get this organization together and get the research park moving.

I believe you were involved from the beginning, were you not?

(C) I became involved in '66. Not the beginning of the idea . . .

(H) No, not the concept but really putting it together.

(C) Yes.

(H) We did put it together and we had no money. We asked the law firm of Grier, Parker, Poe, and Thompson to draw up a nonprofit corporation. We appointed 27 or 28 people, if I remember right — in the beginning about 25 — trying to get representation from all of the banks,

---

[1] Paul Lucas was also a trustee of Charlotte College.

Duke Power, the industrial end of the community, and some real estate people. Louis Rose and people such as Louis were interested in the development and sale of properties of other people in the industrial world. That is why they were considered the best. There was one thing wrong with everything we did up to that point. We hadn't figured out yet how we were going to get the money. Louis Rose, Paul Younts, and several others put together several hundred acres that we could purchase for a reasonable amount of money and Edwin Jones had quite a tract of land out there.

(C) Younts took an option on the land which he sold to Collins and Aikman.

(H) Right, Bill Ficklen of the chamber and I specifically asked him to do this. We were working with Collins and Aikman and they wanted to be in that general area. This piece of property was physically closely related to the university and they were very much interested in that area. I personally think that was the only area in our community in which they were interested. Therefore, it was essential that we get something together or we would have missed this very fine company. Paul took the gamble that we could sell them and if we couldn't we could sell someone else.

Let me go back to the money again because it would never have flown except for the financial plan. We came up with every scheme in the world of how we could put the money together. We figured we had to have a half million dollars. As you do most things in this community, you go to the financial organizations of the community. I told Pat Calhoun, "Well, Pat, there is no point in our talking to anyone except your bank and that is Addison Reese. Set up an appointment as early as you can on Monday morning and I will meet you here and we will go see Addison. If Addison won't do it we can forget about it." We went and I told Addison exactly where we were. I wasn't in his office five minutes. I said, "Addison, it gets right down to this. You have to put up $100,000 so we can get the rest of them to put up $100,000. If you don't do it, it isn't going to fly. It is a worthy thing but you, the financial people, have to back it up." He said, "Well, Bill, you've got it. You go see the rest of them and don't waste any more time on me." I met Graeme Keith (of First Union National Bank), George Broadrick (of First Citizens Bank), and Northwestern Bank and Wachovia people and we got the money. We got some money from Duke Power Company. We acquired the property — some 450 or 460 acres. Then Jones added 700 to 800 acres into the park to make it a 1,100 or 1,200 acre park. As you know at that point in time, we had to have some protection. We got Fred Bryant and his staff from the zoning board to come out and make recommendations for zoning the park.

(C) I think it is probably worthy of note here that simultaneously the university had managed to put together about $25,000 to hire Gouldie Odell as a planner for the campus and was working with the planning commission on planning around the university. So the park and the university were planning with the planning commission at the same time.

(H) Yes, and you came up with a coordinated plan — for the University City.

(C) You indicated that you thought Mr. Reese was the man who really triggered the thing. You and I know that Mr. Reese was a man who helped with a lot of other things, but it was quite an act of faith not only on the part of Mr. Reese but on the part of all of the banks to make this thing float. How much money did they put up initially?

(H) The banks put up $400,000, and we wound up with about $440,000 that different people put up. The memberships, as you know . . .

(C) They tried to sell memberships but that never did go very well . . .

(H) We had a few at $1,000, but not many.

(C) It is worthy to note too that about this time the university ran out of water and had to close down one day.

(H) The wells ran dry.

(C) We got an awful lot of cooperation from both the city and the county. The waterline that came out to the university split off and went out to the park at the same time. We had to put up our own money to get it into the park, didn't we?

(H) That's right. We had to furnish the dollars that it took to put the major trunk line out there. They did not build that trunk line. The University Research Park furnished the money to build from the split off of Highways 29 and 49 up Highway 29 and across the highway to our own property. We were fortunate that Edwin Jones picked up his share of this and Collins and Aikman did the same.

(C) For the record I think it should be clear that this was before I-85 was built.

(H) It was slated to be built.

(C) When we started putting sewer and water out there we were paying for that out of that money as well as buying land, weren't we?

(H) Yes. We made only the minimum down payments on property and paid a pretty low interest rate, 4 to 6 percent, on most of the property. I don't remember who we bought all of the property from but we bought some of it from Dr. Charlie Robinson. Charlie didn't need money so we made a minimum down payment to him. We didn't pay anybody totally. The banks had given us a credit allowance of $400,000 to $500,000 but I don't think we ever borrowed that much.

(C) Let me go back to another individual whom you have mentioned two or three times — Pat Calhoun. If I remember correctly, he became treasurer and was a real workhorse.

(H) That's correct.

(C) You said that Bill Ficklen was a man who liked to do the impossible. Wouldn't you say that Bill Ficklen was a key man in the first ten years of operation?

(H) Yes, without Bill Ficklen it would never have flown, Dean, let's face it. Everybody was important; everybody did their part but there were some key people who would take the time and effort to do things. Bill Ficklen worked as the industrial specialist for the Charlotte Chamber of Commerce. This was over and beyond his job but he gave untold hours. He had an excellent mind as to detail and all of the things that needed to be done.

(C) He also generated a lot of confidence in people who came in to look, they trusted him. He came to see me several times with people like the Westinghouse people who were coming into another part of the city. He told me, "You won't know who these people are and I won't tell you except that they are good people." He was a man whom they trusted.

(H) Bill was a man of absolutely high integrity. His word was his bond and he knew how to handle people such as this without giving away anything that he wasn't supposed to. He trusted you, he trusted me. If he told them that he would not divulge who they were, he wouldn't. He didn't tell his wife; he didn't tell his best friend; he didn't tell anybody. This is the way Bill operated. He really built up confidence.

(C) Including what we owed the banks and what we owed the people from whom we bought the land we were close to a million dollars in debt, weren't we? How did you feel about that when we had been into it about four or five years and we hadn't sold anything?

(H) The bright spot in all of this was that property in that general area was moving up all the time. Therefore, our values were not being depreciated or eroded, they were moving up. This was mainly because you and your group were developing the university at a fast pace and I-85 was coming through and that was certain. I was ready to sell some property; I don't mind telling you. We were not really in the investment business; we were trying the development business for the research park.

(C) Developing an idea.

(H) Right, and we desperately wanted to get started with some good people.

(C) Let me switch to another angle of this. Some other important people came in. How about talking a little bit about them.

(H) Dan Moore was elected Governor of North Carolina. George Broadrick was appointed as highway commissioner. George Broadrick is one of the most capable people that I have ever met in my life. He doesn't do a lot of talking but when he says something, it makes a whole lot of sense. We told George what our needs were and that if we could get the right kind of right-of-way we would give the property if the state would take it and develop it. Of course, the planners showed the need

for the road and their concept as to how it related to the university and to the park and other traffic that needed to move across there. Governor Moore allocated to George certain uncommitted monies and George had a certain amount of authority.

(C) We are talking now about a new road. Highway 49 was a two-lane road; it wasn't a four-lane road. I am glad that you gave George Broadrick the introduction you did here because I think General Younts and George helped greatly.

(H) The university gave its share of the right-of-way facing its property, a 200 foot strip. Collins and Aikman gave a certain amount and the research park gave both sides of the road for quite a ways over there.

(C) Also the foundation of the university owned some land and gave the right-of-way from Highway 49. The county owned Green Acres and it also provided right-of-way. As we stand today we have Harris Boulevard which is a two-lane road from Highway 49 to Mallard Creek Church Road but the state has a right-of-way for a four-lane road which it has had since the very beginning of that planning.

(H) That's right. It was planned from the very beginning as a four-lane road.

(C) With the commitment we have to extend Harris Boulevard all the way over to I-77, which was not in existence then, we have assurance that the time is not very far away when we shall have excellent road connections. For the record, let me say in this connection the appreciation the board of the University Research Park had for your leadership in the initial development of this and for your serving as president for the first ten years was demonstrated by naming that road Harris Boulevard. It will be a more important road as years go by. What can you say about the first contact with IBM which changed things? Did they come to us or did Bill Ficklen find them or what happened?

(H) What we did back in those days, Dean, in trying to secure people was to look at big corporations. Looking at the people who should be ready to expand was the work of the chamber partially and the research park group. We did look at IBM as one of the corporations that should be considered. They had opened an operation in the Research Triangle Park, employing some five thousand people. They had a research center with small manufacturing going on in it. Bill Ficklen went to New York to the research headquarters. This is the way the thing came about. They became interested in Charlotte because they were building places across the country at that time.

(C) Did they come in here and deal with Bill Ficklen in this usual pattern?

(H) Yes, they did. They came and kept talking. Duffy, who is head of the local organization, was one of the men who moved in here and did some looking.

(C) They paid close to $2,000,000 for the land, didn't they?

(H) Yes, they paid about $5,000 per acre.

(C) I remember some of your comments. I think a lot of us shared your feelings that we felt pretty much relieved to finally have a little money and not have any debts. How did you feel about that?

(H) Well, I felt great about it, Dean, as you remember, we paid off all of our debts and had about $1,150,000 left. A lot of us were ready to say that we had pretty well achieved what we set out to do and, therefore, we were going to give this money to the university and get out of this business. That was the way some of them felt. I had a little bit of trepidation about that but I will never forget your viewpoint. You said, "Now, wait just a minute. We have just really started developing the research park and I don't want the money for the university. Take the money and put it in more land and investment." You felt that the greatest investment the university could make was to keep 25 or 30 of the high caliber people that we had on the board working on a research park.

(C) The leadership of this group is important. You headed them for ten years before you retired from the presidency and Dave Taylor has given very able succession to you. We did pay ourselves out of debt; we did buy some more land.

(H) We had people who were bold — Addison Reese, McGraw at First Union, Scott Cramer at Wachovia, and George Broadrick at First Citizens. That was about the time that Northwestern Bank moved to Charlotte and we got Emery Inman in. Those people were people of vision because they had been builders themselves. They were willing to take whatever calculated risks it took to do the job.

(C) We had an economic depression that hit us about 1974. I think that

is one of the reasons that we felt mighty glad to be out of debt.
(H) The economic depression held up IBM and that created some problems. The big deal with IBM, I was told, was that they had a breakthrough in computer sciences. Suddenly, their computer units moved down to about 10% their previous size. They had adequate room for the smaller scale manufacturing process in their whole company.
(C) I remember when we went to New York to visit with them they were very careful not to reveal too much of their future plans. It was clear to us that this breakthrough in technology caused them to need less floor space. When we got the message that they were going to activate this project all of us were very happy. In the meantime we weren't sitting still because we weren't sure that IBM was going to come. Say something if you will about the option we gave Billy Graham.
(H) Actually, we bought an option from IBM for part of the land. The land is where the IBM building is now structured. We were hoping to get the Billy Graham center here.
(C) It was the Billy Graham Library which eventually went to Wheaton College.
(H) I think the future with the leadership that we now have, Dean, is bright. Dave Taylor is doing a magnificent job. He is a very wise man who is well versed in this field of research. Dave is one of the research people who has some practical sense. He is just a great fellow.
(C) One of the very rich set of circumstances that I have encountered here in Charlotte is the kind of leadership from these various groups that I have had the opportunity of working with. We talked about the University Research Park where you were president for ten years and then you were followed immediately by Dave Taylor. Addison Reese

was president of The Foundation of UNCC from the very beginning when I came here. Then Addison became the chairman of the first Board of Trustees that we ever had at UNCC. I worked with him as the president of the foundation and chairman of the Board of Trustees, with you as President of University Research Park, and then Dave Taylor as president of the foundation and the University Research Park.
(H) There is a better understanding of the work of research today. This is the lifeline of the total picture. It is just unbelievable what can be done.
(C) That land that we bought initially — what did we pay on the average for that?
(H) I would say we averaged about $500 an acre.
(C) We are now buying land again and it is about $5,000.
(H) We sold to IBM for $5,000 an acre.
(C) The acreage is being quoted at $25,000 to $30,000 an acre now.
(H) In my judgment we shouldn't get overly greedy because one of the reasons for setting up the research park was to hold some property at a reasonable price and not price ourselves out of the market. Dean, we are talking about a world market now rather than just bucking some southern city; you are raring up against the world. They will move in here from all over.
(C) You have been very much in the life of this community. In the 12 to 14 years that I have been here I have seen you operate as chairman of the Board of County Commissioners, as president of the Chamber of Commerce and as president of the University Research Park. The whole community is better by your having been here. Thanks to you for taking the time to record this information.

EXCERPTS FROM AN INTERVIEW WITH DAVID TAYLOR, NOVEMBER 7, 1983 BY DEAN W. COLVARD

(C) Dave, before we get into talking about the park, how about giving us a little synopsis of what brought you to Charlotte and something about your background in research before you actually got involved in the park.
(T) Well, Dean, I never was longhaired enough to be a good research person, but I had a natural bent in that direction. In '52, '53, and part of '54, I was running a research operation for Celanese in Cumberland, Maryland; and subsequently, was asked by the chairman of Celanese to come to Charlotte and set up laboratories that would be dedicated almost entirely to fiber research rather than that whole gamut that was practiced in Summit, New Jersey, and at the central labs of the corporation. I came in May of '54 and at once started looking for a site that we might use for the labs, a site that was to be remotely accessible from the main office that had just been completed in late '53 and early '54.
(C) The main office was where?
(T) The main fiber operations office was here in Charlotte. The headquarters were in New York, although the building that was built here in Charlotte was to serve for the principal corporate offices which were to move from New York but never did. I found a site out on Reed Road, which is now Archdale Drive, working with Claude Freeman in those days. It was about 114 acres, and I purchased the site for about $98,000. I studied buildings up and down the east coast and finally decided that one in New Jersey operated by Johns-Manville was ideal for us. We had Austin Company of Cleveland lay out all of the buildings which now add up to about three-quarters of a million square feet. After that I left research and went back into product development, process development, manufacturing, and eventually into the manufacturing operations itself.
(C) When you were in manufacturing you were primarily in the administrative side of manufacturing?

(T) I was vice president of manufacturing for the fibers operations. In '60 I became president of the Plastics Company and moved to New Jersey.
(C) One of the things that seems to me to be somewhat related to the University Research Park is the way you designed and planned that layout to protect it on the one hand and to give it accessibility on the other hand. Were you involved very much with the city planners at that time or was the planning as sophisticated then as it was later?
(T) I was not involved with the planners at that time. It is my understanding that it was not as sophisticated. We picked land that was adjacent to county-owned land at that time and well protected along one side. We bought about a half-mile frontage to look after the beauty of the operations. We spent money to design units that were most attractive.
(C) Give us some idea of the scope of this operation during the latter years of your active involvement.
(T) The laboratories eventually housed three independent, yet dependent units; the marketing company, the fiber company and fiber industries. They are now all one unit but at its peak it involved 800 to 900 people and was, and is, one of the great fiber laboratories of the world.
(C) For some years, in the beginning, it was one of the very largest employers of the county, too, wasn't it?
(T) It was. The fibers main office and the laboratory involved about 1,800 people. That put them in the top half-dozen employers in Charlotte.
(C) When did you first become involved with the University Research Park?
(T) I believe I came on the board in 1967.[2]
(C) You came on while Mr. Harris was chairman of the board and served with him most of the ten years that he served and then you succeeded him as chairman. Having been a member of that board, and still a member, I was very much aware of the fact that Mr. Harris had made a great contribution as a leader of the Chamber of Commerce and of the community. Of course, you've been a leader of the Chamber of Commerce, too; but I know everybody felt that your research background was the thing that made you a very unique person among board mem-

---

[2] Mr. Taylor was elected director on the recommendation of President Harris at the board meeting on May 9, 1967. He was presented as a new member at the board meeting on July 5, 1967. The board had met monthly since January, 1967.

bers. The thing that I would like to hear you discuss would be the changes that took place soon after you became president, not only because you were the president, but also because conditions had changed a great deal. How about commenting on the evolution of the park beginning about the time IBM became active. Mr. Harris has recorded quite a bit about how IBM got involved and all of that.

(T) Let's go back to 1977 when I became chairman or president. At that time we had been more or less without movement in the park. We commissioned a study by UNCC on a marketing strategy for the park. We were well pleased with what came out of that study. It showed very, very clearly the strengths and weaknesses that we had, and we set out to make the most of it. As early as '73, Jack Tate had made a strong point about the need for the extension of Harris Boulevard and also the need for residential development that would in some way lead to growth in the northeast. So we went to work along those lines. Before I go further, let me talk a little about the organization itself.

In order to market the park we had made an arrangement with the Chamber of Commerce to pay half the amount for a sales representative, or development representative, who would work generally for the chamber but certainly concentrate on the park. Morris Ewing was selected and for several years, maybe three or four, Morris worked under those particular conditions. Following the growth that came with the announcement of IBM it became very, very apparent that the park could no longer operate as a desk at the Chamber of Commerce. It must begin putting together some kind of organization that would be independent. We needed our own phone; we needed an address; we needed an identity that was not too clearly spelled out under the existing situations. The fact that I headed the chamber in 1978 was a great help in moving for independence. It was not totally achieved in that year, nor in the next year for that matter, but we began moving and breaking away to where much that was being done was done largely through the real estate committee.

(C) Tell us a little about the real estate committee, how they worked.

(T) The real estate committee was composed of Ed Vinson, Louis Rose,[3] and Claude Freeman.[4] With the death of Ed Vinson we dropped it to two members, who were also directors. Basically we had a contract with that committee to guide us in the directions that we might go in the purchases of land, to help us in establishing prices, to promote the park in meetings with prospective tenants and literally to sell and purchase land. Because of the work they did conceptually, putting together maps, contacting people, and one thing or another, they even benefited from sales that were made by other real estate firms within the city or county to one or two percent. At one time we cut back on the commission we would pay outside realtors, but that was a mistake. We very quickly raised that amount up to the standard and the add-on came to the members of the real estate committee.

(C) If any realtor in the city had a prospect, they would join in with either Louis Rose or Claude Freeman and then Claude and Louis would share that commission in some small way?

(T) We had to have some professional advice on pricing, location, and size of property that would not in any way destroy the value of the adjacent property, etc., so the committee has been of immense value to us. I do not believe we have anyone in the city any better than Claude Freeman in the conceptual ability that is required in this kind of work, nor do you have a better sales person than Louis Rose, so the team has worked very proficiently and very successfully for us.

(C) In some instances, I suppose, they have been both the realtor and the representative.

(T) That is quite true, and especially under those circumstances there is usually some modification to the fees that are paid. Eventually, working with Bland Worley, we did break away from the chamber and established our independence, although it was very, very essential that we always be related to the chamber. Indeed, the chamber still nominates about a third of the directors. Looking at the park and its relationship to UNCC and the foundation and with the work that started when The

[3] Following his death, Louis Rose, Sr. was succeeded by his son, Louis Rose, Jr.

[4] According to the records, after his death Paul Younts was succeeded by Claude Freeman, Sr.

[5] Dave Taylor was on the regional board of Wachovia from 1964 to 1981.

Foundation of UNCC got into acquiring land for University Place, I tried to determine whether these two units (University Place and the park) might operate as a single entity.

(C) One of the reasons you are in a good position to do that is because you were president of both of them.

(T) That is true, Dean. A study of what might be achieved by putting them together proved that they would be better to operate independently largely because the park has no problem operating as a nonprofit entity based on cases involving development sponsored by chambers of commerce. The foundation, on the other hand, suffers if they ever go into any kind of a business related operation. While we tried to avoid the tax questions by forming a subsidiary of the foundation, it became very, very clear that these two entities, while closely related, should not operate as a single unit. Following that study I had both charters, that of the foundation and that of the park, redone to correct inconsistencies or contradictions and make them thoroughly compatible. Under the new system, the foundation receives all contributions as well as residuals from the park and, of course, the university is the total beneficiary of both. Those exercises were well worthwhile. We also raised the number of directors in each so that we brought in more and more people and expanded even our banking relationships to include the Piedmont Bank & Trust Company for the first time.

With that background on the organization, we will go back to the problems facing us in order to correct the weaknesses, largely related to residential units for upper-middle income people who might wish to live near developments that were taking place in the park and who might want to avoid the long drive from southeast Charlotte. With the announcement in early '78 that IBM was going to start building that fall in the park or almost immediately, the matter of housing and growth became very critical.

Jack Tate, who had always taken a very active part in the total promotion of the park towards the northeast, especially towards Davidson, where Jack lived and where his bank was headquartered, became more and more active. The two of us set out to see where and what might be done, first of all with the road. We looked at the maps for the extension of Harris Boulevard and saw very clearly that they were drawn in such a way as to cross I-77 between Sunset Boulevard and Reames Road without an interchange at that far end. Because this would bring us into an area that would be harder to develop into expensive homes we insisted on connecting at Reames Road. In order to get this done and change the road plans, to get the governor behind it, we asked Dr. Colvard to visit with the governor and sell the whole idea. He was imminently successful in that and the governor made the announcement. The road went to the top of the list. We see today the complete grading of that road all the way to Reames.

We had some problems with the Davis Store that was an historical monument of sorts and it forced a movement of the road south of Florida Steel. In the long run we did achieve the ability to bring the road into property that the park had acquired for residential development. We had acquired two blocks of land, one with about 120 acres (Fox-/DeArmon) which adjoined the Queens property across Harris Boulevard from IBM, and further to the north the Slayton tract of about 94 acres. The Fox/DeArmon property was for transitional use. The Slayton property was to be largely single family with some multi-family housing allowed. The Slayton property was later expanded to include enough of the DeArmon property and we ended up with about 120 acres for residential use. We had an early proposal from Allen Tate, John Crosland, and Walter Hedrick to put the housing in there if and when we would have water, road, and sewer.

(C) Dave, before you go any further how about backing up just a little bit. You say you land-banked this property. I think it's important that we get in here how it was financed.

(T) About this time we made an arrangement with six banks to have each lend $250,000 for the acquisition of land. This gave us a million and a half dollars to operate with. Wachovia, Northwestern, First Union, NCNB, First Citizens, and Piedmont Bank were the banks involved. Wachovia, because of my relationship[5] with them, took the lead in putting together the instrument that permitted us to literally borrow from these banks at a fraction above prime with the understanding that while we would mortgage land to look after their essential needs, they did not hold us to particular property that we had bought at the time.

(C) They did not take a deed of trust on any particular tract?

(T) That is right. They were extremely understanding and to this day the park would never have been a success if we did not have these banks with their foresight and understanding supporting us in every single way necessary. We have gone into debt, come out of debt, gone into debt, come out of debt and always worked it out for the total good of the park, yet at no time were any of the banks in a problem situation. There was always land, there were always assets to cover any debt several fold. It is a good point always to make clear to anyone, Dean, that the role those banks have played in both the University Research Park's development and the foundation's involvement in University Place, was essential to these important developments.

Having covered the road, Jack Tate and I met with the county commissioners and presented a plan for the extension of the park to an ultimate 3,000 acres. We asked their endorsement for this long range plan and also asked that they put in a sewer down Mallard Creek to the far end of the property that the park owned, which meant that they would cross Harris Boulevard at some point on the Slayton property. The commissioners and the city council both approved this request. We eventually stopped work on Mallard Creek and took the sewer up Clark Creek because that drained the area for the residences that were projected. We also got an agreement to take the water up Harris Boulevard when the center line of the new road was established and also to carry that water all the way over to Highway 115 so that we would interconnect the 24" line going up Highway 115 with that 16" line up Highway 29 and 20" line going up Highway 49. That is presently part of the plan and the bonds we are going to vote on tomorrow[6] are going to cover the costs.

As the development of IBM progressed it induced other people to look hard at the park. IBM was a tremendous catalyst for growth. Their location gave us an anchor, a very attractive anchor, that started other people looking at the park. We saw Verbatim come in from Sunnyvale, California. They make floppy disks. They bought about 33 acres across from the entrance of IBM. We saw Fairfax Properties come in to take the corner because they hoped to build a building that might house some of IBM's support structure that IBM might not want to build for themselves. We saw ADP come in and buy land on the other side of Reeves Brothers. Union Oil of California that had part of their chemical division in Charlotte with a plant on Mallard Creek Road built a unit on Research Drive to service their customers and do lab work. We also had EPRI, the Electric Power Research Institute, put in a nondestructive testing unit on Queens property that is operated by the J. A. Jones firm for the electric utilities of this country.

(C) I think it's important to note here that the Queens property was a part of the park for planning purposes from the very beginning so it's on their property but it's still in the University Research Park.

(T) It is definitely a part of the park and a very essential and very large part of the park with the park ownership adjoining them on both sides. They are in the section zoned for research, whereas the property we bought for residential and for that part in between was not in those days zoned for research. We always tried to make it clear that while we would not gain from a sale of property that was owned by Jones or Holtzman, nevertheless, we promoted that land as being available. Whenever there were roads, sewers, or other things involving Jones and the park, a proportional part was paid by both. They have been marvelous to work with and are good neighbors. They are well represented on the board and, in fact, Jones has sold the park land from time to time so that the park could benefit.

(C) Just for the record here — although none of these new installations have gone on the property owned by Collins & Aikman, they likewise have been partners in the park development from the very beginning, just as Queens Properties has been.

(T) That is quite true, although, to date they have acquired more property and have sold none. There is the possibility at the moment that they will be selling some because they are now in excess of 100 acres.

(C) That might be modified slightly by an earlier action they took to sell to the Allstate Insurance Company. They did sell that property to them earlier, didn't they?

(T) Yes. That Allstate property is about 33 acres.

(C) It would be interesting to put in the record some ideas of how the values of this property have varied with the passage of time.

(T) Dean, the park enjoys tax-free status, largely because it is devoted to economic development. In order to achieve that situation, we are supposed to, on occasion at least, sell land for less than we have in it if the benefits to the community exceed any desire we might have for holding onto that property. In '70, IBM bought the land largely for around $5,000 an acre. The Fairfax property which is across the road and on the corner sold at a bargain price of $45,000 an acre. Prices go up and down with needs and location. Verbatim got a bargain at $23,000 an acre, Southern Bell paid $40,000. The latest price offered to a prospect for a building on Harris Boulevard was $70,000 per acre. It may seem like these numbers are beginning to go up quite high, but the cost of water, sewers, and roads — the roads within the park are paid for by the park — takes a tremendous amount of money. We got about $22,000 an acre for ADP but, on the other hand, the bulk of land they bought was in a flood plain. Flood plain can still be used for a parking lot, but you certainly cannot build on it.

We have asked that the state put in an interchange on Mallard Creek Road. While it is not in their plans, we expect it to go in because the amount of traffic that is now being generated in the park is in excess of existing highways.

(C) How about picking up where you left off when you talked about the separation from the Chamber of Commerce and tell us how you went about that and what happened.

(T) Dean, what was happening was that I was coming closer to retirement from Celanese and once I was out of my business office without secretarial help, phones, and all of that, I could no longer spend the time, which was often running four hours a day on the park. We began formulating plans to get a part-time director. Rusty agreed to take the job in early 1981. I would step down to become chairman of the board and Rusty would become chief executive officer and president of the park. With that position, which would carry a salary, the need for help arose and we got a part-time secretary. Under Rusty's direction we put together a conference room that for the first time enabled us to really display the maps and the paraphernalia necessary to sell the park to potential tenants. The offices the park acquired were next to those of First Charlotte Corporation where Rusty continued to be active, but it was very, very clear that at least his time was required to proceed with this thing. Working with outside help, he has put together a brochure that is very well done. We have a slide show that is very good and we have bought to bear a more sophisticated, competent and devoted organization that continues to plan, to sell, to promote, to do those things which bring success a lot quicker than they would if you continued with the operation that was largely handled by members of the board on particular assignment. It has been a very happy move as far as I'm concerned, and I just think that in Rusty we have a type of individual that flourishes with a challenge.

(C) You reached a point that he moved first as a part-time person and then eventually devoted more or less full-time, didn't he?

(T) At the present time, Dean, Rusty devotes full-time to this thing.

(C) After you became president, if I remember correctly, you became aware of a certain amount of lost motion in dealing with the entire board on all matters and you brought about a change in the organization of the board and the distribution of the authority of subcommittees. Tell us about that.

(T) First of all, I never worried about the large board. We had an executive committee that was composed principally of the chancellor and, of course, the six bankers. If you have six bankers on the executive committee you never have money problems, but what we have here is a difference in style of management. I have never worried about the degree of information going to large numbers of people and have always enjoyed throwing out an issue for a strong discussion, with every point of view and everybody there aware of the situation. On the other hand, once you got into some of the requirements of tenants and you needed quicker action, it was always an awkward thing to get on short notice a quorum on a large board that would take action and occasionally we've had to demand that the total board approve a certain stipulation in sales contracts. Again, it's a matter of style of management. I always thought we did best when we had many people involved and more meetings, but on the other hand many a director has told me, "I can never operate with more than five or six people and get anything done." We have, in the present structure, two major committees. The principal one is the Operations Committee headed by Rusty that in-

---

[6] The bond vote passed.

cludes Bill Lee, Chancellor Fretwell, Cliff Cameron, Jack Tate, Dave Burkhalter, and myself. There is also a Financial Committee composed of the bankers with Rusty on it and I act as chairman of that group. I also act as chairman of the Audit and Compensation Committee. It has worked out very, very well in practice. It allows you to conduct business with strong support of key directors and allows you to drop the meeting of the main board to about once a year, which is again a matter of choice.

(C) You still have the membership of the board elected from nominations submitted by the chancellor of the university, the Chamber of Commerce, and the Nominating Committee of the board itself?

(T) That's correct.

(C) In the final analysis those different nominating groups have a great deal of veto power; if they felt something was going wrong they could nominate different people but they've never had to exercise that.

(T) This is very true. It's been a situation that after about 17 years or so we've never had a basic disagreement nor a confrontation nor do I think we've ever made a basic strategic mistake. Everything so far has stayed within the quality requirements that the board has always viewed as essential for success.

(C) By the way that study — you said it was made by UNCC — was made by the Geography Department of UNCC, wasn't it?

(T) That is correct and remarkably well done. It is our bible. Long-range plans are marvelous things to make. You should never follow them too closely because they will often stop you from a certain tactical opportunity, but you should never go against them deliberately. One of the things that it stressed was the need for some relaxation of existing requirements. In the case of Verbatim and Dow-Jones we saw nothing very wrong with their presence and an awful lot right with their presence. I think if we were looking at things today, we would say that if the prospect is a multinational or a national company of considerable stature, and if their operation was essentially dry, we would welcome that unit in the park. A chemical company with pollutants and sewer problems would not be accepted. Each one is considered on its own merits.

(C) For that matter, I guess a small concession was made to IBM.

(T) Yes, but IBM, of course, has 440 acres within the research zoning and about another 1,000 outside. This is typical of what happens at parks. The line is crossed and expansion proceeds in two environments.

(C) Having been privileged to serve from the beginning with Bill Harris and you, I think it's a fortunate sequence of leadership of very different styles. When you put together the University Research Park and the foundation and the university and look at the planning that's been done in cooperation with all the agencies of government from the very beginning, I wonder if there's been any development of this kind that has had a more complete planning by a lot of different planning agencies than this four or five thousand acres that's involved here.

(T) Dean, I think you are right on this. What is happening is that we've got a textbook case here that is now getting international attention. Doug Orr and Jim Clay are just back from Barcelona and this combined operation — University Place, the park, the university, and University City — is being followed in Europe. It is unique. It's very rare that an urban university gets a chance to become involved in the planning of its environment in any way. It is often situated where it is boxed or where it's really in conflict with business or development and with not the happiest of relationships. We have here three units that are so devoted to a common objective that you're seeing a decided influence on the northeast. Because of our total control of probably six square miles, that influence is going to expand for another 30 square miles. The tone is set and the centerpiece, of course, will be University Place, between the school and the park. We were very, very fortunate in having total support from the county and the city on the things that we have tried to do. We have not received money from them other than $70,000 from the state to help on one road and, of course, some trunk lines for water

and sewer from the city council and the county commissioners. We have not had people giving us public money to develop roads or anything of that nature. Sewer and water connecting lines are paid for by the park.

(C) It would be correct to say, though, with reference to roads, that the planning of the highway commission has been another very important element in the planning of the whole area.

(T) It has been of tremendous importance to us. I was thinking more when I said roads, of roads within the park that are paid for by the park rather than the main arteries such as Harris Boulevard. The highway commission, starting with the work of George Broadrick to get us an interchange at Harris Boulevard, has been so, so supportive.

(C) It is almost dramatic to recall that when this idea was being developed that I-85 was not there; Harris Boulevard was not there; Highway 49 was a two lane road; and I-77 was not there. There has been a great planning input. My hat is tipped to the city-county planning commission in the early days who helped protect that area when the university first came here.

(T) The zoning has been the key to the protection that we've had out there.

(C) We are certainly greatly indebted to the leadership that you have given to it and that you continue to give both to the park and to the UNCC foundation.

(T) One other thing I might mention, Dean, is that we are now even crossing beyond the park, beyond the university and beyond the Foundation when we see that the county and Memorial Hospital are building within the environs there. This is another huge plus for us, and we are grateful to Memorial for selecting the site and to the county for supporting us. I cannot help but think that that unit, working cooperatively with the nursing school, will lead to many doctor's buildings. As you know, Dave Carley is going to put one in for about 40 doctors immediately. Also, of course, further up Highway 49, we are seeing John Crosland's commercial development that will add some of the essential amenities to the university.

(C) The foundation is sound and there has been a willingness of the various constituencies to stick with a sense of purpose and carry this out. To me it has been one of the most exciting things that I've had the privilege of observing, and I believe that long after you and I are no longer a part of it that it will be greater than it is today and probably greater than we could visualize.

(T) Of course it will be, Dean. One of the essentials of good long-range planning is that you don't live to see it completed. I don't think it means that you should die early, but rather that planning for this area should cover several decades.

(C) That reminds me of a spot that some of my colleagues at UNCC put me on because I had said consistently that one element of a long-range plan should be that you provide latitude for future planners for things that we didn't have imagination to visualize. In a sense we have done that with what has now become University Place. When Doug Orr and Jim Clay started wanting to use the area that I had set aside for future planners, they convinced me that the future was here.

(T) That was a stroke of conceptual genius for them to come up with the switch. It's turned out to be sheer delight.

(C) There's one other aspect of this physical layout that involved the county that Mr. Harris included to some extent. Initially, there was a close relationship between the university and the county when the county did, in fact, give the university much of the land that it now has, which was originally the county farm and county home. They still had this acreage that was Green Acres, which is now the location of the hospital. They had on record a commitment that the land would go to the university, but the need for the hospital was so much a part of the total plan that the university was quite happy to give up any claim it had by their previous commitment to get them to do the thing that benefitted the whole. Let me thank you for putting this in the record.

EXCERPTS FROM AN INTERVIEW WITH SEDDON GOODE, JR., AUGUST 21, 1985
BY DEAN W. COLVARD

(C) I'm with Rusty Goode who has been the chief executive officer of the University Research Park for some time. He's been deeply involved in many of the most significant developments that have taken place and in plans that have been laid for the future. Rusty, tell us something about your career that led you in the direction of becoming involved with the park.

(G) Following five years at Southeastern Factors I moved over to NCNB as a commercial loan officer. I guess I actually moved to American Commercial Bank but it was soon to become NCNB. Part of my responsibility at NCNB was industrial development. During that period I became very well acquainted with Bill Ficklen, Charles Crawford, Bill Harris, and Pat Calhoun.

I left NCNB in the late 1960s and went to work at Interstate Securities. I became chairman of the economic development committee at the Charlotte Chamber of Commerce and became very much involved with the University Research Park and the general economic development activities that were taking place in Charlotte. About that time I met Cliff Cameron who has sort of been my mentor in civic involvements. Also, at that time I got to know Dave Taylor. In the early 1970s I went on the board of the University Research Park, was elected a vice president, and was put on the Executive Committee.

(C) Were you working in industrial development and with the Chamber of Commerce in 1966 when this thing was first being talked about?

(G) As a matter of fact, I was involved but not from that standpoint. I was a commercial loan officer at NCNB and Jack Tate, the city executive at NCNB, brought a file folder to my desk and asked me to get together with these Charlotte banks — First Union, Wachovia, NCNB, and First Citizens. I handled the first loan to the University Research Park and syndicated it out to those banks.

(C) After determining that NCNB would handle this, you were the officer in the bank to work with it?

(G) That's correct. I just happened to be handling the loan.

(C) You were elected to the board prior to Dave Taylor's succeeding Bill Harris as president at the end of the first ten years. How about picking up at the time Dave Taylor became president and take us through the change in the corporate structure of the park that led to your presidency and Dave's chairmanship.

(G) I always had an interest in the park and talked with Dave Taylor about requesting that some of our community's business leaders hand carry us to some outstanding firms in the nation to encourage them to move into the park because in the '70s it was pretty dry up there. One of the companies that I was very interested in was Eckerd's. Ed O'Herron and I felt that they would have certain leverage with the pharmaceutical industry.

IBM in the Research Triangle Park was started when Governor Hodges (after retiring as secretary of commerce) picked up the phone, called Tom Watson and said do you remember that plant you promised me, we're ready for you to build it in North Carolina now. I know enough about the way decisions are made to know there are more made that way than scientifically.

Verbatim had come to Charlotte and there had been an awful lot of confusion. The park was being run out of the bottom desk drawer at the Chamber of Commerce and we had a real estate committee that was quoting prices. The sum and substance was that Verbatim was quoted three different prices for their piece of land. Verbatim was one of the two companies that Governor Hunt had enticed into North Carolina from Silicon Valley where his big push was then. At that time, there were 36 board members. In order to make changes or approve a purchase or sale, the bylaws required a complete meeting of the entire board and this was clumsy and unwieldy.

In the late '70s, Dave Taylor, Claude Freeman, and I were talking at the City Club and Dave mentioned that we needed a full-time director. We were embarrassed about what had happened with Verbatim. I agreed with Dave but it didn't ring any bells with me. We had some vacant space next to our office at First Charlotte and I probably suggested to Claude Freeman during the following two or three weeks that we move a park office there and I would devote some of my time to the park and try to make some things happen. Claude passed that on to

Dave Taylor and he seemed very enthusiastic about it. Dave and I talked about it and I told him that I felt the present operation was unwieldy, that we needed to make some bylaw changes and that we needed someone who could speak with authority for the park and run it like a business. That was when we decided to have an Operations Committee, as well as a Finance Committee. The Operations Committee has the full powers of the general board. I am chairman of that committee. Other members are Cliff Cameron, Bill Lee (chief executive officer of Duke Power Company), David Burkhalter (retired city manager, now employed by the Belk organization), Dave Taylor, E. K. Fretwell Jr. (chancellor of UNCC), and the chairman of the Chamber of Commerce rotates on this committee on an annual basis. This committee is where the functions of the park are run. They have set guidelines for acquisition of property and other transactions, so I have a broad leeway in operating and have never felt encumbered by them. I probably talk to Dave Taylor on a weekly basis and while Claude Freeman is not on the Operations Committee, I think of him as the father of the park and talk with him on an almost daily basis. Our Operations Committee is involved in our long range decisions. Our property is priced and is public information, so if a company comes in, meets our qualifications and wants to buy a lot we don't have an Operations Committee meeting for that. If negotiations are required, such as those with Charter Properties, we meet.

(C) Do you feel pretty good about the structure of the organization as it's now working?

(G) I feel very good about the structure of the park, it's working very well and I'm very comfortable with it. I get a lot of pleasure out of what has taken place out there.

(C) How about starting about the time Verbatim and you came into the park. Sketch the things that have happened since, in terms of new clients, and then I want to ask you some general questions that apply to all of them.

(G) Verbatim was on board before I got involved with the park but when they opened their doors for business I had the responsibility for the park. Then Union Oil came along and bought five acres. I was not involved in that negotiation but that went pretty smoothly and I was on board when Union Oil opened its doors.

(C) Who was the principal negotiator with Union Oil?

(G) I don't know but Union Oil was already in Charlotte, located on the Cabarrus/Mecklenburg County line. They moved into the park to serve the textile industry and I don't remember who was involved. The Dow Jones/Wall Street Journal situation was something that Louis Rose had worked on. I was involved in the closing of that situation but was not involved in the decision to change the zoning to permit Dow Jones to come in.

Incidentally, I was not involved in changing the zoning to permit Verbatim to come in. Our earlier zoning would not have permitted them to be in the park because they are actually manufacturers. But when you looked at their operation you thought you were in a hospital's operating room because everybody was in white gowns and it looked very technical. It's a good employer but their salaries are really not that high. It was on the cutting edge of high technology and that's what we wanted and certainly everyone wanted the Wall Street Journal published at the research park.

My first real involvement was the location of Southern Bell's data processing facility in Charlotte. It was 1981 or '82, I was in Raleigh for a Board of Transportation meeting. Louis Rose called and said he thought Southern Bell was really interested in locating at the park but they were concerned about where their employees would eat and the lack of housing on that side of town. I called Frank Skinner, a close personal friend and president of Southern Bell, at home that night and told him that we wanted that facility in the research park. Frank, as any good executive would do, said he was not going to make the decision about the location, that he had a program out and that he thought it was probably going to Atlanta. Following that, Southern Bell got pretty interested and I talked with Allen Thomas, Frank Skinner, and Louis Rose. They've got one of the prettier facilities in the park with the capability of expanding by about twenty more acres. I'm constantly reminding my friend, Frank Skinner (who now appears in our slide show), of the need to put another nice facility there and I think we'll get it.

About this time, I became close friends with the management of the IBM facility and discovered they had a lot of traffic problems, Governor Hunt had recently put me on the Board of Transporation as the minority political party member which was required in North Carolina. Governor Hunt and I turned out to be cousins and we had a good relationship with each other. I took the IBM folks to see him. They explained to him that IBM's payroll in North Carolina was in excess of $500,000,000 annually. When they left the room the Governor pulled me by the arm and took me back into his office and said, "Rusty, do you realize that the payroll for the IBM company in North Carolina is approaching the tobacco-growing income." At that time, I think tobacco was somewhere in the neighborhood of $700,000,000 to $750,000,000 annually. That visit really rung his bell. I got Billy Rose, highway administrator, in touch with Jim Webb, facilities man at IBM, and things began to happen as far as the roads were concerned. Among the old tenants that I didn't work on, IBM is the only company who needed problems solved.

(C) Rounding out the picture, you didn't mention EPRI.

(G) EPRI was there and finished before I got involved. I went to EPRI's groundbreaking as a member of the board of the park. Fairfax had been sold and was a completed transaction before I got involved with the park but I was very much involved in causing and helping IBM to decide to locate that building on Fairfax property. I talked directly to the management of IBM and told them how important it was to me and the park to have that building located on Fairfax's property.

(C) The Fairfax building you referred to is the office building IBM rents?

(G) IBM leases it and it's located at the corner of I-77 and Harris Boulevard on what was probably our most attractive lot.

(C) The debt that had been incurred at that time — tell us about that. It is based primarily on two things, as I recall. One is development, such as roads, sewage lines, etc. and also the buying of property for future housing.

(G) Prior to my involvement, the park had an opportunity to buy several tracts of land — the DeArmon property at the corner of Mallard Creek and Harris Boulevard, the McMillan property, the Belk/Black property and 120 acres of residential property on Harris Boulevard. Our basic method of operation was to make a down payment and have the seller finance the remainder for us. At the same time, we had to develop Research Drive and bring some water and sewer into the area. The decisions to purchase that property were very wise but a $2,000,000 loan at 22% with no way to pay it off for a nonprofit corporation was a little frightening.

(C) Did you borrow that $2,000,000 from essentially the same banks who had put up the money to start the park?

(G) That's right, except at this stage of the game Wachovia was the managing banker for our consortium of loans and has been for many years. They petition out the loan. I believe the move from NCNB to Wachovia happened when Dave Taylor became president of the park. He was a board member at Wachovia and chairman of the UNCC foundation. Today, the chairman of the park and the chairman of the foundation are the same person. As far as I know, Wachovia has been the lead bank in the park's credit for at least the last ten years.

(C) I believe you would agree, however, that from the very beginning the backing of all of the banks was one of the sources of strength for the park.

(G) Without question. If you go back and look at the success of it, Jack Tate, from NCNB, and Pat Calhoun were major forces in the park. Also, Bill Bowen, at Wachovia, was very active and, of course, Cliff Cameron in his last few years at First Union has been a strong, dominant force that has made the park a success.

(C) To round out the record, there's one man from First Citizens who has been a director from the very first day and that's Harry Nicholas. George Broadrick was quite involved along with Harry.

(G) When Northwestern moved to Charlotte and Ben Craig became the chief executive officer we added them to our list and Ben Craig to the board.

(C) Say something about the decision to buy land to be held for residential development and how you executed that plan.

(G) That's one of the unique things we have done in the research park.

The park bought 120 acres of land in the middle '70s and then convinced the North Carolina Department of Transportation that we should have a main arterial road from I-77 to I-85. One of the most satisfying things I've been involved in at the park was a meeting held in our little room on the 24th floor of the First Union Tower including city officials, county officials and the state department of transportation officials. During this meeting we worked out an arrangement to have the state build a portion of Harris Boulevard and to have the Charlotte/Mecklenburg Utilities Department, Duke Power, John Crosland and Allen Tate put in a residential development. It was started a full eighteen months ahead of time and today every residential lot in that 120 acres has been sold and we have people living there. In fact, the managers of AT&T, EPRI, and the EDS division of General Motors have bought houses in that residential area. We have made a giant step in having a place where you can live and work. The dramatic process that has taken place at University Place provides shopping, hotels, etc.

(C) I know that you gave some tribute to Governor Hunt. I personally had the opportunity of being involved with him when the decision was made to extend Harris Boulevard to I-77. I think that it's important to remember Governor Moore through to George Broadrick.

You've bought a good bit more acreage for the park. How much acreage do we have in the University Research Park now including the area held by cooperators and people who've purchased it and what the park itself owns?

(G) The park itself has 2,600 acres under what we call the RE2 zoning umbrella.

(C) That does not include the 120 residential acres?

(G) That doesn't include the 120 residential acres but it includes IBM's 1,300 acres, Queens Properties property, Collins & Aikman, and Allstate on the east side of I-85. I think that one of the really significant developments that Dave Taylor and I worked out was an arrangement with W. H. Barnhardt and his partners, James G. Cannon and Jimmy Harris, relating to approximately 200 acres that they owned on the north side of Mallard Creek but didn't want to sell. The park owned a couple hundred acres and Queens Properties owned a hundred acres on the north side of Mallard Creek. I felt that the park should not build a bridge and a major road to open our two hundred acres and Jones' one hundred acres because they would also open up the Barnhardt (I refer to this as Barnhardt land because he was president, but Jimmy Cannon and Jimmy Harris owned equal portions of the land) land totally. After several months of negotiation we reached a unique arrangement which has been interesting. The Barnhardt group put all of their land in a trust at NCNB. The University Research Park gave them $200,000 cash and pays the taxes on that land. We have the sole decision-making power about that land and are obligated to give the trust department at NCNB approximately 40% of the retail sales price when we sell, but no less than $15,000 an acre. At the time we gained control of these two hundred acres, they would have appraised at around $7,000 an acre. The first acreage was sold in January 1985 to AT&T. The Barnhardt group received approximately $22,000 an acre for their property and the park received approximately $25,000 an acre for its share. We hope that other major landholders in the area will work with this arrangement because we don't have to put up much cash, it controls some acreage and the folks can participate in it. The acquisition of the Barnhardt property enabled us to open up five hundred new acres on the north side of Mallard Creek.

(C) Rusty, there's been a lot of cooperation with all of the governmental agencies — the city council, the county commissioners, and as you mentioned, the governors. If I remember correctly, initially, the total capitalization was $52,000. Are you aware of any other source of capital, other than generated capital, that's gone into the park?

(G) The only thing I know of that would have gone into the park is the agreement by the North Carolina Department of Transportation to spend $70,000 out of a total of $300,000 to build an industrial access road to the Wall Street Journal. As far as I know, there has been no injection of any other funds of that type in the park.

(C) It's truly a creation of the community and of the leadership that's been involved. It's been especially active during these last eight or ten years that you've been involved with it. Of course, I give you a lot of credit for that. I think that we should remember that it was ten years before the Research Triangle Park really got going well. I would like for you to touch on the total planning that's taken place involving the city

/county planning commission, the university's planning, University Place, the highway commission, and the park. Do you know of any other development anywhere that's been more completely planned than this?

(G) I certainly don't. It's really beginning to pay off.

(C) What is your appraisal of the impact that the University Research Park and university planning (in conjunction with each other and developing together) have had on the property values of others in that area?

(G) There's no question that it's gone up dramatically. Residential land that would have sold for $7,000 an acre three or four years ago is currently selling at $20,000 an acre. There is no certainty that this land can be zoned for anything other than single family but some of the people that have bought it are going to try to have multi-family.

I'm beginning to communicate with the YMCA and would like to see a commitment by the Y on a piece of University Research Park property within the next eighteen months. I think an amenity similar to the James J. Harris Y in southeast Charlotte will be great. We're spending $30,000 ourselves to put in jogging trails. These are the sorts of things

that will attract the decision-makers of the future to locate in the park.

One thing we might add. I believe that you mentioned to me that the current governor was instrumental in helping the park get water or sewer when he was chairman of the county commissioners.

(C) During the very first years of the park and the university, when Dr. Jim Martin was chairman of the Board of County Commissioners, we ran out of water. Our present governor was one of the people who helped to break one of those very elementary bottlenecks. It would be nice if we could round this out during his administration because he has been involved, as have the mayors and others.

Rusty, I appreciate your taking the time to chat with me about this.

(G) Dean, I want to thank you for taking on this project.

(C) It is interesting that each president of the Chamber of Commerce since 1966 has been a member of this board. That's twenty leading people selected by the community. Add to that the leaders in the banks, the corporations and the park and other leaders in the community and you have a very clear story of a park that's been developed by this community.

EXCERPTS FROM AN INTERVIEW WITH JOHN A. (JACK) TATE, JR., NOVEMBER 7, 1983 BY DEAN W. COLVARD

(C) Jack, you were with North Carolina National Bank when the University Research Park was being organized, weren't you?

(T) Yes, my involvement really dates back before the park. Addison Reese was very involved in everything at UNCC and perhaps was one of the key people who asked you to come to UNCC. I went to work for Addison in the latter part of the 1950s. I was fresh out of the real estate business and was close to Romeo Guest and the Research Triangle Park through Claude Freeman. Because of my real estate experience I was involved with Reese in the real estate end of locating UNCC. He was one of the pillars out there.

(C) He was on the Board of Charlotte College. He was chairman of the Board of Charlotte College before UNCC's days.

(T) He was very much a deciding factor in who the real estate agent would be and where the original UNCC location would be. At that time we realized that we would have to locate the university in north Mecklenburg. I was involved with the park in two or three different ways before the park was proposed.

(C) I'm very much interested in that. I was involved when I was at N. C. State with Governor Hodges' committee, which was chaired by Bob Hanes, who was head of Wachovia. I was one of the three people from State along with three from Chapel Hill and three from Duke who wrestled with that conceptualization about the time that Archie Davis came in.

(T) I'm not sure that Claude would have told you, but at one time he was offered the job of going up there and running that. This was before the days of Huffman.

(C) George Simpson was the first person hired there. It might have been about that time.

(T) I do think that Claude's background was important. He was from Raleigh and knew a lot of the people who were involved in the triangle area. He was very close to Romeo Guest and, of course, Guest was very much involved there. Ironically, I think more than any one person he probably instigated that triangle facility. Then from a business standpoint got less out of it than most anybody I know.

(C) I think he is generally given credit for being the originator of the idea. Hodges was the developer and promoter of it. Were you involved directly when the Chamber of Commerce began to promote the idea of the University Research Park?

(T) I don't remember exactly how I got involved in the park. I know Bill Harris, as president of the Chamber of Commerce, picked up and pushed the idea. I associate him, before anyone else, with the idea of a research park in Mecklenburg County. The idea might have come out of some industrial development committee.

(C) Let's get back to the beginning as far as the bank is concerned. You were in charge of NCNB's Charlotte office at that time?

(T) That's right. I was running the Charlotte office.

(C) As the chief executive officer of the Charlotte office of NCNB, what do you recall as the first involvement that you had with the financing, putting up of the money to buy the land that was bought in the early days?

(T) I remember very specifically that one day Bill Harris called me and said that he wanted to see me with Paul Younts. Since they weren't regular customers of the bank I knew something was up. This was the first I'd heard, specifically, of a given piece of real estate related to the university area. They wanted money to get the research park started. They needed money as down payments on contracts that General Younts thought he could get. At that time they wanted to borrow what I thought was a significant amount of money. It was either $200,000 or $300,000.

(C) They approached about four of the banks and according to Bill Harris they thought that your bank was a key and whether the others came in or not might depend in large measure on your involvement.

(T) In all fairness to NCNB, to history, and to Addison Reese (you know that I left NCNB three or four years after this took place), the financing arrangement asked of NCNB was not for participation. We were not asked to lead a group of Charlotte banks. We were not asked for any participation or help; we were asked for a commitment, period.

(C) At any rate we do know that they came to you, that you made a commitment, and that you were not participating. You were simply lending them the money.

(T) That's right. It was a loan, pure and simple, although it was a loan that would have violated any sound business principles. It was what I would call a community-type loan. It was like lending 100 percent purchase price. In fairness to the other banks at that time, NCNB was by far the largest bank in the community. We were one of two home grown banks, so it was a lot easier for NCNB to say yes than it would have been for other banks. The buck stopped with Addison Reese. I wish I could have said "Gentlemen that was my decision; you've got the money." I did not say that. I could not say that, but I did recommend to Addison that we do it because I could see the opportunities we had in the community. I was sold on the fact that for Charlotte over a period of time this would be a sound proposition. So I think Addison was really the one who made the decision to put the money on the barrel head.

(C) I suppose it was in the minds of all of you that with the university coming in to that area we had a new dimension in the community that would at least encourage development along those lines. Is that right? To what extent were you influenced by the fact that UNCC was about to be developed?

(T) I don't think there's any question that Bill Harris and Paul Younts would not have considered the research park had UNCC not been there. It was tied in, I think, from the very start in terms of the land acquisition and it was tied in from the standpoint of Addison Reese's interest. His interest in the university was probably stronger than it was in the industrial development of Charlotte at that particular time.

(C) Nobody else has said that but knowing him as I did I think you're probably right.

(T) He was very wrapped up in the university and sold on what it meant to Charlotte. I think he felt a strong responsibility toward the university since he was chairman. He was really the daddy rabbit that got it from Charlotte College to the university.

(C) When I came here in 1966, about the time this conversation was taking place, Addison Reese had been chairman of the Board of Charlotte College and was one of the people in the community who was regarded as a leader on behalf of the new university. One of the very first dinners I had in Charlotte was with you, Dolly, and Addison and Gertie Reese at the City Club.

(T) I remember that very pleasantly. I think one of the interesting things as I look back on it, Dean, was the development of the relationship between the bank and the park. Addison was extremely busy. He was very much involved at UNCC. He wasn't involved in the day-to-day workings of the bank in Charlotte. By virtue of my position, the loan processing, lending and extension of credit were my responsibility through loan officers. Later the other banks came in and participated with the park and in the liabilities. I certainly wouldn't say anything derogatory about the other banks.

(C) They were all very cooperative.

(T) I think the way that we've gotten First Union and Wachovia and later First Citizens and the other banks has been very productive. I don't remember how I got involved. I do know that it was my recommendation that we go to Joe Grier. He was selected for three reasons, all of which were known to me. One, Joe had an outstanding law firm; two, he was a University of North Carolina man, which I thought was important; and three, his family had a lot of property there at Newell, so he was interested in the northeast quadrant of the city as a landowner, as well. Joe was probably more responsible than anybody for working out the bylaws and legal instruments which gave birth to the park. The University of North Carolina at Charlotte was made beneficiary at the time but it was not given the prominence or the importance that it was accorded later. Some day it is going to be the beneficiary of millions of dollars as a result of what's in that instrument.

(C) The instrument, as you know, was modified in more recent years.

(T) There was no question from the first, Dean, and I think the history of the project ought to show this — the research park and the university were inseparable in terms of our objectives. We wanted to put in the bylaws that the university had direct representation on the board. We wanted to put in the record that any money made (if the park was liquidated or any significant distribution was made) would benefit the university.

(C) Studies that I have made supported that intent, although as you say, the document was little less than absolutely specific at that time.

(T) I'm sure that The University of North Carolina at Charlotte is in the first document.

(C) Yes it was in there more than anybody else but there was a little "or" which was changed in more recent years. For a while the park was borrowing money from you to pay interest on borrowed money. Do you have any memory of some anxious moments?

(T) I don't think that anybody at NCNB was worried about that loan. When the loan was made it was recognized as a high-risk, community-type, nonpolicy loan. The question was not if we would be paid but when we would be paid. Over the years there have been very slow periods in the park and periods when we have been discouraged. But I don't think anybody has ever thought that the park would not move forward. I don't know of any time, any president or anybody on the Board of Directors who ever waivered in their faith that the park would be a viable, ongoing enterprise.

(C) You're basically right but there were some pretty anxious people on the board in 1974 when the crash came and we still hadn't sold anything and were paying interest on a lot of money.

(T) I wasn't in that bank in 1974 so I wasn't responsible for collecting the loan that I'd made seven years earlier.

(C) At any rate, the important point is that if the banks had not taken the leadership to make the money available from the beginning, it probably wouldn't have been started.

(T) I don't think there's a question about that.

(C) Jack, I think that you can provide better insight on the idea of developing the county to the north away from South Carolina and toward Davidson and Lake Norman and the central part of the state. After you were disassociated with NCNB and had your own bank, Piedmont Bank, you lived at Davidson and became a very active advocate of the northern tier of the county. Pick up there and say what you'd like about that.

(T) I've had two or three different thoughts as a board member about the park and the university as they relate to north Mecklenburg. First, I had an idea that hasn't worked out the way I thought it would or should. Mecklenburg County owned about 400 acres of land on the I-77/115/21 highway where Huntersville Hospital is located. At one time it was a major parcel of land for the county and only a small part was used for the hospital. We've got the large acreage above UNCC at the 49/29/I-85 intersection and in that general area. I always thought that these two parcels should be connected in some way and that it would be to the advantage of county, state, and city governments to connect those parcels for some sort of joint use. Before the ECU issue came up I thought that we were a logical candidate for a medical school (if there was another one adopted in the state) and that it could be tied with the hospital system in Charlotte. Memorial Hospital has always been sort of an outpost of the medical school at UNC-Chapel Hill anyway. I envisioned that somebody would tie that hospital to UNCC and Memorial Hospital into a medical school. Maybe this was thinking too far down the road. Now Memorial Hospital is building a university hospital annex next to the campus and Harris Boulevard extension goes in that direction. It is a partial answer to my idea. Another factor that was necessary for growth in this area was the extension of water/sewage into north Mecklenburg. Our efforts regarding this started about the same time that the park did. Water and sewage have always been a major factor, particularly since I have been living in north Mecklenburg. We now have the 201 sewage development which I think is the greatest thing to happen to north Mecklenburg.

I thought for the park to prosper we had to have strong residential development in that area. I have been in the real estate business in Charlotte and am very aware of how much prejudice there is about living north of I-85. People in Charlotte think there's no place to live except southeast Charlotte. IBM's development has been an unbelievable revelation to a lot of people. A lot of people prefer to live in areas other than southeast Charlotte and are quite happy.

Getting back to the research park, in the early '70s when things were slow, I thought we should do something to get strong residential development. I thought the only way we could get residential development was to make water and sewer available. It had to be large scale.

(C) I think you, probably as much or more than any other individual, have been promoter of doing something to get residential development going. As Dave Taylor said, the park helped to make some land available to get that underway. That, with the development of the road and water and sewer, has promoted that idea.

(T) Let me make two comments, Dean. Somewhere we should put in the history about Dean Colvard. I don't think you're one to . . .

(C) This is not designed for that purpose.

(T) In a true history we should recognize that during the years you made a contribution as the head of The University of North Carolina at Charlotte because it was a joint enterprise in a real sense. You'll do yourself and the history a discredit if you don't put that in. Over the years Bill Harris gave us leadership. Dave Taylor was an important factor in being able to give the time and effort to get a lot of things done and to get ideas translated into action. As you write the history there is nobody that is more related to the park and its beginning than Bill Harris. You are an important factor in giving us support over the years. Addison Reese and Dave Taylor have been important factors.

(C) Dave provided a very different style of leadership, coming from a research background and an industrial background. Bill had been in business mostly but had been locally involved in leadership and politics.

(T) I'd like to say something else, Dean, and I want to say this in a positive manner. I think there have been relatively few people on the park board who have really seen a big picture. Because of your, my, and Claude Freeman's exposure to the Research Triangle, I think we thought bigger in terms of scale, mass, and impact than other people who came on and off the board. We still haven't had an impact on Charlotte. We've got IBM but the potential of the park is just beginning.

(C) Dave Taylor would fit in that same category. He was not personally involved with the Research Triangle but a colleague of his was on that board originally. He was on the planning committee. I believe it was Dr. Armstrong. He was involved when I was working with Bob Hanes and Governor Hodges in trying to further conceptualize the thing. I would be very interested in your comments regarding the fact that city, county, state highway, UNCC and research park board planners have been involved . I have ventured the opinion that this is much more completely planned than the triangle ever was. The triangle was planned for the triangle itself. You've introduced the housing element. The zoning of University Place, the university itself and the University Research Park goes all the way back to the city-county planning when it zoned University City to protect the future. There has been an enormous amount of planning.

(T) That's true. I think one reason is because Claude Freeman is a planner. He thinks in those terms and he's had a relationship with a lot of people on the planning commission. This park has been a bridge to Raleigh probably more than anything in our lifetime. Governor Hunt is with us on what we're trying to do. We've cut off two or three years on Harris Boulevard through his personal backing. I think the fact that the research park has been a generator of jobs and the type of industry that Raleigh has turned to now has done a great deal to bring Mecklenburg into the State of North Carolina.

(C) Are you satisfied with the direction that developments are taking now?

(T) I think so, Dean. I get with Rusty, as I guess all of us do, about getting something going on that residential development. This can be more important to Mecklenburg County than a lot of people realize. I sure hope that it goes the way we have planned. As I sign off, I hope I have been helpful. I would like to suggest, Dean, that no one is more qualified than you to talk about both The University of North Carolina at Charlotte as well as the University Research Park. I think both of these enterprises are very vivid and dramatic illustrations of this community and what makes it tick. There would be no research park if there hadn't been an unbelievable amount of cooperation and dedication by a large number of people. I think the same is true of UNCC. I hope that somewhere, as you write this history or go back, you wrap into it what I call the spirit of Charlotte. That's what really made the University Research Park.

(C) I've worked with universities in several different communities and observed a lot of the universities around the country. At no place and at no time have I seen this kind of total community involvement.

(T) Whether it's been Addison Reese at the bank, Dean Colvard of the university, Jack Tate at the bank, Claude Freeman, Bill Harris, or Dave Taylor — nobody has used this as a vehicle to get glory or make money. Basically 99% of the leadership has come by people who are just interested in the community.

(C) I think it is a rare community.

(T) I don't think this community realizes yet what UNCC has already meant to it and that someday UNCC might be the most important thing around here. Maybe it is already. I don't know.

(C) Well, I'm too biased to make a comment on that and since it's a little off the subject, too . . .

Thank you very much for coming over.

EXCERPTS FROM AN INTERVIEW WITH CLAUDE Q. FREEMAN, SR., NOVEMBER 8, 1982 BY DEAN W. COLVARD

(C) Meeting with me today is Claude Freeman, Sr. who has been involved with the University Research Park from the beginning. He has had a very rich experience as a realtor, not only in the Charlotte area but in other areas of the state, and I'll let him tell that. Claude, it's good to have you share your experience for the record of the University Research Park. Will you begin by telling us something about how you got involved in the early history of the Research Triangle in the Raleigh/Durham area and how you got into the University Research Park?

(F) The research park has been quite a challenge since I've been on the board. As to the Research Triangle, I was on the original board. Carl Robbins, you may remember that name, a textile giant in North and South Carolina, was the principal for the up front money in assembling the property.

(C) Was that assembled for a research park at the time he put it together?

(F) Absolutely. Romeo Guest of C. M. Guest & Sons, general contractors in Greensboro, conceived the idea. I don't think Romeo received the proper recognition for his leading roll in making the triangle a reality. My association with Romeo prior to the Research Triangle was in the move of Celanese to Charlotte some thirty years ago. He asked me to serve on the initial board of the Pinelands Company, Inc., which acquired the land that is the Research Triangle. I can't remember all the directors, but, of course, Luther Hodges was a director as well as Durham banker, George Watts Hill, and Collier Cobb of Chapel Hill. The assemblage of 3,000 acres of land was much easier in those days than it is today. But we found that in going public with the Research Triangle as a private enterprise venture, we would be competing with the same sources of money sought by the Research Institute. After much thought it seemed expedient for the Pinelands Company to turn the land over to a State Government committee that ultimately developed the trian-

gle. There was pressure from the business community and the state for this, and I think it was with wisdom that it was done. The stock of the Pinelands Company was turned over to the newly formed Research Triangle group at a luncheon meeting at the Sir Walter Hotel in Raleigh. Governor Hodges presided. Immediately after the turnover, Bob Hanes, president of the Wachovia Bank in Winston-Salem, gave something like $150,000 to the triangle for its first building, the Research Institute.

(C) I worked with Bob Hanes on the committee appointed by Governor Hodges consisting of three people from N. C. State, three from Duke, and three from the Chapel Hill campus of the university to give further attention to forming the basic ideas and structures. I think it's very significant that you had that depth of background before you got involved with the research park here. Now tell us about your very early involvement and the beginning of the research park era as you know it.

(F) Having the triangle background and enjoying that type of challenge, I was quite pleased and ready to accept the invitation when I was asked to take Paul Younts' place on the University Research Park Board in 1970. I was not on the initial board. Paul Younts, Louis Rose, Sr., and Ed Vinson, Sr., were the first members of the board involved in real estate. When Paul died I was asked to take his place.

(C) You're the surviving senior member of the realty group since Louis Rose, Sr. and Ed Vinson, Sr. are no longer with us. Tell us something about the way you, Louis, and Ed worked together in relation to the research park in handling the real estate transactions.

(F) Back then there were no real estate transactions. Again, I draw the comparison between the triangle and the park. Nothing happened at the Research Triangle to my knowledge other than the Research Institute Building and perhaps the Dreyfus Building, until IBM made a move. There may have been some other tenants that I don't remember, but the big shot in the arm as far as the triangle is concerned was when

IBM moved in. We had the same thing here. Back in those early days, Bill Ficklen was the executive secretary of the park, and all business was conducted through the chamber. There were unsuccessful efforts to recruit firms to move into the park. I think we were noted in the early days for what we didn't accomplish. For instance, Ciba-Geigy was very interested in a research facility in the park and talked about an option of 30 acres. It so happened that they found exactly what they needed between Greensboro and Burlington, an existing research facility which they bought from Burlington Mills. The Yale-Town division of the Eaton Company wanted to move into the park but they could not meet our qualifications. Homelite took a sharp look at us, decided against the park, and went out on Carowinds Boulevard. It was said that one reason they located there was because they had a manufacturing plant in Gastonia. Also, some of their executives wanted to live in River Hills on Lake Wylie rather than in north Mecklenburg. Incidentally, this is one of the problems we've had with the park from the start. In those early years the better commercial and industrial facilities that had moved to Charlotte settled in the south and southeast. The real estate trade in Charlotte had more or less turned its back on what the park offered because of its location in the north county. This is something we have had to live with, but thank goodness we have now overcome it.

(C) When you came on the board the water and sewage were already out there, so you worked with it after that had been basically accomplished.

(F) As I said before, in the early days we really lay dormant. Just after I went on the board in 1970, I remember distinctly that IBM came to see us saying that immediately after buying the land they were going to start construction of their first building, but they had a technological breakthrough which changed their plans. They had started a facility in the Washington, D. C. area and wanted a similar operation here. They were manufacturing a chip about the size of a match box. Of ten such chips that they made, their mortality was eight. One day's production could be carried in a valise. The breakthrough was their ability to grow something the size of the head of a straight pin and, out of ten such particles, the mortality was only two. So they immediately called off their plans for building in Charlotte at that time.

(C) That, I think, was related not only to the technology per se but to the fact that it required so much less floor space than the other things they had been making. I went to New York with John Belk, Bill Harris, and a group of people on a follow-up of that meeting trying to persuade them to move.

(F) Also, I remember that the Billy Graham organization took an option on some of the IBM land after IBM deferred their building plans. It was a little difficult for some of us on the board to figure out exactly how the Billy Graham organization was research, but nevertheless it seemed like a worthwhile thing. As it turned out they didn't exercise the option, and the land went back to IBM.

(C) I think it's fortunate that Billy Graham's group did not come, but I think they found a setting which was more suitable to their particular interests although I was involved in that and agreed that it might be all right.

(F) When IBM decided not to build immediately, they asked the park to buy back 150 acres, which was all of the frontage they had at that time on I-85 south of Harris Boulevard. Bill Harris, Pat Calhoun, Bill Ficklen, Louis Rose, Jr., and I went out to walk the land to see whether or not the park would like to have it back. Of course, the park at that time didn't have much money. Also, we weren't too anxious to acquire the IBM land because of its topography. It is well we didn't buy and they didn't sell, because you can see now what a lovely thing they have made out of the entrance to their facility on part of that 150 acres.

(C) Claude, there is one rather crucial point here I think that more or less molded the park's future in the early days. When the University Research Park was in debt to the banks, and I think it is in the record elsewhere and I'm sure you concur, that the leadership of the banks, their willingness to loan the money with only the land as security, was the thing that made it possible for this thing to go. Bill Harris recorded that very clearly in an interview I had with him. During that 1974 depressed period when we owed the banks close to a million dollars and borrowed money to pay interest on borrowed money, it created a pretty good feeling on the board when we finally made a sale for two million dollars. Do you recall that?

(F) Yes. That's when we got out of the woods.

(C) I think that's what really got us out of the woods, and then we turned around and invested some of that money in more land.

(F) The unusual thing about the Charlotte business community, particularly the banking industry, is they were willing and continue to be willing to encourage progress in the park in spite of the risks. It has paid dividends not only at the park, but in other places around Mecklenburg, as you know.

(C) IBM did buy and finally did build. This created the stimulus to which you alluded. The board called you back into action in a rather substantial way with plans to buy more real estate and sell the park, too. For instance, I remember your involvement with the "dog and pony show" very well. Tell us about some of the more recent developments after we got out of the financial problems back then.

(F) Once the IBM move was made, and Dave Taylor came on board as president, it was obvious that we needed to do something about the housing industry. Jack Tate was appointed as chairman of a committee to figure out some way to find land for housing. This involved the extension of Harris Boulevard from where it presently dead ends at Mallard Creek Road, and if extended, to where it would terminate to the west. A lot of planning was done to determine the proper route as far as the park and north Mecklenburg were concerned. For the park, the I-77/Reames Road interchange seemed to be the logical point of termination. Bill Lee (of Duke Power) was very helpful. He assigned some of Duke's engineers to help with the mapping of the route. That route was then presented to the Department of Transporation in Raleigh as the desired extension of Harris Boulevard. The DOT had in its long range plans an extension of Harris Boulevard, but it was far from being a matter of top priority with them. I remember trips that we took to Raleigh. I went a couple of times with you and others to see the governor. I can say, Dean, I have never in my thirty odd years experience in the real estate business in Charlotte seen the amount of cooperation that has been given the park and the university. The concept, that's no longer a dream but a reality, of the orderly development of north Mecklenburg has had unusual support from all governmental agencies on the municipal, as well as the state, level.

(C) I think that has been a very strong feature. I agree with you completely that the City-County Planning Commission, the university, the Highway Commission, and others were most cooperative and helpful. Of course, that was true to some extent even before this latest period. George Broadrick, who was then a highway commissioner, played a very important part earlier in having the Highway Commission help with the planning and actual construction which converted Highway 49 from two lanes to a four-lane University Boulevard.

(F) And the interchange of Harris Boulevard with I-85.

(C) That's right. The interchange was not there originally. George helped bring that off.

(F) I think we can tip our hats to the planning commission and the whole planning process of Mecklenburg, for their foresight in seeing the potential of north Mecklenburg long before other people were willing to admit it. The road systems around UNCC and the park will never be another Independence Boulevard or Wilkinson Boulevard. There's no chance of this because of zoning and good planning. In this area we have five radial roads going north and south, compared to southeast Charlotte with only Providence Road. With Harris Boulevard, as extended, acting as the circumferential road, I think the accessibility of this area is something that is unique.

(C) The planning that took place even before the park was developed preserved the Highway 49 area. And, again, this involved the Planning Commission.

(F) Yes, but you can't overlook the tremendous contribution Addison Reese made to this whole concept. Nor will we ever discount what your contribution was as the chancellor of the university and how you bulldogged important things that came to reality. It again stresses the fact that in Charlotte-Mecklenburg we've got a business community that is willing to stick its neck out. Addison stuck his out. You stuck yours out. And there are others of us still sticking our necks out.

(C) I think that is true. I'm not seeking any accolades for myself, but I think it's very true that it couldn't possibly have happened without a lot of cooperation. A recent example is the transfer of land for University Place. The county had given the university much of the land that it owned to build the university; but the county had given that land with a reversion clause which said that if any of it ceased to be used for university purposes, it reverted to the county. But in plans for the development of University Place, two or three additional organizations have been involved. First of all, the county had to be willing to relax its restrictions to the extent that we could swap and buy land. All of this had to be approved by the Council of State, which involved every elected top official of the state. In addition, there was the building of the road. The UNCC foundation played a substantial role in this and is continuing to do so by putting up some front money, negotiating University Place, and that sort of thing. You mentioned Bill Ficklen. Along with Addison Reese and others, he was one of the very important people in this development.

(F) Yes, he was. Bill gave unselfishly of his time to the park as he did other things connected with his Chamber of Commerce duties.

(C) Tell us a little bit more specifically about the most recent real estate activity in the park.

(F) The park is a nonprofit organization whose sole beneficiary is the university, so we are in business as long as the chancellor wants us to remain in business. I hope he wants us to remain in business for a long time, because in order to buy land we must sell land. We've been very fortunate since the IBM move, in that we started getting the proper inquiries from such people as Verbatim, which now owns about 35 acres of land. At this point, they have built an 80,000 square foot building. It should be occupied within the next three or four months. That is one of two or three buildings of equal size which they have planned. Union Oil of California came in on a five-acre tract with a 25,000 to 30,000 square foot research facility. ADP, Automatic Data Processing, has bought ten acres of land for a 60,000 square foot facility. Dow Jones has bought ten acres of land and will print the Wall Street Journal there. Fairfax Properties has bought 35 acres at the corner of Research and Harris Boulevards for 300,000 square feet of office space. The latest one we have gotten is Southern Bell. They have under contract 27 acres of land on which they will put approximately a 300,000 square foot facility. All this happened after the move by IBM. The only thing the University Research Park doesn't have yet, which maybe we will have someday, is the clout to get both state and federal facilities. If you drive through the Research Triangle you see a lot of state and federal buildings. I hope ultimately we will get some government buildings. We have been acquiring more land as we've been able to afford it. The six banks still offer us a line of credit, and fortunately we don't owe them a

cent and have some money in the bank. In the immediate future we will file a request for research zoning on land we have purchased that is contiguous to our present holdings. We work very closely with the planning staff and they remain very cooperative.

(C) What about the acquisition for land to be reserved for residential purposes?

(F) We have a consortium of five builders in Charlotte who told us about three or four years ago that as soon as the western extension of Harris Boulevard was started, they would buy from us land that we have been inventorying for that purpose. It will involve the acquisition of other land besides what we are holding for them, to make it a really worthwhile housing development. It's significant that on Mallard Creek Road just beyond our acquisition of land for builders, the school board has purchased acreage for an elementary school.

(C) The University Research Park, with the help of the bankers, bought this land and held it for residential purposes so that the entire community could be planned. This constitutes one of the major differences in the planning of this park compared with some others that I've observed.

(F) Also, we must not overlook what has, for some time, been called University City.

(C) University City was zoned earlier.

(F) And University Place on the east side of I-85 also has housing in its plans. Land north of University Place will be used for residential development. I can't think of a better nucleus around which to build a new city, and that's what it's going to be, than the university, the park, and University Place.

(C) Claude, you don't have any doubt in your mind about the continued growth and development of this, do you?

(F) None, whatsoever. Dean, there are utilities in place to support a 75,000 people city. All that is needed is the extension of these utilities. I think in the next two decades you'll see this size city develop in north Mecklenburg.

(C) Claude, are there other comments, generalizations, or specific things, that you'd like to make about the park?

(F) Being a part of it is one of the most exciting things that has happened in my real estate career. The orderly growth of the park, University City, and north Mecklenburg is going to have a very positive impact on Charlotte and its environs.

EXCERPTS FROM AN INTERVIEW WITH J. NORMAN PEASE, JR., DECEMBER 13, 1983 BY DEAN W. COLVARD

(C) Norman, how did you first become involved with the University Research Park?

(P) The first contact I had with the University Research Park was through General Paul Younts. That was an informal contact — our firm designing the Allstate Insurance Company building at that time. Later, my contact was with Graeme Keith who was serving in a capacity with the Chamber of Commerce. That was when we officially had a relationship with them doing the master planning for the research park.

(C) Actually, Allstate was the second building in the park. The first one was Collins & Aikman. So this was in the early days after the park was organized. You were not in on the very first organization of it but you got in very early.

(P) I checked my files and the first correspondence we had with the park was in June of 1967.

(C) Well, that's quite early.

(P) The first written contact is a letter that I wrote to Graeme Keith in June of '67. That letter had to do with the way of master planning. After we received that letter, we entered into a contract with the park in October of 1967 and they we began the master plan.

(C) What did you do in the early stages of the planning of the park?

(P) Well, in the early stages we assembled all of the available information — maps, topography, property line data and all of that. We tried to decide what the park should be and work with Claude Freeman who had the experience of working earlier with the Research Triangle. We worked with Claude and Bill Harris trying to determine our planning direction.

(C) What did you do? There were three different owners of the property, weren't there?

(P) While meeting with the owners it was explained that it was necessary to view the property as a single entity and all the owners were agreeable to this approach. Once it was decided essentially what the park would be, we proceeded with the site analysis and an eventual preliminary plan of road, utility requirements and eventually indication of parcels. At that time we had established minimum and maximum tract sizes.

(C) You said a minimum tract. Do you recall what the minimum might have been?

(P) The minimum was initially established as four acres. There were actually two schemes developed for the park. The first used the minimum of four acres with many small acreage parcels, four to eight acres. The second and later scheme revised the planning to establish a five acre minimum with very few of the minimum parcels shown. Parcel size then ranged from 5 to 25 or 30 acres. A site model showing topography, property lines, existing utilities, existing roads, proposed roads and proposed parcels was built.

(C) You were involved in the planning for the sewage and the water. Would you say something about the conditions that prevailed in that respect when you first got involved.

(P) The park was located ideally in respect to the total area of the county, in that the city-county had already planned certain waste disposal facilities in that area. The park has good natural drainage. The Charlotte-Mecklenburg Utility Department worked very closely with us. We are fortunate in having capacity beyond our present needs in that part of the county.

(C) You say that we're fortunate that we have adequate sewage facilities, take if from the first plant and follow it through just a little bit.

(P) Dean, I don't remember the numbers but the first plant, as now designed, can be doubled in capacity. Right now it is not taxed as far as its abilities to take care of what's out there is concerned.

(C) Did you and your associates have very much involvement directly with the City-County Planning Commission or was yours primarily restricted to development of the park plan which would then be looked at by other planners.

(P) Our involvement was primarily in the park. We did have an excellent relationship with various city-county agencies. We worked very closely with the Charlotte-Mecklenburg Utility Department.

(C) Has your firm designed some of the structures for the individual companies other than Allstate?

(P) Yes we have. We designed the Electric Power Research Institute building; Southern Bell Corporate Data Center, now under construction; and we are associated with an Atlanta firm in the design of the Fairfax building.

(C) You've continued to be involved as the park has been developing rather rapidly in recent years What do you regard as some of the more significant developments that have taken place in the last two or three years that have enlarged and changed the whole outlook of the park?

(P) I'd say the opening of Harris Boulevard all the way through to I-77 has been the most recent thing. Then the development of IBM has spurred the entire park. I also believe that expanding to the north, going across the creek and opening that area will be one of the biggest things.

(C) Have you been involved in the planning of this expansion?

(P) Yes, we continue to be planning consultants for the park.

(C) To be a little more specific here for the record, and I doubt if this appears elsewhere in these interviews, President Rusty Goode asked Dave Burkhalter and you and me to explore the possibility of having a chancellor's home established in this area where the residential development is occurring. When you and I went out and looked at it I think we were something less than overwhelmed by the possibilities that were laid out there.

(P) Yes. Particularly in the area that one of the developers wanted us to consider. We initially did consider it, but further study showed that there were better places elsewhere on our property.

Besides the initial planning study we've made a secondary study to consider possibilities for expansion of the park. This was done quite some time ago but it was to consider how we wanted to grow in the future. That's when we first considered the "Barnhardt/Harris" property.

(C) I know your firm has been involved not only in the planning but in the interpreting of these plans. Would you say something about the development of the visuals, the slide show, as Claude Freeman called it "the dog and pony show," because you were deeply involved in that.

(P) We were. As a matter of fact we got so deeply involved in it that between Claude and our office we developed the first "dog and pony show." It served its purpose at the time. Later I recommended that we employ a professional and put together a real show. Yes, we did develop the first show with the help of the university. The university people took the first show, upgraded it put sound to it, and we worked on script with them, then they produced it. As you know the show was designed for several different types of viewers but some who see it know very little about Charlotte or North Carolina. The show must say something about the immediate neighborhood, the city, county and state. Hopefully, the current show reaches those who know Charlotte, as well

as those who are complete strangers to North Carolina.

(C) Have you been involved very much with the prospective clients when they've been identified by the Chamber of Commerce or by Rusty Goode or by anybody else? Do they come and talk to you about sites?

(P) Dean, I think the answer to your question is both yes and no, depending on the circumstances. If the proposed purchase is confidential, the prospect may not even want the park to know who they are. So at times we are not involved; and if we are, we may not know anything about the person or the company they represent. When we do get involved, their position of confidentiality is respected and rigidly adhered to. Some prospects, on the other hand, are very open, identifying their firms, the processes or services, and their needs, and at times we have worked very closely with such persons in their site selections, and perhaps later in their site planning. An example of this would be EPRI.

(C) EPRI for the record is Electric Power Research Institute.

(P) We also worked very closely with Fairfax when they were looking at the area. With Southern Bell we were very much involved. Bell had many people, as you know, trying to sell them property, and the park was only one of several sites being considered. We wore two hats really. We have worked with Bell on over 300 projects through the state, and site was a major consideration for most. With the owner's representative I did go out and look at several proposed sites in the park and as you know, they purchased about 27 acres for their Corporate Data Center.

Before the park had its own office, we had no place to take people; so we would set up the "dog and pony show" and maps and drawings in our conference room and meet there. At that time I tried my best not to wear two hats. I wore the University Research Park hat and often they didn't even know when they left that we would be interested in working with them in a second capacity.

(C) I'd like to ask you something about your views of the park over the long term. What do you see as its significance and its potential development?

(P) I think what we are seeing now is little more than a tip of the iceberg. Because of the growing economy in this particular area, nothing should happen to the park except good things. It will continue to grow.

(C) History will probably show that the total planning involved in the development of that side of town is probably greater than the planning of any other area because we've had so many different people involved. You've been involved, the planning commission has been involved, the university planners have been involved, the highway commission has been involved, so that the total of the planning effort which you've been a part of there from the very beginning is a large effort.

(P) I think the development between Highway 29 and I-85, Harris Boulevard, University Place, the new hospital, etc. is going to make that area bloom and I think it's going to be a major part of the city in a very few years. The park will have to get more land. We can go north and across I-85 as a possibility. I believe we're going to need that property before too long.

(C) We've been more or less limited to date to the Toby Creek watershed. Are there other aspects of the park development that you would like to comment on?

(P) Dean, I believe that the park has acted very wisely through its real estate efforts and through its board members. They've been very sensitive to the neighborhood and tried to work well with people that live and work there now. When we were buying some houses very recently, it was handled extremely well. I think people ended up feeling good about the transaction and good about the park.

(C) The people who own the land have been very adequately compensated.

(P) We have not condemned any property. I don't believe we have the eminent domain power or authority. You mentioned that fact and I hadn't thought of it in just this way, but it is quite remarkable that in all of this negotiation concerning the property we've never had and real knock-down, drag-out nasty situations.

(P) In the expansion study that we did, we estimated that we should acquire about 2,500 acres. At that time IBM had not developed. We were still estimating a 2,500 acre expansion so, as you see, we've still got to go north and, I guess, west.

(C) Well, Norm, it's good of you to come in.

(P) Thank you for asking me to meet with you. I enjoyed it.

INDEX

UNIVERSITY RESEARCH PARK
THE FIRST TWENTY YEARS

Dean W. Colvard

Chancellor Emeritus Dean W. Colvard, the first chancellor of The University of North Carolina at Charlotte, has been a member of the University Research Park Board from its beginning. In the 1950s he participated in launching the Research Triangle by serving on Governor Hodges' Working Committee. He has emphasized the university's role as a partner in the quality development of Charlotte-Mecklenburg. He has received awards for service and leadership to three institutions of higher education. As a former dean of the School of Agriculture and Life Sciences at North Carolina State University, he co-authored a book entitled *Knowledge Is Power*, covering the history of agricultural education and research in North Carolina. He is also the author of *Mixed Emotions: A University President Remembers*, dealing with the integration crises of the 1960s while he served as president of Mississippi State University.

Douglas M. Orr, Jr.

Douglas M. Orr, Jr., Vice Chancellor for Development and Public Service at the University of North Carolina at Charlotte, gives leadership to the University's outreach and development activities. A prime mover with the team which envisioned and launched University Place, he has served on the University Research Park board since 1984. In 1987 he and Chancellor E.K. Fretwell Jr. received, on behalf of the University, the American Association of State Colleges and Universities' award for innovative university-community development for the institution's role in the development of University City. A geographer and former recipient of the University's teacher of excellence award, Orr co-edited the widely acclaimed *Metrolina Atlas*, *North Carolina Atlas*, and *The North Carolina Urban Economic Atlas* series. He is co-author of a forthcoming book on the United States South.

Mary Dawn Bailey

Mary Dawn Bailey, Associate Director of the Urban Institute at the University of North Carolina at Charlotte, heads the organization's publications' program. She is author of *Urban Environment*, UNESCO's environmental education text for teachers and students worldwide, co-author of *Man and Environment*, a Gale Research Company guide, and a co-author of the *North Carolina Urban Economic Atlas* series for the North Carolina Department of Commerce. As an initiator of university-community public affairs programs, she has been intimately involved in researching and disseminating information for the Urban Institute for 15 years. In addition to her writing skills, she brings to the project an important public affairs perspective.

Urban Institute
University of North Carolina at Charlotte
Charlotte, North Carolina 28223

ISBN 0-945344-00-7

The University Research Park is a non-profit corporation, its sole beneficiary being the University of North Carolina at Charlotte. Its directors are leaders in Charlotte business and industry who volunteer their time, influence and energies to managing the park and promoting its benefits to tenant prospects around the country and indeed, the world.